Tri-Tuning

Harmonizing your Mind, Body and Spirit to Live Beyond Fear

TRI-TUNING

*Harmonizing your
Mind, Body and Spirit
to Live Beyond Fear*

A QUEST FOR THE KEY TO **KI**;
THE ESSENCE OF LIFE

Hilda Neff Perkins

Foreword by Gerard Lamothe

UNIVERSAL QUEST PUBLISHING
Vero Beach, Florida

Copyright © 1999 by Hilda Neff Perkins
Published and bound in the United States of America
All rights reserved. Except as permitted under the Copyright Act of 1976, this book may not be reproduced in whole or in part in any manner without written permission by the author.

Library of Congress Catalog Card Number 97-91369
Library of Congress Cataloging-in-Publication Data
Perkins, Hilda Neff
Tri-Tuning – Harmonizing your Mind, Body and Spirit to Live Beyond Fear

ISBN 0-9662618-0-1

1. Fear, 2. Mind and body, 3. Spiritual life, 4. Ch'i (Chinese philosophy), 5. Aikido (*Ki*), 6. Self-actualization

10 9 8 7 6 5 4 3 2 1

Cover design and text layout by Flying Dutchman Productions
Author's photo by Suzan Phillips
Instructional Art by Jason Kofke

Note: The instructions in this book should be performed at the discretion of the reader, in accordance with personal health and professional recommendations. The author and publisher hold no responsibility and are not engaged in rendering medical, psychological, financial, legal or other services that should be sought from professionals in any field.

The subject matter has been extensively researched to insure accuracy and no responsibility will be assumed for errors, inaccuracies or omissions. Any slights of people, places or organizations are unintentional. Please bring to the attention of the publisher any names of authors listed as unknown or any material thought to be printed in error. Send to:
Universal Quest Publishers, P.O. Box 1393, Vero Beach, FL 32961.
Phone: (561) 562-3031 • e-mail: hildaper@sunet.net

Dedication

To my sons,

Kenneth and Stephen,

with the wish
that I had been aware of and had practiced tri-tuning
during their youth, when I was so futilely trying to
be the perfect mom.

and

To my grandchildren,
who are part of the next generation bestowed with a potential
to create and enjoy a better world.

In memory of my dear friend

Joe Sherry

and

*in memoriam to
all those whose virtues
helped to set standards for the
privileges enjoyed around
the world.*

Foreword

It is the way of the West—

When we are born, our parents seek to provide a better life for us: a better home, better food, more security, more choices, and more education. They seek to encourage us to internalize these choices into a maturity that will follow us into the journey of our adult lives. There, they hope we will be able to seek for ourselves a better life, healthier relationships, a better job, a bigger home, more security, greater leisure, more pleasure, deeper happiness and even more love.

Generations of this cycle have evolved into a culture that nurtures and promotes this kind of growth in spiritual, political, educational, and social settings. For the most part, we see this as *good*. We call it progress. We separate what is good from what is not good. We question progress, reform it, recreate it, but we cannot rest. *More* becomes the object of power, enlightenment, and holiness. It is the Way of the West.

It is the way of the East—

When we are born, our parents seek to introduce to us our place in life. They guide our eyes to gaze inwardly. We find there within ourselves a home, a source to nurture ourselves and an emptiness of desire. They trust that we will seek mastery of the knowledge that all we need to know is within ourselves. They encourage us to internalize this discipleship throughout our lives. Their aim is that we will achieve an emptying of the desires and thoughts that cloud our destinies; to be at one with nature, peace and love.

Generations of this cycle have evolved into a culture that nurtures and promotes this kind of inner growth in spiritual, political, educational and social settings. For the most part, we see this as the way it is. It is neither *good* nor *bad*. We need only recognize it. We call this Enlightenment. Philosophy, religion, patriotism—all are empty idols. We do not need an answer to find peace. We need only surrender to our existence and cease the needless, empty questioning. *Less* becomes the object of our reality; the source of inner power, holiness and enlightenment. It is the Way of the East.

Here is a book that bridges West to East. A book that connects the languages and methods of both Eastern and Western approaches to the human heart. A book that integrates the search for greater love with the quest for the surrendered self. A book that welcomes the accumulated human knowledge and wisdom of both cultures in the human drama to experience the Spirit of power, Holiness and Enlightenment. We are, after all, brothers and sisters.

This is the way of the human heart.
This is the Way of the Spirit.

Gerard J. Lamothe, M.Div.
Director, Pastoral Counseling Center
Vero Beach, Florida
April 15, 1998

Guide to Symbols and Terms

To understand the meanings of foreign or newly coined words, please read the following:

The coined words **Tri-tuning, Spirergy, Triality** and **Holitude** are keys to better understand the text. They represent Eastern concepts that no one English word adequately defines. These four words will appear in **bold letters** when first introduced in the text.

Tri-tuning – mind, body, and spirit; the art of developing a synchronized flow of living.
Spirergy – spirit-energy; an English interpretation for *ki*
Triality – three-dimensional thinking; the blending of mind, body and spirit.
Holitude – an attitude of oneness; a holistic view.

Foreign words included in the ***Glossary of Foreign Words*** will be printed in ***bold italics*** the first time they appear in the text. Afterward, they will appear in regular *italics,* along with other *italicized* foreign words. Example: The word ***ki*** (above) would be printed as *ki* after its first appearance.

Japanese names and titles are reversed. The title is placed after the name; i.e. ***sensei***, meaning teacher or doctor, appears after the name. Example: ***Tohei Sensei***, rather than Professor Tohei or Nakamura Sensei instead of Dr. Nakamura. Among Western martial arts organizations, "sensei" is often used the Western way, i.e., Sensei Simcox, or he might simply be addressed "Sensei."

BCE – Before the Common Era (same as BC – before Christ)
CE – Common Era (same as AD, Anno Domini – in the year of the Lord).

If neither indication is used in the text it means CE and AD.

References in the text to topics listed alphabetically in Part II, indicate where further information can be found concerning that subject. Refer to them as you proceed or chronologically as you read Part II.

Tri-tuning Symbol

The tri-tuning emblem symbolizes three-dimensional living; the synchronizing of mind, body and spirit; a harmonious unity of diversity:

- The thin square indicates order and organization.
- The pointed square means change and increased intelligence.
- The larger circle represents a complementary balance of the never-ending cosmic circle and the Oneness of all things.
- The triangle unites the circles of mind, body and spirit.
- The tri-tuning circle represents our potential to achieve higher personal understanding and intuitive knowingness.

The Triangle:

- symbolizes the number three.
- in the ancient association of numbers three; God in humanity.
- in Christianity; the Holy Trinity.
- in Buddhism; the buddhas, the scriptures and the monks.
- the upward apex represents aspiration to higher unity.

- illustrates activity and dynamism, or pure spirit.
- within a circle, means the spiritual principle within totality.

The Circle:
- is a ring symbolizing circumference or unbroken continuum.
- means unity from multiplicity; heaven, perfection and eternity.
- represents the ultimate state of Oneness.
- is the sum of two equal parts of positive and negative; the universal energy.

The Square:
- symbolizes the number four, earth, firmness, order, stability and intellect.
- represents the four points of the compass and the four seasons.
- when resting on one corner, implies dynamic change in fundamentalism.

– from *A Dictionary of Symbols* by E. Cirlot, translated by Jack Sage

Words of Gratitude

WHEN I BEGAN LISTING those I wanted to thank for their contribution to this book, I was reminded of Gregory Alan-Williams, author of *A Gathering of Heroes*. After he became a hero in 1992, during the Los Angeles riots, he realized that what had prompted his brave reactions was the culmination of influence, guidance and the molding provided by so many caring people during his lifetime.

My *gathering of artisans* includes the nurturing influence of parents, family, teachers, friends and relationships. I am grateful to the *Oneness* of existence; God, *ki*, cosmic consciousness or whatever name best fits each reader's concept of the vital spirit-energy that pervades the cosmos. I feel indebted to the *All* of Nature for the inherent gift of mind, body and spirit bequeathed me for this short walk on planet earth.

I am thankful for the childhood religious and spiritual contributions by my family, community and church; especially our Lutheran minister, The Rev. S. Wallace Berry. During middle-age, my childhood impressions were matured by another Lutheran minister, the late Rev. Henry Schumann.

My interest in mystical teachings was enhanced by Unity minister The Rev. Robert Marshall. My perspective on world religions and human relationship was broadened by Professor Gerard Lamothe, whom I thank for contributing the Foreword. The main source of encouragement, especially during the early challenging years of compiling this book, came through insight by my spiritual counselor, Robert Conrad. Plans and schedules were influenced by astrologers Dorothy Turner and Jacqueline di Carlo.

I feel that *God, It, What* and *Whomever,* directed me to the wealth of knowledge I received as a student under *Koichi Tohei* at *Ki no Kenkyukai* (Ki Society International) in Tokyo, Japan, from 1986 to 1988. I feel fortunate to have learned about the non-violent ideals held by the late *Morihei Ueshiba*, founder of the martial art *Aikido*. Without the knowledge I gained through *Koichi Tohei's* modification of the ancient wisdom concerning *ki*, I could not have arrived at the conclusions prescribed in this book.

In addition to my own experiences as researcher, instructor and healer, I gained valuable knowledge from my colleagues, students and clients.

Their interest and questions stimulated my quest to further analyze what I had learned in Japan.

I thank the authors who gave permission to quote their words of wisdom. Without all the literary contributions passed down throughout history that aided my teachers, as well as the insight I gained through my own research, I could not have attempted this writing. I wish I could include the name of every author, living or dead, who influenced my thinking and added to my understanding of the questions that perplexed me as I compiled this publication.

I hesitate to list all my benefactors by name because, among the long list, I might accidentally omit a worthy contributor. I will, however, introduce my assistants in this undertaking.

I am grateful to the many Japanese and other nationalities who contributed to my well-being while in Japan. Besides those in Japan already listed, I want to thank: Koretoshi Maruyama, *Ki Development* and *Kiatsu* instructor; author William Reed and his wife Kumi, who were my classmates at Ki Society International.

I thank my manuscript critics: writing instructor Kay Odekirk; author and behavioral counselor Michael H. Greene; Chief Instructor for the Virginia *Ki* Society, George Simcox; *Ki-aikido* brown belt Pat Worster; author and *Ki-aikidoist* Carol Shifflet; *Aikidoist* Rabbi Jay R. Davis; alternative physician Peter R. Holyk, MD; Soto Zen Priest Shohaku Okumura; special education teacher Nancy Sherry; writer and poet Betty Neff Dickens; teacher and world traveler Rachel Dooley; retired military officer Jack Romney; English professor Jane Whitehead; artist and proofer Connie Harper; Eastern culture advisor Donald Whittaker; author Nancilee Wydra; art historian Willie Quade; and my teenage grandson, Shawn Smith.

Marian Christiansen acted as a partner to verify the instructions for *ki* tests and skills.

I was most fortunate to have Holly Addonizio choose a portion of my manuscript to fulfill her assignment for certification as an editor. I thank her mother and father, Frank and Norma Klobucher, along with other members of our comparative religions discussion group called Quest, who helped critique portions of the manuscript: Harry Anderson, Tom and Betsy Smith, Cecele and Roland Proteau, and Alma Krumm.

Besides those listed on the copyright page and the many friends who gave me encouragement during this project, some others who assisted in various ways include: Dan Mack; Jon Ward; staff members at the Indian River County Main Library; co-members of the Vero Beach Branch of the National League of American Pen Women; Lauri Tagliaferro; Linda Knolls; D. A. Taft; Cricket Pechstein; Pete Sharman; Marsha Damerow; Gary Oberholtzer; Jane Marsh; Deborah Kilcollins; Olske Forbes; William Hunt; Mariam Plans; Virginia Knudsen; Barbara Matuszewski; June Page; Faith Mitchell; Betty Komarisky; Marilyn Blauman; Faith and Glen Swift; Kate Romney; and Kelly Moriarty.

Quotes on Fear

"We don't gain through fear, we gain through understanding."
Author unknown

"We crucify ourselves between two thieves; regret from yesterday and fear of tomorrow."
Fulton Oursler

"There are very few monsters who warrant the fear we have for them."
Andre' Gide

"The First Law is that you can be and do and have whatever you can imagine. The Second Law is that you attract what you fear."
Neale Donald Walsch, Conversations With God, book 2

"The greatest mistake you can make is to be continually fearing that you'll make one."
Elbert Hubbard

"When fear comes our vision is clouded, and it becomes difficult to distinguish between the guilty and the innocent."
Jawaharlal Nehru

"Let not your heart be troubled, and do not be afraid."
Holy Bible, John 14:27

"To conquer fear is the beginning of wisdom."
Bertrand Russell

"When a man has quietly made up his mind that there is nothing he cannot endure, his fears leave him."
Grove Patterson

"Sometimes when I get in a nervous dither over such current problems as inflation, war, taxes, crime, pollution, political intrigue, urban sprawl, population and whatever, I find myself yearning for 1933, when all we <u>had</u> to fear was fear itself."
Oren Arnold

"Don't be afraid to enjoy the stress of a full life nor too naïve to think you can do so with out some intelligent thinking and planning. Man should not try to avoid stress any more than he should avoid food, love and exercise."
Dr. Hans Selye

Table of Contents

Foreword   vii
Guide to Symbols and Terms   ix
Tri-tuning Symbol Defined   xi
Words of Gratitude   xiii
Quotations on Fear   xvi
Introduction   xxi
Preface   xxvii

PART I: What is Tri-tuning?

A Reminder to review the Guide to Symbols and Terms

Chapter One: Three-dimensional Living

A Look at Fear   1
Complementing the Opposites   4
Tri-tuning   7
Universal Vital Energy   9
Tri-tune Your Posture   10
Getting Beyond Fear   13
Student Experiences   17
Tri-tune with a Partner   18
The Enemy   20
A Fighting Conscience, A Slave Conscience or A Triality Conscience   23
How to Tri-tune Your Life for Easier Living   24
The Logic of Tri-tuning   27
Accepting Foreign Influence   28

Chapter Two: An Eastern Orientation

Two Years in Japan   31
The Martial Art Aikido   32
What is Ki?   33
The Use of Ki in Everyday Life   35
Tohei Sensei's Ki Development Training   39
New Aikido Organizations   42
Ki Exercises   44

Ki Meditation 46
Kiatsu Healing Art 47
Whole-Body Breathing 49
Practical Application of Ki 50
Choose Your Perspective 51

Chapter Three: The Paradox of Opposites

East and West as Opposites 53
Teaching Ki Development to Westerners 55
The Mind of a Martial Artist 58
An Attitude of Holitude 61
Positive Thinking 62
Unity of Calm and Action 67
Yin/Yang 70
Western Dualism 72
Opposite Extremes 74
The Ball of Knowledge and Awareness 77
Beyond the Opposites of Positive and Negative 81
A Magic Wand 83

Chapter Four: Gleaning the Best from East and West

My Introduction to Ki Society International 87
Subconscious Fears 88
Intercultural and Universal Understanding 90
Aikido Tenkan Technique 92
Verbal Conflict 94
Relationships and Family Conflict 95
Blend and Mend 98
Three-dimensional Programs 104
Blame and Shame 107
The Epitome of Tri-tuning 110
Bridging Western Logic and Eastern Feeling Nature 112

PART II: Ways to Tri-Tune Our Everyday Lives

An Alphabetical List of Reasons and Ways to Tri-tune

Anger 118
Balance 120

Breath   122
Change   127
Consciousness   131
Death   133
Defense   136
Dualism   136
Ego   138
Exercise   138
Fair-mindedness   140
Fear   140
Fighting and Slave Conscience   144
Flow   145
Freedom   146
Guilt and Punishment   149
Habits   151
Happiness   153
Harmony   157
Healing and Health   158
Holitude   163
Intuition   165
Kiatsu   167
Kinesiology   167
Love   168
Magnetism   169
Materialism   173
Meditation   174
Mind/Body Coordination   178
Nature   178
Opposites   180
Peace   182
Posture   183
Power   184
Spirergy   185
Spirit   185
Stage Fright   187
Thanks   190
Thoughts   192

Time   193
Triality Conscience   194
Tri-tuning   195
Truth   197
Western Religions   200
Win-Win   202
Personal Tri-tuning   205

PART III: Creating a Better World

My Introduction to Ki and Aikido   209
Creating the Future   210
Turning Fear Into Care   216
Changing the World by Changing Ourselves   220
Doing Our Best in the Best of All Possible Worlds   226
All is Well   231

Afterword   235
Glossary of Foreign Words   237
Bibliography   261
Index (includes list of the graphics under Illustrations and the tests under Tri-tuning skills/Ki tests)   267

Introduction

WHEN THE TWO-YEAR COURSE in *Ki Development* and *Kiatsu* healing art in Japan ended in 1988, the instructors asked how we planned to use our training. Along with specific intentions, I added that I would like to be a Johnny Appleseed for the spread of *ki* awareness. This puzzled the Japanese and amused my American classmates. An interpretation of that American pioneer story brought smiles and nods of approval from the Japanese students.

I have put my impression of what I learned into print as a means of planting the seeds of *ki*. How each of us uses this unlimited awareness will determine the results of its widespread possibilities for a bountiful harvest.

A life-long curiosity about the *whys* and *wherefores* of life led me to Tokyo, Japan, in 1986. I studied under *Koichi Tohei* at Ki Society International, which he had established in 1971 to teach *Ki Development*, and the *Kiatsu* healing therapy training course that he had added in 1980. Both evolved from his training in the martial art *aikido* and through his personal research into the philosophy of *ki*. Beginning in 1939, *Koichi Tohei* had practiced under *Morihei Ueshiba*, who in the early 1900s had founded a martial art that he later named *aikido*.

This book provides an awareness of how to access the endless potential of spirit-energy that the Japanese call *ki*. Even though I have studied, researched, taught and experienced *ki*, I do not refer to myself as an expert on such a profound subject.

Ki is the elusive energy, spirit or vital essence that continually produces, sustains and recycles all forms of life. This energy, as seen from an Eastern perspective, is a frontier that modern Western physicists are beginning to analyze with the hope that eventually it can be scientifically and spiritually defined. Surmounting the need for logical interpretation, Eastern *and* Western mystics have examined and used this phenomenon for ages, labeling it differently through various interpretations and practices.

For the purpose of explanation, I will equate *ki* to electricity. No one can explain exactly what electricity is or why it works. We can enjoy the many electronic inventions but we must respect the adverse side effects of electricity. These factors enter into the opposing aspects of *ki*.

Ki, like the relative world it pervades, manifests the opposing energies that Benjamin Franklin designated as positive and negative electricity. Electricity encompasses both matter and motion. The theme of this publication is: how to sense and utilize positive and negative *ki* in the same complementary way that we reap the usefulness of electricity.

The terms "male plug" and "female plug," though they are diametrically opposite, do not render one gender dominant over or inferior to the other. Like negative electrical current, negative *ki* cannot be discarded as useless while exalting the positive *ki* to a place of prominence. Mutual, but opposite, actions are necessary to produce the desired results. How we handle the everyday opposites in our lives affects not only our individual lives but the future of the world as well.

Appropriate thinking, or what we call "positive thinking," is vital to our present and future existence. Learning to deal with the *fears* that we associate with good or bad—is equally essential. A better understanding of the everyday usefulness of *ki* will help ease our fears and put them in perspective. With more awareness of the quintessential potentiality of *ki*, we can improve and simplify our daily habits.

First we must recognize and compare the differences between a Western mind-set, which encourages positive versus negative logical thinking, and the Eastern mind-set that is based on *Taoism's* holistic outlook and the complementary *yin/yang* concept of the opposites.

Tohei Sensei defined and emphasized the Western mind-set as plus *ki* and minus *ki*. He also demonstrated the unity of calm and action through the Eastern mind-set.

After much research into the sources of these two mind-sets, I concluded that each outlook can be more useful if both Eastern and Western views are better understood. My venture to reconcile the two mind-sets sent me out on a limb of contemplation.

When I attempt to explain, or when I observe someone else trying to convey Eastern concepts to Westerners, I realize that it's like trying to describe a lotus blossom to someone who equates that explanation to a rose. The lotus blossom is the spiritual symbol of the East. The rose is symbolic to the West. Both are flowers, just as the basis of both Eastern philosophies and Western religions are essentially the same—yet each is perceived differently.

Westerners often ask "What is *ki?*" and expect to be enlightened by a one-sentence answer. An Eastern view of life is holistic; recognizing the interconnectedness between all things. This insight is confusing from a Western standpoint. Our Western view stems from a dualistic division of the opposites; the historical scientific and religious aspects of separating the mind and body.

To blend the blossoms of *Eastern philosophy* and Western religion into a balanced bouquet of harmony, I weighed the merits and hindrances of both mind-sets. For Westerners to grasp the full meaning of Oriental thought, we need to learn more than just a few superficial facts about a particular *Eastern philosophy.* My aim is to help clarify the misunderstandings about the Eastern spiritual paths by comparing and blending Eastern and Western approaches.

When I become impatient with individuals who are biased against Eastern ways, I have to remind myself that thirty years ago I, too, was a biased Westerner who rejected any acceptance of Oriental philosophy. I was curious, but noncommittal.

It was not until 1970 that I began to cut the cords of suspicion and to open my mind to the depth of Eastern philosophies. When my late friend Ann, a member of the Theosophical Society, began talking about reincarnation, I responded, "You know that I am interested in religions and metaphysical subjects but I cannot accept the theory of reincarnation." I felt that coming to terms with the various Western religions was enough challenge, without adding the confusion of *Eastern philosophy.*

She asked, "What do you know about reincarnation?"

The question jolted me into the realization that I knew nothing except that it was a Christian virtue to regard reincarnation and foreign religions as heathen beliefs. I told her my thoughts.

She answered, "I didn't ask you what someone told you to believe. Examine reincarnation and if you still disagree, that's your privilege."

That conversation launched me into a quest that eventually led me to put my experiences in writing. After researching the various beliefs in reincarnation, I came to no definite conclusion as to which of the various versions of reincarnation might be correct. At present I espouse no particular *Eastern philosophy* or Western religion. I do have great respect for, a curious interest in, an eagerness to learn more about, and a willingness to participate in all of them.

I have, however, concluded that *nothing*—neither motion nor matter—is ever really destroyed. All *energy* continuously changes form, from motion to matter and from matter to motion, throughout the universe. My greatest satisfaction *and challenge* came when I concluded that my thoughts and actions, along with the accumulated results of *all thought* throughout time, constantly creates the present and the future.

I resolved to learn about unfamiliar subjects with an open mind and to keep it open so that I can continue to learn and grow intellectually. I have concluded that everything is relative—even truth. A particular viewpoint can be gospel to one person or group, but blasphemy to another.

We cannot be certain of the *truth* about anything we hear or read, either ancient or modern. Even the Bible, which some regard as infallible, has prompted numerous interpretations. Any concept that is new, old or foreign to us requires study and testing by experience before it can be intelligently lived by.

We are living in an "instant era." The tolerance of impatience in personal, business or government practices has enabled small immature mentality to have a major impact on our lives, as well as on the destiny of our planet and the cosmos. The tendency to rely on quick but inadequate explanations and remedies, denies us the satisfaction of learning and relearning through personal experience.

My objective is to relate my own learning experiences through simple examples of the basic patterns that concern philosophy, scientific discoveries and religious practices. I simply want to convey a means to help minimize fear of the known and unknown through the complementary merging of Eastern and Western thought. I have refrained, as much as possible, from condemning or condoning any specific belief, philosophy, religion or culture—Eastern or Western, ancient or modern.

I invite each reader to broaden his or her scope of understanding. Simply become aware of both sides of each issue and draw on your own intuitive conclusions. Refrain from reading this text with the usual perspective of either being dogmatically close-minded or hypnotically persuaded.

The explanations and suggestions are meant to inspire all of us to *examine* our fears. Tri-tuning can help us face, and live beyond, our fears that lead to stress and worry. The simplicity of calm-alertness can replace our usual sense of either sensational alertness or collapsed calm.

Amid the clamor of Western hyper-physical positive thinking, we have forgotten the value of calm and quietude. Tri-tuning is a way of merging tension with calmness to attain harmony. It is a way to experience the euphoria of well-being.

The extreme imbalances we experience daily, occur when we succumb to "socially correct" demands for sensationalism and hyperactivity. We are in need of a means to rebalance our habits of extreme. Valuable energy is wasted on any devastating egotistic drive for material ownership and the selfish motives for personal power that result from the attitude that "I am #1," or "I must win at all cost."

The misuse of "positive thinking" causes negative results for everyone, including ourselves. Our entertainment world all too often leads us to believe that nothing less than winning with super-human destructive actions is worthy of applause. Balance, through a tri-tuning sense-of-being also reduces stagnation, indecision or inaction. Practical awareness creates a rebalance of extremes through harmonious solutions.

The basic tenets of our Western Judaic-Moslem-Christian Scriptures convey that good can manifest when we put God first. From an Eastern perspective, that same advice is expressed: Honor the Oneness of the Universe and good fortune will follow. Both tell us to balance our outer and inner lives through respect for others while maintaining self-respect.

Many religious groups claim that only supernatural miracles and supra-human deeds are connected with God. Therefore we tend to separate mundane everyday occurrences from our spiritual lives. From a tri-tuning perspective—when Oneness is created, separation simply disappears.

During the 1960s, an interest and awareness in *Eastern philosophy* was sparked. Many of the New Age pioneers swung to passive extremes in their attempt to convey Eastern thought.

A more balanced, "action within non-action" interpretation of both Eastern and Western philosophies is emerging. Twentieth century scientific discoveries, especially through modern physics, are bringing old revelations concerning spiritual mysticism to light through new insight into scientific revelations.

This book takes you beyond the mind/body connection. It provides a means for three-dimensional living—mind, body and spirit. This three-fold tri-tuning, a triad state-of-being, will simplify and improve the daily habits that govern our lives. We *can* learn to understand, and to live beyond, our fears.

Preface

One reason for the publication of this book is to acquaint more Westerners with the meaning of *ki*. At present, this Japanese word is as foreign as *chi* and *prana* were twenty-five years ago. My main purpose, however, is to share the concept of *ki*. *Tohei Sensei's Ki Development* program and my version, *Ki Wellness,* provide a means or tool to meet and handle the conflicts of everyday life with less fear. It is a way to create more harmony in the world.

My quest for *ki* began on Thanksgiving Day in 1981, after viewing a TV program on which George Leonard explained *ki* through a demonstration of the Japanese martial art, *aikido*. This encounter led me to a 1982 phone conversation with Virginia Ki Society Chief Instructor, George Simcox, who was referred to me through the Japanese Embassy. In 1983, after reading several books on *ki,* I attended a seminar in Virginia that was conducted by the chief instructor, Koretoshi Maruyama, from *Tohei Sensei's* Japanese headquarters for Ki Society International in Tokyo, Japan.

In 1985, I returned from Florida to my native state to study with the Virginia Ki Society under George Simcox. This move to Virginia would determine whether my increasing desire to study *Ki Development* and *Kiatsu* healing under *Koichi Tohei* in Tokyo, Japan, was compelling enough for a senior-aged adult to make such a quantum leap.

William Reed, one of George Simcox's former students who visited from Japan that same year, gave a seminar for the Virginia and Maryland Ki Societies. He answered questions about the requirements for the two-year certified courses of study under *Koichi Tohei*. Choosing between either *Ki-Aikido* martial art training and *Ki Development,* or the *Kiatsu* healing art and *Ki Development*, I opted for the latter and moved to Japan in 1986.

The founder of *Ki* Society International, *Koichi Tohei* or *Tohei Sensei* (teacher), instructs *Ki Development* through what he defines as mind and body coordination with *ki* extended. By using this method as a practice tool, our uncoordinated thoughts and actions can be replaced by synchronized habits of balance which help us cope with and ease the conflicts of everyday life.

This book reflects the unfolding of my personal conclusions, both during my studies in Japan and while adapting the potentials of this Eastern philosophy to Western understanding. When I returned to Florida and began teaching *Ki Development* classes in 1989, I found it challenging to explain the Eastern concepts with words that were readily comprehensible to the Western mind-set. These two points-of-view are in many ways exactly opposite; two sides of the same coin.

To aid in the understanding and blending of Eastern and Western mind-sets, I coined new words. Sometimes foreign terms are impossible to adequately translate from one language to another. Using English words that only partly relate to the Eastern meaning distorts the translation. Review the Guide to Symbols and Terms to help clarify the language barrier before reading the text.

Many years of intrigue concerning the role that opposites play in our lives had led me to examine the *Taoist* theory of *yin* and *yang*. I equated this complementary relationship toward the opposites with *Tohei Sensei's* mind, body and *ki* concept. I named the similarity between these and the mental/physical/spiritual triad—tri-tuning. It is a way to handle the fears caused between our Western dualistic belief in the separation of mind from body and the fears often associated with spirit.

I compared the Eastern philosophical sense of *universal oneness* with the Western religious and scientific doctrines of dualistic separation of the mind and body. I envisioned, like many others before me, the advantage of merging the merits of both worlds into something greater than either.

From an observation of humanity's wide-spread arguments over *truths,* I began to recognize the similarity between a fear-ridden human fighting conscience or a slave conscience, and the term fight/flight syndrome. Without a sense of personal serenity and courage, there is a tendency to meet conflict by either fighting, fleeing or freezing—all derived from fear. A sense of *flow* is created by meeting daily challenges with *Tohei Sensei's* "mind/body coordination with *ki*" approach, or what I have translated as the tri-tuning of mind, body and spirit. Tri-tuning extends the options of fight or flight or freeze—to the synergy of a mind/body/spirit—*flow.*

We are living amid the aftermath of eons of human thought and actions. We do not know exactly what transpired in prehistory that made humans the world's most dreaded predators—feared by each other and all life existing on earth. We have exceeded the limits of hierarchical brutality practiced among the lower kingdoms that inhabit our planet. The human race has warred over territorial control and boundaries with unmerciful maiming and killing.

Historically, our cultures have consisted of hierarchically governed groups consisting of leaders and followers, lords and subjects, masters and slaves with reigning titles such as monarch, ruler and sovereign. The present wave of pro-democracy began when, in 1776, the American patriots attempted to resurrect a republic patterned after that of ancient Greece. The successful establishment of a democratic government, now taken for granted by so many, was predicted to be impossible by the Europeans of that day.

The possibility for a democratic world of the future, is being fueled by the increasing demand for individual freedom and by the spread of technology and education. The age-old patterns of dictatorial kings with absolute authority over their subjects are crumbling into inevitable chaos among citizens who have little experience in coping with the freedoms that they are gaining.

The advantages of both democracy and technology inevitably create their opposites. Neither a national republic nor a world democracy can endure without governing representatives who are reliably honest, and citizens who are responsible and self-reliant.

It is not the extent of technology and education associated with democracies that will determine their success or downfall. If we do not create a balance between technology and Nature's universal laws, we will self-destruct. If, through technology, we continue the attempt to make Nature our slave, both will be lost. A complementary approach to the two provides hope.

Although we have not achieved absolute democracy, even limited forms of representation will help eliminate the age-old pattern of dictatorial lords with absolute authority over their stifled subjects. Pure democracy will not be possible so long as humans live by a fighting conscience versus a slave conscience. This pattern needs replacement by commendable and appropriate human interaction.

I have termed this possibility a *triality conscience*; a mind, body and spiritual synergy of good will that can lift humanity above the flaws of injustice—and toward universal integrity. The goal of tri-tuning with a triality conscience is to enjoy life's journey as a challenge, rather than through habitual fear.

To convey this supposition, Chapter One of Part I explains the use of spirit-energy and its potential in everyday life from a Western interpretation, without the confusion of foreign words. Chapter Two is a background account of spirit-energy or *ki*, from an Eastern view and interpretation. Chapter Three includes my own insights concerning a complementary view of the paradox of opposites through a blending of Eastern and Western thought. Chapter Four contains a series of examples of professional programs that relate to this same trend of thought among Easterners and Westerners. Unusual experiences of bravery by ordinary people are also included.

In Part II, words or subjects touched on in Part I are elaborated upon to further explain their particular usage in the context of this book.

Part III contains inspirational motivation for betterment of the human condition at present and in the future, as well as examples of human integrity inherited from the past.

A glossary, giving background definitions of foreign words, has been added to help clarify unfamiliar Eastern philosophies and practices.

The instructions in this publication do not completely follow *Ki* Society training. My *Ki Wellness* tri-tuning program is based on a compilation of *Ki Development* training as well as other Eastern and Western practices. While many examples are included for applying the concept of tri-tuning, the main thrust is freedom of choice. By personal decision, each reader can develop his or her own beneficial ways to use this information in everyday life.

PART I

What is Tri-tuning?

*"**Tri-tuning** is the sense-of-being that those who live beyond fear have experienced throughout the ages."*
The Author

Reminder: To gain a better understanding of foreign and newly coined words, read the Guide to Symbols and Terms (pg. ix) before reading the text.

The mind is the pathfinder for the human brain.
Both are fueled by the human spirit—
A trilogy of God-given energy.

Betty Neff Dickens

CHAPTER ONE

Three-dimensional Living

> "The thing that numbs the heart is this:
> that men cannot devise
> Some scheme of life to banish fear
> That lurks in most men's eyes."
> James Norman Hall

A Look at Fear

> "The experience of overcoming fear
> is extraordinarily delightful."
> Bertrand Arthur William Russell

FEAR CAN BE THE ULTIMATE four-letter word—or a godsend. When the warning benefits provided by fear are misused, they become the underlying causes of such fear-filled conditions as anger, anxiety, stress, phobia and chronic worry. Vital energy is wasted.

We attempt to disguise our fears by the many masks we wear. When **tri-tuned**—a state of mind, body and spirit connection—we tune-in to both our fears and to the solutions that will help us *live beyond fear*. In this state-of-being, fear serves its intended purpose; an internal alarm system that alerts us to danger.

Our useless hidden fears can be detected through simple muscle testing. To her amazement, Amy passed the **tri-tuning** test when she was told to think a pleasant thought. During the prior testing, when I had instructed her to think of something fearful, she was easily moved off balance. This weakness indicated that she was not mind/body focused. Amy was both puzzled and elated that her thoughts could determine the strength or weakness of her body.

Mike volunteered for the next class demonstration. He was a pushover when tested with his shoulders raised. The body language of shrugged shoulders indicates insecurity and instability. When re-tested after releasing the shoulder shrug, Mike remained steady and balanced.

After each demonstration, pairs of students practice simple muscle-testing techniques to detect each other's reaction to stressed, limp and stable composure. They learn quickly to detect whether or not the one being tested is responding from a **tri-tuned** state-of-being.

To validate again the extent that we are affected by our conscious and subconscious fears, I asked John to walk past me. As he went by, I put out my arm and stopped him with very little effort.

"Walk by me again and resist my stopping you," I said.

Again I stopped him, but it took more effort. "Now choose a stopping place and focus on that destination while you walk by me again." This time I could not stop him.

In the first instance, John displayed no concern about the outcome, relying completely on my instructions. During the second test there was physical stress and mental concern about possible failure to meet his goal. John was determined to win, but harbored subtle *fear* that he might lose. In the third testing, he was aware that I would attempt to stop him, but John's attention was focused beyond that fear—upon his destination.

Whether we anticipate a situation fearfully or advance beyond fear, depends on how we perceive the situation and how we react. On the third attempt John had **tri-tuned**, a word I coined to define *our natural ability to coordinate mind, body and spirit with focused intent.*

In Western terms, when someone is clumsy we say that they are uncoordinated. When we are uncoordinated, the body and mind are not in sync. When we act with ill intent, consciously or subconsciously, we ignore our potential for tri-tuning. We resort to some form of fear. The first demonstration revealed Amy's attitude and intent. Mike's shoulder tension was a physical reaction. John showed a mental response.

The triad of **tri-tuning** is a three-dimensional tuning-in to the harmony of the cosmos. We "tune into" a third dimension by integrating not only the *mind* and *body,* but *spiritual* intent as well. You will come to understand and enjoy this integrating concept as you read and learn by participating in the various demonstrations.

Living beyond fear does not mean that we erase the word *fear* from our vocabulary or from our minds. Tri-tuning balances danger and opportunity. It is a way to benefit from fear, rather than fighting it or becoming its slave. It isn't the fear itself, but how we handle our fears, that makes the difference.

When we are afraid that we cannot handle a situation, fear is our body's way of rejecting the mind's demand for perfection. Conflict takes over when the mind and body are out of tune. The fear might be caused by the fright of giving a speech, the first attempt at bungie jumping or from an unconscious memory stemming from past failures or abuse.

When mind and body are in harmony, we are automatically synergized rhythmically with cosmic spiritual energy. Using the psychology term, we are *transpersonalized*—mind, body and spirit—to a higher level of awareness. Instead of ordering, the mind will lead the body in a united manner. Through correct practice, using this sense of unified *attunement,* we can learn to achieve anything more easily.

We experience fear when we become involved in horrifying events such as terrorism, brutal physical attacks or natural disasters. Fear sends our hearts racing, provokes terror and creates pain. Fear can send us into a state of shock or possibly result in death.

We are less likely to recognize the fact that fear is the source of such problems as chronic worry, low self-esteem and needless stress. We overlook the link between these low-key fears and such devastating habits as anger, hate, pride, defensiveness, jealousy and abuse. All of these are grounded in and result from fear.

Most of these underlying fears are created and fed by unfortunate social rules, unduly controlling family traits and undesirable personal habits. Recognized or unrecognized, unnecessary fears gnaw away at our mental and physical well-being. If not corrected, they are perpetuated from generation to generation.

Each of us harbors unnecessary fear. This book was born out of the mini-fears I faced during my studies in Japan. Fear's challenges continued to loom during my trials of adapting these teachings in a manner that could be readily understood from a Western perspective. My attempt to write about what I had learned through the experience of teaching, lured more dragons out of their long-time residency in my psyche.

From the other end of the spectrum, without a sense of fear we might walk off cliffs, feeling no sense of danger. We might even think we can fly. How we deal with real or imagined fear, largely determines the results of our everyday living.

Although tri-tuning may seem strange at first, its value will soon become clear. It is a practical way to uncover, examine and attempt to remedy our chronic fears. As we proceed and experience this simple, subtle, yet effective method, its purpose and benefits will be better understood. Tri-tuning is a means of turning conflict into harmony and fear into caring.

Tri-tuning is a simultaneous blend of mind and body awareness with vital life energy. Like a 3-way light bulb, dim creates light and medium creates more light. The full spectrum of illumination requires all three levels of intensity—just as it takes the combination of mind, body and spirit to tri-tune.

Chapter One reflects the results of my own development of thought and the conclusions I drew from training, teaching and personal experience. It is presented from a Western perspective. Chapter Two will trace the Eastern sources, evolution, practices and explanations of this knowledge from an Eastern way of thinking.

Complementing the Opposites

> *"The way I see it,*
> *if you want the rainbow,*
> *you gotta' put up with the rain."*
> Dolly Parton

The lure of our personal quests can propel us beyond the fear of failure or censure. My quest for better understanding of Eastern and Western philosophies motivated me to examine fear and its relationship in the world of opposites.

We live in a world of opposites, but we do not have to be victims of either side of a situation. All too often we allow the conflict of "good versus bad" to become chronic fear, rather than using both as stepping stones toward a better future. What is appropriate in one situation can be untimely in a different setting. What is good for one person or group may prove to be disastrous for another.

All of us can recall situations when a seemingly good course of action ultimately proved to be disastrous or when a regretted action eventually ended as the best choice after all. When we learn to respect and complement the opposites instead of fighting them, we will recognize the possibilities and usefulness existing on both sides of any situation. Proverbial sayings, such as "it takes sun and rain to make a rainbow" or "when you're dealt lemons, make lemonade," illustrate this point. We do not have to destroy one side of these opposites to enjoy the other.

Complementing the opposites does not mean that we become passive, allowing others to take advantage of us. It also does not mean taking over or demanding undue submission to our control. These opposite reactions reduce us to a slave mentality or to a fighting mentality. Rather, when we honestly examine both sides and listen to our intuition, it becomes easier to act responsibly.

A complementary view of the opposites does not mean that we submit to mediocrity or stay on the fence of indecision. It also does not mean that we cannot disagree with an opposite view. Complementing the opposites is a posture that lifts us above petty arguments and defensiveness–to understandings, negotiations and solutions that benefit both sides.

An ancient Eastern story about an old man, his son and their horse, serves to explain how we can complement the opposites.

> The son used the horse to till the land while his father planted and cared for the crops. Together they made a modest living for their families.
> One day the horse ran away and could not be found. Everyone in the small village became alarmed. They asked the old man, "What will you do? You cannot work the land and feed your families without a horse. This is terrible."
> "Maybe so, maybe not," said the old man, as he continued his work.
> A few days later the stallion returned with a young mare by his side. The people in the village rejoiced. "Isn't it wonderful! Now you can raise twice as many crops and soon you will have a colt. You will be rich."

The old man answered simply, "Maybe so, maybe not."

Early the following morning when the son tried to break-in the mare, she threw him and his leg was broken.

The villagers moaned, "You are worse off than ever. Your son cannot work, you are too old to do all of the work and now you have more mouths to feed. It's your son's fault. He never broke in a horse before. You should punish him for being so foolish."

The old man muttered, "Maybe so, maybe not."

The next day, government officials came through the village conscripting young men for military service. The son was left behind because of his broken leg.

This story could go on and on, like the unforeseen to-morrows of our lives. Exactly where any event in our lives will lead us is unpredictable. We are easily hypnotized by the extreme pendulum swings of public opinion. Unwittingly, we can become slaves in bondage to the see-saw of ups and downs in our lives.

Our underlying fears are caused by depressing memories from the past, anxiety about the future and our chronic grumblings concerning the present. Such fears sap our energy and make us ill. We defend ourselves by desperately attacking or slinking away in fear, wasting even more valuable energy.

Like the villagers, we tend to see events either from a wonderful or dismal point of view. We fail to grasp opportunities that sprout from the terrible. We close our eyes to future adverse changes seeded by the wonderful. Even while gloating over rosy predictions, we are secretly haunted by the fear of losing a precious moment or a special relationship—only to find that our fears become self-fulfilling prophesies. If we could live life with a sense of challenge and adventure, our fears would be replaced by courage.

By taking life in stride, the old man took advantage of the tides of ebb and flow instead of fighting the waves. He rode the ups and downs of everyday stress. He ignored the frustrated villagers, caught up in fighting the pendulum swings of opposite views. He dealt with the opposites by considering the possibilities on both sides, instead of fighting them.

He did not feel compelled to side with one extreme conclusion while opposing the other. He evaded over-confident speculation, but did not waste time feeling sorry for himself. He was neither slave nor fighter; he lived beyond mundane fear.

Suggestion: Reflect on your feelings about the various roles you play in life. List the habits that make you feel uncomfortable and fearful. List replacement habits that would ease your fears. Balance these lists by making a third list; the habits you are thankful that you have improved upon during your lifetime.

Tri-tuning

> *"As body, mind and spirit weave together, we find ourselves rediscovering knowledge that's as old as humanity."*
> Joy Gardner, *Colors and Crystals*

Tri-tuning is a heightened sense of awareness that is more easily experienced than explained. When learning anything from a book, however, ample explanation is necessary to help the reader grasp the instructions and the value of experience.

Tri-tuning is not only a mind-set; it is using the sense-of-being that John felt when he set his intentions beyond fear. (*Refer* to page 2.) We become stable and balanced when we are mind and body coordinated by simultaneous *thinking and feeling*. After following the instructions and explanations for tri-tuning, you will be able to experience its benefits in the workplace, at home or during any activity.

Tri-tuning is a focused coexistence of the opposites with appropriate intent. It is a natural reward that occurs when we complement the opposites. We tri-tune naturally and easily when we use our talents and skills to perform our daily routine with a sense of flow.

In this writing, "normal" refers to contemporary beliefs and culturally accepted norms. "Natural" means the action and results of tri-tuning. It goes beyond the shackles of fear by allowing the fusion of mind and body to react naturally with vital life energy. (*See* Illustration.#1.)

Tri-tuning is useful when we think, feel or act. It is a three-way involvement between mind, body and the spirit of harmonic cosmic

Illus. #1

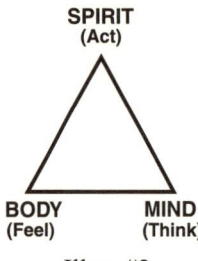

Illus. #2

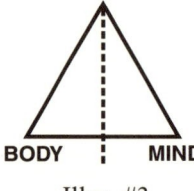

Illus. #3

energy. We can experience tri-tuning physically, mentally and in accordance with our individual moral and spiritual pathways. (*See* Illus.#2.)

A tricycle analogy helps beginners grasp the three-way combination required for tri-tuning. The two rear wheels represent the balance of mind and body, while the third (front) wheel represents intention and action. The three create balanced performance. Using only the body and intent, or just the mind and intention, is like the hypotenuse of a triangle. Only half the triangle of mind/body and intention, or cosmic energy, is utilized. (*See* Illus. #3.)

Riding a bicycle is natural tri-tuning. If we aren't balanced with mind/body coordination and motivation, fear takes the place of the missing element of the triangle. We become either too stiff and scared, or too limp and afraid. Our energy is wasted and the bicycle falls to one side or the other.

I experienced this lesson as a child, during my first attempt at riding a bicycle. I panicked when it was time to stop and get off. I fell sidewise into a rambler rosebush!

When we practice riding a bicycle until it becomes an ingrained habit, the tri-tuning becomes second nature. Any way we choose to tri-tune should be practiced until it becomes a subconscious reaction. Otherwise, we revert back to our usual stressed or aimless habits. The chief requirement to become skilled at anything holds true with tri-tuning: practice, practice, PRACTICE—with one added requirement—be certain it is being practiced correctly.

Since mind/body unity with intent is a natural state, tri-tuning may occur unexpectedly. When I returned from my training in Japan, I demonstrated a technique for Jane, a friend who asked what I had studied. Shortly thereafter, she endured a CT Scan medical test. When asked whether she was claustrophobic, Jane looked at the large drum and assumed that there would be plenty of open space. Once inside, however, she opened her eyes and realized her nose was four inches from the top of the tube. She panicked.

Without realizing why, Jane suddenly recalled the technique I had shown her. She connected her index fingers and thumbs of each hand and concentrated on them. Slowly her heart palpitations began to ease. She relaxed by deep breathing out and in until the test ended. Jane had tri-tuned by coordinating her mind and body while concentrating beyond her fears.

While tri-tuning, nothing is eliminated, not even fear. Rather than being overwhelmed by fear, we balance caution and courage in perspective with the situation. Awareness of the problem is essential, but the emphasis is put on a solution.

Suggestion: Make a list of the ways you would like to use tri-tuning to ease your fears. If you do not already keep a journal or diary, this is an ideal time to begin. By recording the desired habits, you can appreciate the progress made while proceeding through the choices of suggestions you decide to develop.

Universal Vital Energy

"Life is not a problem to be solved but a mystery to be lived."
M. Scott Peck

Tri-tuning lets us reside in natural *attunement* with ourselves and our surroundings. In addition to mind/body coordination, tri-tuning requires vital life energy. This energy has already been referred to as focused intent, action, spirit and concentration.

The entire universe is made of an elusive, rather indescribable, unlimited vital energy. It shifts back and forth—forever interchanging itself between motion and matter. It exists in both positive and negative forms. Electricity is an example of this energy, as well as magnetic fields and the energy aura that exists around every object or form.

What we call our sixth sense, along with other paranormal phenomena yet to be explained by science or religion, is an expression of this energy. It encompasses all that we can and cannot see; both the invisible cells and visible fibers of our bodily makeup. Scientists do not fully understand the source, existence or the changing forms of this elusive *it*. The study of this complex universal energy, referred to by scientists as matter and non-matter, is a frontier yet to be adequately explored and understood. Comparisons and differing interpretations from both scientific and religious points of view, make it even more complicated and complex.

The English words *spirit* and *energy* come closest to describing the infinite fullness of this all-encompassing mystery. Neither the word spirit nor energy, alone, is an adequate means of expressing this broad perception of energy. Combining the words spirit and energy into a new word, **spirergy** (pronounced spear-ergy) helps to explain this vital flow. This combination can help reconcile religion and science with compatible understanding. **Spirergy** is the dimension beyond the connection of mind and body that Westerners are just beginning to understand. It is another way to visualize spirit. (*See* Illus. #4.)

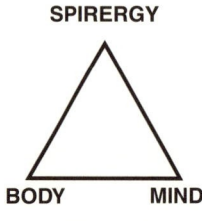

Illus. #4

We are made of, and are a part of, this spirit-energy whether we believe it to be created by a Living God or through any other explanation. Whatever we believe or do not believe, our actions can be improved upon by utilizing this vital spirit-energy, or spirergy, in a three-fold unity with mind/body coordination.

Suggestion: Summarize what the words energy and spirit mean to you. Do your definitions relate to spirergy? Its meaning in this text will be demonstrated and explained further as we proceed.

Tri-tune Your Posture

> *"Posture isn't just about appearance*
> *It's an expression of an underlying*
> *functional quality."*
> Neal Schapero

You may choose to practice the tri-tuning techniques as you read or you can carry out the instructions later. We will begin with simple, but important, basic tri-tuning.

Observe Your Posture

1. **Stand in your normal stance.** Mentally observe yourself. How do you feel?
2. **Now stand in erect posture and look straight ahead.** Feel the subtle differences between the first and second position.

Note an added feeling of confidence that the improved posture provides. If you did not feel better, it was because your body is habitually accustomed to a slouched position or you may have held your stomach in. Both of these habits put the body into a state of stress. Release the abdomen and straighten your shoulders to a comfortable position. This will flatten the stomach somewhat, depending on your particular physique. More importantly, when the shoulder position is comfortably lowered, your body will not be stressed.

This natural posture promotes you to a special state-of-being—tri-tuning. You naturally *think and feel* at the same time when you become aware of and correct your posture. Your mind and body are in tune with each other. You have a simultaneous sense of alertness and calmness.

In this state we are focused and primed to perform with appropriate action. Our chronic fears, doubts and uncertainties diminish. We haven't done anything magically different but we feel surprisingly energized when we are tri-tuned.

Switch back and forth between these two postures: first your normal stance and then erect posture. Which is the easier way to face the day? Naturally erect posture may not produce an earthshaking difference. However, there is a sense of serenity and well-being that will develop more fully with awareness and practice.

Our normal stance either tends to be slouched, lackadaisical, nonchalant, collapsed or—we are tense and stressed. We revert to these uncoordinated and energy-wasting postures much of the time. Natural posture is automatic tri-tuning that provides a subtle, but special, sense of clarity and confidence. Even though you already have relatively good posture, you will recognize the difference between normal and tri-tuned posture.

Do not confuse naturally erect posture with an exaggerated or military stance. For the sake of comparison, stand with rigid posture (belly in, shoulders back) and observe how you feel. This is a military stance.

Now repeat the natural posture. Sense the added balance and stability. It's an extra-good feeling that can be savored often with awareness and practice. We underestimate the value of erect posture in ways over and above good physique. In contrast, however, a chronically frozen or stooped posture does not prevent us from experiencing this difference when coordinating mind and body. An awareness of how to improve each of our own postures, through tri-tuning, can help to improve the worst of postures.

Logically we think of rigid muscular action as the best means of physically defending ourselves. Now notice the increased stress when you stand once again in rigid posture. The military teaches "attention" and "at ease" postures, both of which provide group control for eliciting trained responses to specific orders. This training serves well in special group situations where rigid conformity is essential. We are aiming toward individual everyday confidence and stability.

Another type of rigid posture results from chronic shrugging of our shoulders. Without realizing it, many of us habitually lift our shoulders when we are stressed.

Shrugging of the Shoulders

1. **Lift your shoulders and walk a few steps.**
2. **Now walk with natural posture for a few steps.**
3. **Feel the difference.**

The term "uptight" well describes "shoulder shrug" problems and their detrimental results. This test was demonstrated with Mike.(*Refer* to page 1.)

When I ask students how they have tri-tuned since the last class, often one will say that it's easier to take the lid off a jar when tri-tuned. We tend to raise the shoulders when we perform tasks with our hands. This weakens the entire body. When the body is weak, we use tension to compensate, creating a cycle of chronic stress. We lift our shoulders when stressed; stress, in turn, causes our shoulders to rise.

Three-Dimensional Living ▲ 13

Shrug your shoulders and peel something, a potato or a stick. Release the shoulders and repeat the task. Observe what happens. Tension makes the task more difficult and saps energy.

If you automatically shrug or tense your shoulders, you may be walking around in habitual stress much of the time. Become aware of your shoulder position as you go about your daily routine. If you are a chronic shrugger, practice releasing your shoulders to natural posture.

Set a timer. When it rings, observe whether you feel mentally or physically stressed. Are you standing in normal or natural posture? There is a very subtle, yet profound difference between normal and natural posture. It goes beyond our bodily physique and reaches into our attitudes and reactions. Posture is a form of body language that reflects what we think and feel. Natural posture incites our best responses.

Suggestion: Be aware of your posture as you go about your daily routine. Practice natural posture and record the difference it makes in your life. When engaged in any activity, notice whether your shoulders are raised or natural. Practice releasing shoulder stress.

Getting Beyond Fear

"Fear is the seed of every worry."
Author unknown

Mental worry triggers a rigid body. If we are rigid when thinking, feeling or performing in any way, we react defensively. If we are limp, we react through insecurity. Both are the result of some form of fear. When we react rigidly, we are alert, but not calm. As we relax, we become limp or collapsed. We are calm but we lack alertness. A calm mind is like the smooth surface of a lake. It remains smooth, despite undercurrents. A frustrated mind resembles choppy water.

The combination of calm-alertness gives us a clarity of mind *and* an alert body. We are aware of danger, but our fears are put in perspective. Mental clarity automatically helps us make quicker and better choices in any situation. Visualize a triangle with *alert* at the right corner, *calm* at the left corner and *calm-alertness* at the top. (*See* Illus. #5.)

Illus. #5

This combination enables us to perform with the extraordinary euphoria that we feel when everything is in sync. We are complementing the opposites with dynamic results that go beyond fear. All activities through which we flow smoothly and skillfully are natural tri-tuning. This three-way focus of mind/body coordination with universal spirit-energy, or spirergy, adds vitality and balance to our lives.

A student aptly labeled this "gentle strength," as opposed to brute strength. The opposite of brute strength, using no strength at all, is a limp, relaxed or collapsed state. Gentle strength lends a balance between mind, body and spirit that transforms us beyond fear.

When we are tense, we are often instructed to "relax." This is intended to bring us into balance. Instead, we lose the alertness we had when we were tense. What we need is the balance of tension and relaxation that creates tri-tuning.

An example of this accomplishment is the strength employed by an apparently sleeping cat, when it suddenly springs upon an escaping mouse. Animals still use this natural response that our ancestors lost when they became top-heavy with logical reasoning. With awareness and practice, we can regain this lost art without sacrificing reasoning. We can fuse logic with our latent instincts to form incredible intuitiveness. To visualize this sense-of-being as a triangle, think of logic on the right, instinct on the left and intuition at the top. (See Illus. #6.)

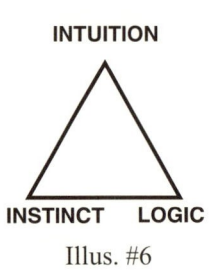

Illus. #6

Babies tri-tune naturally to support their weight while grasping your fingers, even when you lift or swing them gently back and forth. Try prying a baby's fist open when it chooses not to cooperate. This is only one example of the instinctive tri-tuning with which we are born. Babies lose most of this natural ability, little by little, as they subconsciously mimic our fear-filled reasoning. Their naturally cautious instincts concerning fear are replaced with uncoordinated fear.

If we depend on our thinking only, without attention to body actions, we become stressed with the fear of failure. When we depend upon brute bodily strength alone, we are fearful of being overpowered. Tri-tuning permits us to become focused, centered and united with the flow of the universe that propels us beyond fear.

After we learn the *feel* of tri-tuning, we can retrieve, at will, that sense-of-being. Focus at the center of your being. Imagine yourself as the figure in the Leonardo da Vinci drawing of the encircled human figure. The center would be somewhere in your lower abdomen. (*See* illus. # 7.)

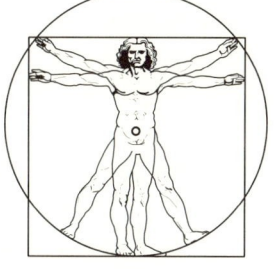

Illus. #7

When your mind is focused naturally at your center, it is coordinated with your body. You *think and feel simultaneously.* Now, release your body weight to gravity. Relax, but do not hunch. Carry out your intended thoughts or actions.

Learning to Tri-tune

1. **Be aware of your mind and body.**
2. **Focus at your center.**
3. **Release your body weight to gravity.**
4. **Use spirergy to accomplish your objective.**

Enjoy the euphoria of the moment and allow yourself to feel as good as you can imagine. Retrieve this *gentle strength* when you find yourself "uptight."

If you felt tense, it was because you *tried* too hard to *make* it happen. Instead, let go of fear and *let* it happen; *allow* peace of mind. When you practice tri-tuning, avoid trying to make it happen. Focus on letting and allowing it to happen. *Trying* wastes energy; *allowing* utilizes energy.

Repeat the above instructions; enjoy letting it happen. To practice the next exercise, have someone read the instructions for you while you visualize them with eyes closed.

Enjoy the Experience of Tri-tuning

1. **Tri-tune and imagine this pleasant feeling permeating your entire being.** Feel and remember the euphoria of this moment. Practice until it becomes an immediate and natural reaction.
2. **Retain this pleasant feeling while changing your thoughts to some worrisome problem.** The euphoria has, no doubt, vanished.
3. **Continue to worry with a tensed body.** It's very tiring.
4. **With muscles still taut, again coordinate mind and body.** You probably had an overwhelming desire to release the tension. If you released it and tri-tuned, you overcame the stress naturally.
5. **Now imagine yourself limp with fear, experiencing a physical or verbal attack and wishing for a way out of the situation.** This may be an actual fearful abuse that you often experience.
6. **Now retrieve your tri-tuning and ease the fear.**

This is a more detailed version of Amy's test. (*Refer* to page 1.) First, she had envisioned a fearful thought, then a happy one.

When tri-tuning is practiced to the point that you become familiar with that feeling, the tri-tuning sense-of-being can be retrieved at any time. When we find ourselves in a defensive state-of-mind, we have forgotten to tri-tune. It's easy to see why chronic fears cause us to succumb to defensiveness and fighting. When we *tune-in* with tri-tuning, we do not have to "tune out" the world.

Suggestion: List your chronic fears and review how you react to them. Practice tri-tuning as a means of replacing them with desired habits. Do not become discouraged if your old habits recur when you forget to tri-tune. You may not have practiced enough to permanently replace the old habit. List the fears that you have overcome during your lifetime and how you managed those accomplishments.

Student Experiences

"The rain in our lives helps us grow."
Author unknown

Students have related various ways that tri-tuning has helped them through difficult times.

Dolores, whose husband was elderly and quite demanding, said, "I don't know how I managed before I learned to tri-tune." She was learning to help her husband without being devastated by his anxieties and unnecessary demands for her attention.

Walter had the opposite situation. His wife was dying of cancer, and he couldn't imagine life without her. She had always done everything for him. "I practice tri-tuning and it does help, but I'm going to need it a lot more." Walter tri-tuned to ease his grief and to get the most out of each moment with his wife. It also helped him concentrate on learning how to take care of himself.

Barbara tri-tuned before calling her mother about an issue she was sure would provoke an argument. "I couldn't believe it. We had a good conversation. I tri-tuned my thoughts the whole time. I'm convinced that the kind of energy we send out will be received, even at great distances." She had acknowledged her mother's viewpoint while retaining her own independence.

This testimonial led to discussion about how our thoughts are transmitted endlessly. Prayers and meditative thoughts that are directed to specific distant situations are examples of natural tri-tuning.

Suggestion: Everyone has habits they would like to change and situations they would like to meet in less threatening ways. In the beginning, choose simple inclinations you want to replace. Tackle your mental tapes of long-standing and major undesirable habits later, as you progress.

Observe and record how often you think about tri-tuning. List the ways you recall having tri-tuned naturally before you had heard of the word tri-tuning. Your list will likely include special talents or hobbies such as playing an instrument, a sport or any art form. Add and compare a list of things that are very difficult for you to achieve. Practice replacing these fears through tri-tuning.

Tri-tune with a Partner

> *"True strength is very delicate."*
> Louise Nevelson

There are ways of testing to determine whether we are tri-tuned. Now that you have a general idea of how to tri-tune, let's experience the testing. All tri-tuning can be tested by a partner who places his or her flattened fingers on your upper chest between the neck and shoulder and presses gently. (*See* Illus. # 8.)

Illus. #8

For inexperienced or older students, I suggest that the tester holds his or her free hand near the testee's back. This will lend support in case the partner loses balance to the extent of possibly falling.

This testing must *not* be done with a jerk or shove. Instead, the tester should press just enough to observe the testee's balance and stability. Both partners can easily detect the degree of tri-tuning that is being achieved. If the one being tested remains stable, he or she has passed the test. After some practice, you will begin to recognize when you are tri-tuned, without having to be tested.

To avoid embarrassment or physical injury, always remind a new partner that this is a test of comparative accomplishment. It is *not* a test of brute strength. You and your partner are a team, intent on helping each other, rather than contestants in competition. Only after you practice and develop tri-tuning as a subconscious reaction, can you deal with severe brute strength. The question is: Am I more stable when I react with muscle power (uptight with tension), or when I am tri-tuned? You will appreciate the advantages of tri-tuning when you can recognize this difference.

Ask your partner to test your stability in all three forms of posture: stressed, limp and natural. Exchange roles and test your partner. Discuss your thoughts, feelings and reactions before proceeding to the next tri-tuning skill.

Natural Tri-tuning with a Partner

To experience how we tri-tune naturally, ask your partner to test you.
1. **Raise your arm in front of you to shoulder level, palm down, and resist your partner's attempt to push your arm down.**
2. **Your partner will place his/her hand on your arm just above the wrist and will push down only enough to test.** More than likely your arm went down or your body tilted at least to some degree. The extent will depend on the difference in your physical strengths.
3. **Again, raise your arm to shoulder height.** This time point toward, and concentrate upon, an object some distance in front of you. Ask your partner to test again with the same amount of pressure. If you maintained your concentration, you both experienced your increased stability.
4. **Retest, keeping your mind on the fact that your partner might push your arm down.** Most likely you were unable to resist. You became stressed with the fear that your partner might succeed.

Both stress and tension are necessary, but they need the balance of calmness. Alone, either stress or calm leads to and results in a form of fear. Calmness alone is immobility. Tension and calmness together equal *gentle strength*. Exchange places and discuss your experiences.

Shoulder-shrugging Test

Now experience another test of physical balance:
1. **Ask your partner to shrug his/her shoulders and hold that position.** Test by placing your flattened hand on his/her upper chest between the shoulder and neck. Press just enough to test for stability. No doubt he/she failed to stay balanced.

2. **If he/she leans forward to resist, test with your other hand from the back and he/she will tend to fall forward.** You can see for yourselves that raised shoulders cause tension, which imbalances the whole body.
3. **Tell your partner to stand with natural posture.** Again, test front and then back. What a difference! Your partner remained stable if he/she concentrated on natural posture.
4. **Change roles and have your partner do the testing.** Discuss situations that cause each of you to shrug and why these actions weaken the body.

Sometimes we habitually perform our daily routines with shrugged shoulders, which leads to chronic neck problems. When we hold telephones with our head and shoulder or carry shoulder bags, we put our bodies in a stress mode. It is little wonder that our necks ache and we get so tired.

Doctors call this shopping-mall syndrome. If you are not in a dangerous area, subject to purse snatching, put the shoulder strap over your head onto the opposite shoulder and across the chest.

When we shrug, our bodies are weakened by stress. When we are stressed, we tend to raise our shoulders. Any kind of fear will tend to put us into this stress mode when we are not tri-tuned. Fear is one of our most common causes of fatigue.

Suggestion: Practice these examples of the numerous tri-tuning skills that can be used to reduce unnecessary stress. How many undesirable habits have you decided to change so far by tri-tuning? List your own discoveries and experiences with tri-tuning.

The Enemy

> *"Spend less time worrying who's right, and more time deciding what's right."*
> H. Jackson Brown, Jr.,
> *Life's Little Instruction Book*

When seeking or concentrating upon a solution, we need to be aware of—but get beyond—the fears that accompany the problem. If we fight a problem, we create an *enemy*. This enemy is whatever underlying fears we associate with the problem, trouble or obstacle.

When we put our main attention on the aggressor, we are weakened. If we concentrate on a solution, we remain tri-tuned just as John did to overcome the *enemy* that he perceived. (*Refer* to page 2.)

When we rely completely on muscle power or mental stress to resist an assault, we are physically and mentally weakened by fear; an uncertainty concerning the outcome. Our thinking becomes rattled and either we rely on brute strength or we try to escape the threat. The enemy, *our own fear*, takes over.

Psychologists call this the fight/flight syndrome of stress; the animal instinct to fight or flee. Wild animals know instinctively how and when to react for their survival. Meanwhile, the animal rests and releases the stress until the next attack.

As humans, we have succumbed to habitual stress modes. We allow chronic anxieties, phobias and other extreme habits to dominate our time. There is a saying, "If you can't fight or flee, just flow." When we are in a severe state of fear we sometimes *freeze*; become immobilized instead of flowing. Tri-tuning is the ability to flow instead of any of the other three. (*See* Illus. #9.)

Illus. #9

Tri-tuning allows us to achieve the balance of thinking and feeling simultaneously. It sets the stage for easier action; to achieve our intention, goal, objective or solution. Minimize the attention you give the attacker and concentrate on your objective. Be aware of what you can do to resolve the situation. Replace fear and conflict with care, caution and alert-calmness.

Imagine an attacker coming toward you. Instead of preparing to either fight or flee, surprise him or her by pivoting to the side just as he or she is about to strike. You have flowed with the attack. In a dire situation, you might even trip him/her or give a push as your opponent's momentum carries him/her past you. Hopefully this will give you more time to escape in a physically threatening situation.

By tri-tuning ourselves, we automatically become one with the vibrational flow of the cosmos or what we are calling spirergy. When we attune ourselves with this flow, life becomes easier. *When we flow, we glow!*

The problem we face is how to maintain or retrieve tri-tuning. Imagine that you have stumbled and are falling. Think of retrieving your tri-tuning and you may be able to regain your balance or fall without injury.

A student was leery of participating in a rolling exercise because of her back problem. My suggestion was: close your eyes and imagine that you are rolling with the group. Later, she enthusiastically reported that she had stepped backward and stumbled over a rake lying in the grass. Before she realized what happened, she had sat down, rolled back and sat up, just as she had imaged in class.

Practicing or thinking about tri-tuning is similar to a fire drill. If the information is needed later, our subconscious minds will recall the solution. When our normal reaction to either fight or flee takes over before we remember to tri-tune, it is not too late to retrieve our gentle strength. By conscious intent, we can coordinate mind and body to retrieve a state of tri-tuning.

Even when tri-tuning, patience and practice are required to permanently replace old fearful habits. Those mental tapes have become almost indelibly fixed in our minds. I say almost, because we can change anything if we apply enough thought, feeling and active practice to achieve our goals.

Suggestion: List the unnecessary fears that you have allowed to escalate into the chronic habits that prevent your achieving what you would like to accomplish. Choose one at a time and replace your dragons of fear with appropriate habits. Again, encourage your self-esteem by listing and appreciating what you have already accomplished.

A Fighting Conscience, a Slave Conscience or a Triality Conscience

"Man's mind, not his master, makes him slave."
Robert Johnson

We can easily become slaves to our fears. Often we compensate by fighting the fear, blaming someone else or holding "pity parties" to nurse our "why me?" frustrations.

When we respond through anger or vengeance, we expose our fighting conscience. When we exhibit weakness or self-pity, we reflect our slave conscience. If the fact that you disagree with some of the information in this book compels you to consider it all rubbish, you are reacting through a fighting conscience. If you feel obligated to agree with every point in order to benefit from this information, you convey a slave conscience. Tri-tuning with a triality conscience leads you to draw your own conclusions through self-reliance and personal integrity.

Humankind has wallowed in the inevitable results that come from see-sawing between a fighting conscience and a slave conscience. Either of these extreme reactions will enable those with power to subject the powerless to some form of slavery. Such action has been degrading in all types of slavery—to the point that some have lost their human identity.

Power and slavery are not limited to masters and their subjects. We are slaves to any unwanted or harmful habit we do not correct. We also become dictatorial lords and masters ourselves, when we control others by dishonest and unfair practices. Unwarranted treatment toward each other, or any creature, creates a monster/slave relationship. When we subject an animal, another human being or even a plant to our will, we are responsible for its survival and well-being.

Tri-tuning rewards us with what we will call a **triality** conscience; the harmony of mind, body and spirit. A triality conscience lifts us above fighting or dueling the opposites, to a sense of respect and responsibility. It creates a "serve while leading" and "lead when serving" attitude. Both leaders and followers are a *necessary* part of society. Able leaders know how to serve others, as well as give instructions. Followers with integrity, carry out only responsible and credible instructions. A triality conscience invites our deep-seated human desire to give and receive through the wholeness of integrity.

When humanity as a whole chooses to complement the opposites and practice tri-tuning, we will live by the triality conscience that many already practice. A triality sense-of-being will enable humankind to live in relative harmony instead of chronic conflict.

Some cultural traits have subjected us to habitual conflict. The compulsion to see the opposites only as duality—keeps us dueling any opposing thought or activity. Instead of enjoying competition with a triality conscience, many are drawn into the dishonesty of "win at all cost." Tennis champion Martina Navratilova once remarked, "The moment of victory is too short to live for that and nothing else."

Fortunately, many competitors still carry the torch of fair play through an old-fashioned concept called sportsmanship. Radiance on the faces of Olympic athletes who testify that camaraderie is an essential part of the games, exemplifies the essence of tri-tuning. Fair-mindedness balances the opposites with a win-win triality conscience.

*Suggestion: List ways you now respond through a **triality** conscience. Sometimes we get so caught up in the task of self-improvement that we forget to be happy about what we have already accomplished. Add a list of new habits you would like to form and enjoy the practice.*

How to Tri-tune Your Life for Easier Living

> *"The unexamined life is not worth living. It is time to reevaluate your past as a guide to your new, fresh future."*
> — Socrates

Before I further explain the evolution of thought that led me to formulate such new words as **tri-tune**, **triality**, and **spirergy**, I want you to experience more of their benefits. The usefulness of this book as a means of self-help, depends upon the practice of tri-tuning to develop a triality conscience. As we proceed to learn more about its unlimited usefulness in our daily lives, I will suggest various ways that you can become familiar with the *feel* or *sense* of tri-tuning.

Three-Dimensional Living ▲ 25

The explanations and tri-tuning skills may seem simplistic and redundant but the results are extraordinary. Whether you are practicing the tri-tuning skills as you read this book or plan to review and practice them later, give some thought to the instructions. Utilize them as you go about your daily activities. If you are keeping a journal, continue adding your experiences after you have completed the book. You will be surprised by the ways in which tri-tuning will help you ease through each day.

Even if you limit your practice to improved posture, you will benefit yourself and everyone around you. Using the basic formula of tri-tuning in the manner best suited to your needs is more important than following these specific examples.

When observing or experiencing a situation from both sides, you may realize some of your own frailties. Do not become disappointed or feel guilty about your actions. It can be disheartening to recognize undesirable habits that we have unconsciously practiced for years. One function of the human ego is to protect us from awareness of our shortcomings. With the courage provided by tri-tuning, we can untangle our webs of conflict one strand at a time. In the long run, this practice will prove to be better than hiding behind an ego mask to cover up underlying fears.

After any regrettable thought or action, mentally reenact the scene. Visualize your actions happening the way you wish that you had performed. In so doing, you will imprint the desired reaction onto your brain. Corrected enough times through tri-tuning, it will become a new and more acceptable habit. Do not blame yourself if it takes more time than you expected to replace an unwanted habit.

A tennis instructor explained a technique for mentally dealing with losing shots. He said that instead of faulting yourself about a misplay, quickly replay the shot in your mind. *See* the ball land where you had intended. Whether in our golf game, our routine activities or in the workplace, when we recall this idea we can use it to replace our everyday shortcomings.

To practice a visual use of tri-tuning, think of some facet in your life that elicits fear and procrastination. For example:

> June had developed such a fear of flying that she could not board a plane without the aid of tranquilizers or alcohol. She had experienced several frightening flights, especially one in which the door flew off a military cargo plane. After practicing tri-tuning to get beyond her phobia, she succeeded in flying again with minimal fear.
>
> If she began to panic before or during a flight, she would practice tri-tuning to retrieve her triality state-of-being. She would recall how she had enjoyed flying before those fearful incidences. She thought of the advantages of fast transportation and the added time she would have for memorable experiences at her destination. Reminding herself of how useless and fear-provoking her worried thoughts were, she replaced them by reading and entering into conversations. She practiced deep breathing to help her relax.

Choose a major or even a minor fear of your own. Imagine facing this fearful situation in each of the three ways: *alert* (rigid, ready to fight); *calm* (limp, ready to flee); and then with *alert calmness* (limber, ready to flow and resolve). How did you react to each segment? Which response would help ease your problem? Alert-calmness, of course. You were able to regain confidence and self-esteem. Image these reactions in triangular forms as in the illustrations.

Can you imagine how much energy we waste when we become defensive or remain frightened? With combined alertness and calmness, we can face life from the viewpoint of solutions rather than remaining stuck in the problem. When that situation is encountered again, our subconscious minds will be more likely to recall the solution and react with ease. Each time we visualize a correct solution, the severity of fear will lessen. Practice until the desired habit automatically replaces the former habit. The balance of fear and courage gives us a new perspective.

Tri-tuning can make life easier when it is used to dispel the fear associated with any fearful situation. It can help when undergoing dental treatment or while enduring the trauma of major surgery. Tri-tuning can save energy if applied during the performance of a simple chore or something as taxing as enduring a marathon race.

Suggestion: When you are cooking in your kitchen, driving a car, working in an office or performing manual labor, become aware of ways you can use tri-tuning to decrease your waste of energy. Observe and acknowledge your unnecessary stresses and worries. Correct them by tri-tuning. Also list the ways you have already replaced some of your fearful or phobic habits by tri-tuning.

The Logic of Tri-Tuning

> *"No one cares how much you know, until they know how much you care."*
> Author unknown

Tri-tuning may be confusing when first experienced. It contradicts our normal thought patterns and our usual approach to everyday problems. As the wise man in this Oriental story advises, keep an open mind until you understand the insights behind the instructions.

> A man, seeking advice from a wise counselor, kept rambling on about what he believed and what others had advised him. The counselor began refilling the man's tea cup and continued when it overflowed.
> The man jumped up and asked, "What are you doing?"
> The counselor explained that there was no room for more advice when, like the tea cup, he was too full of his own conclusions already.
> "When you can return with an open mind, I can advise you."

I make no claim of being a wise counselor. I do, however, recommend thinking of these instructions as the three A's: Awareness, Analysis, and Application. Listen to the instructions and explanations. Analyze them and choose what is best for your self-improvement. The most important part of this advice is that you *apply,* through practice, what you have chosen.

Continue to journal your tri-tuning accomplishments. If you feel that you are not advancing as quickly as you wish, compare your former habits with recent tri-tuning successes. Move ahead from where you are at present without regrets about what you have not accomplished. Do not expect so much self-improvement that you blame or shame yourself for your failings. Visualize yourself living the role of your expectations and, sooner or later, they will come to pass.

When we overcome and live beyond our own fears, we automatically help others. There are times when controlling measures are necessary and beneficial to keep order within both group and individual situations. Done through a triality conscience, authority is more likely to be respected. When we exercise unfair control over other people—we are not tri-tuned.

Suggestion: Use the tri-tuning skills as an activity that the whole family can enjoy and appreciate. Share tri-tuning achievements with friends and co-workers. Form a discussion group to share each other's tri-tuning experiences. Use tri-tuning in any manner that will turn conflict into harmony.

Accepting Foreign Influence

> *"Man is disturbed not by things, but by his opinion of things."*
> Epictetus, Roman Philosopher

Chapter One has provided an exposure to basic Eastern philosophies without the confusion of Oriental terms. Tri-tuning can be practiced with or without the specific rituals of any custom or religion. What you have learned is a cosmic formula for potential harmony in the world. The following chapters will provide interesting insights into the historical precepts of both Eastern and Western mind-sets.

In the West, there is an ever-growing interest in Eastern ideas. For hundreds of years, Easterners have been pressured by foreign governments and religious groups to accept Western ways. As a result, Easterners have blended some aspects of Western politics and religions into their native cultures.

In recent years, Westerners are being influenced to examine the ancient Eastern philosophies. Dr. Marcus Bach, a pioneer in the field of inter-spiritual and inter-cultural relations, wrote *Strangers at the Door* as a means to help Westerners understand the increasing Eastern teachings in America. His answer to concerns about the arrival of spiritual messages from foreign lands:

> "...the more truly spiritual we are, the more truly compassionate and understanding we will be. The deeper our spiritual convictions, the better can we enjoy the luxury of what others have found. The greater our loyalty to the basic teaching of our churches the more equipped will we be to meet and influence those who have come to influence us.

The more we know about their beliefs and their intentions, the more honestly will we be able to evaluate our own."

A better understanding of Eastern thinking that has motivated a change in Western thinking has been termed "the mind/body connection." Today, Eastern practices of meditation are recommended by many Western professionals in addition to Western prayer.

After much scientific testing, the author of *Beyond the Relaxation Response,* Dr. Herbert Benson, has concluded that meditation and prayer are equally effective. Through a method he termed the "relaxation response," Dr. Benson has determined that we have an inborn capacity to enter into a special state that slows brain waves, metabolism, blood pressure, heart rate and breathing capacity. This response counteracts the harmful effects of stress. For optimal results, he recommends a combination of the relaxation response and what he calls the Faith Factor (your personal philosophy or religious faith). This, he says, can achieve "remarkable feats of mind and body that many only speculate about."

Some Western scientists have examined the merits of blending Western and Eastern knowledge. Technical advances have increased the speed of global communications. The speed of communication and transportation appears to shrink our globe. The ever-growing human population increases faster than human tolerance and understanding between cultures.

I purposely omitted Eastern terminology in Chapter One. Westerners who are not familiar with Eastern philosophy tend to become confused and sometimes threatened by misunderstood meanings of foreign words.

Unfortunately, Westerners have been influenced to reject Eastern philosophy; to view it as mystical and incompatible with our Islamic and Judeo-Christian inheritance. When yoga began its climb to popularity in the 1960s, the Hatha yoga, or physical part, was more acceptable. The spiritual—meditative—side was viewed by many as mind-threatening. Consequently, it was sometimes eliminated from, or slowly incorporated into, the yoga practice. Upon my return from Japan in 1988, I was surprised when, at one Western martial arts school, I was asked to exclude meditation from my workshop.

While attending a writer's course, I supplied classmates with copies of a sample brochure about my Eastern training classes for their evaluation. One student apologized when she returned the copy, saying that she could not critique the material because it was considered mind-altering by her religion.

Such culture shocks jolted me into the realization that I should learn to interpret my instructions in a way that they could be understood and accepted from a Western perspective. The newly coined words served as a way to translate the Eastern mind-set into a more concise and acceptable meaning that Westerners could understand. Explanation of Eastern concepts, in a manner that can be comprehended and appreciated by Westerners, became my goal.

Tri-tuning is not based on any particular religion, nor is it a doctrine to replace any spiritual path. It is a tool to be used in conjunction with any personal conviction. It is a simple means to help reduce fear and bring harmony into anyone's daily routine.

In Chapter One you have experienced a mainly Eastern mind-set, through a Western interpretation, without the confusing Eastern terminology. Now the explanations of Eastern philosophy in Chapter Two can be interesting and enlightening. With a better understanding of the differences between cultures, we can better appreciate the many ways we *all* think alike.

A Review of the Tri-tuning Tests and Skills in Chapter One:

1. Observing your posture, p. 11
2. Shrugging of the shoulders, p. 12
3. Learning to tri-tune, p. 15
4. Enjoy the experience of tri-tuning, p. 16
5. Natural tri-tuning with a partner, p. 19
6. Shoulder-shrugging test, p. 19

CHAPTER TWO

An Eastern Orientation

"When you become so absorbed in your work that
beauty flows naturally from within,
then, your work becomes a work of art."
Kanjiro Kawai
We Do Not Work Alone

Two Years in Japan

"The old ways persist in Japan,
and for those who are enchanted with them,
this is good."
Richard Holloran
Japan Images and Realities

A GOLDEN RISING SUN peered over the horizon just as I ventured into an empty Tokyo street to survey my new surroundings. A fiery blaze traveled down each story of the varied architecture that lined *Okubo-dori* Avenue, replacing dawn's dullness with a brilliant bathing of light. I stood awestruck while streaming rays completed their illumination of the quiet street with a mass of glowing, orange-red sunlight. Its brilliance temporarily obscured the scene from my blinking eyes.

Soon the whole area would be crowded with activity. Several miles toward that rising sun I would live and study for two years. Still groggy from jet lag and a reversed sleep pattern, I returned to the *rhokan* (Japanese inn), promising that I would capture that scene on camera the next morning. Unfortunately, the sun moves each day. I was left with an unforgettable memory of what I trusted to be a good omen for my stay in Japan.

Our class introduction to the courses we would study at **Ki no Kenkyukai** (translated as Ki Society International) was conducted in a small room, compared to Western standards. There was the customary array of flower arrangements equal to an American funeral. Flow-

▲ 31

ers are a significant part of the many festivals and gatherings in Japan. Floral decorations on street lampposts indicate upcoming celebrations in the community.

I was there to study **Ki Development** and a healing art called **Kiatsu**, under **Koichi Tohei**, who founded *Ki no Kenkyukai* in 1971. In 1974, this organization for *ki* (life-energy) research was combined with *Tohei Sensei*'s (teacher) newly-formed *aikido* martial art school. This form of *aikido* is now known as **Ki-Aikido**.

The Martial Art Aikido

> "Aikido, like dance, involves blending
> with someone else's movement and energy."
> Robert Stone and Ron Meyer
> *Aikido in America*

Tohei Sensei first studied aikido in 1939, under **Morihei Ueshiba**, who had founded the martial art in the early 1900s. *Ueshiba Sensei* mostly drew from *jujitsu* (empty-handed fighting) and *kenjutsu* (Japanese sword fighting) for the physical movements of *aikido*.

More importantly, for those of us who see the philosophy of *aikido* as useful in ordinary living as well as for self-defense, *Ueshiba Sensei* added a deep moral and spiritual dimension. Although most Eastern training in the **martial arts** includes responsibility for personal conduct through **Eastern philosophy**, *aikidoists* put an even greater emphasis on creating harmony between self and an opponent. *Ueshiba Sensei* defined his new martial art: "*Aikido* is a martial art of harmony and accord."

The meaning of *aikido* tells the story. Reversing the syllables in the word *aikido* as read in Japanese: *do* means a way or path, *ki* is life flow or creative energy and *ai* means harmony or love. Combined, *aikido* can be described as a way to create harmony.

The word *ki* was introduced to the West mainly through *aikido*. In 1953, *Tohei Sensei* began to teach *aikido* in Hawaii, then continued teaching in the United States and around the world. He promoted his *Ki Development* program of training to help students better understand the meaning and use of *ki* in daily life as well as for *aikido* training.

What is Ki?

> *"Ki is the infinite gathering of infinitely small particles. ...Ki has no end; its absolute value neither increases nor decreases."*
> Koichi Tohei, *Ki in Daily Life*

Ki is a many-faceted and elusive concept that has been interpreted from different points of view. Most languages provide a word that is at least similar to *ki's* elusive meaning. There is no one word in English that adequately describes *ki*. Peter Payne, in *Martial Arts, the Spiritual Dimension,* describes *ki* as usually applying to both breath and spirit; linking the material and the immaterial.

The most common English translations for *ki* are spirit and energy, though neither really suffices. The word *spirit* is associated with most everything from ghosts to gods and from intoxicants to medicines. These definitions fall short of the in-depth meaning of *ki*.

Energy, to a Westerner, seldom means more than the physical energy used to move about and exercise. Otherwise it is seen as the electrical energy needed to obtain instant lighting and to run machinery. Lacking an inclusive English word, *ki* is usually interpreted as energy.

Among Webster's dictionary listings under the definition of *energy* is spirit. One meaning of *spirit* is breath. The Latin word *spiritus* means breath. Listed under *breath* are spirit and life.

Beyond our limited view of energy, a *ki* perspective would embrace the flow of life, rhythm, balance, sleep, breath, nourishment, exertion, motion and matter. To classify spirit as an English equivalent to *ki*, we must emphasize its deeper meanings: courage, vigor, valor, breath, soul, virtue, divine and life principles, over popular connotations such as alcoholic beverages or evil spirits.(*See* Part II, SPIRIT.)

English phrases that closely describe *ki* are: vital energy, vital life flow or creative energy. Sometimes "life force" is used to describe *ki,* but force conjures up an impression of stress and aggression. In-depth connotations of *ki* energy are also expressed by Anton Mesmer's "magnetic fluid," Wilhelm Reich's "orgone energy" and Baron Von Riechenbach's "oric force." Russia's Victor Inyushin called it "bioplasm." To describe this phenomena, other scientists have used such phrases as bioplasmic energy, etheric energy and electron emission.

No matter what definition seems most appropriate, life would not exist without *ki*. When I say life, I am referring to its broadest sense. Even a rock has life from the standpoint of molecular change. This energy that is constantly changing from matter to motion and from motion to matter, is never destroyed—never completely stagnant—forever changing.

An atom has its own building blocks of energy or *ki*. When we add scientific revelations, such as splitting the atom, this vital energy is studied from another dimension. Some nuclear scientists, especially quantum physicists, are amazed to find that their resent discoveries closely parallel the insights of the ancient Eastern mystics. So far, the scientists can only speculate on the source of this ancient knowledge.

An actual experience led Fritjof Capra to write *The Tao of Physics*:

> "As I sat on that beach, my former experiences came to life; I 'saw' cascades of energy coming down from outer space, in which particles were created and destroyed in rhythmic pulses; I 'saw' the atoms of the elements and those of my body participating in this cosmic dance of energy; I 'felt' its rhythm and I 'heard' its sound, and at that moment, I *knew* that this was the Dance of Shiva, the Lord of Dancers worshipped by the Hindus."

The *Tao of Physics* is his attempt to improve the image of science. He suggests that this field of modern physics has surpassed technology, and can be a *Tao* (way or path) of physics; "a path with a heart, a way to spiritual knowledge and self-realization."

Ki and its cousins, **chi** and **prana,** are words not readily comprehended through Western thinking. *Prana,* an ancient Indian **Sanskrit** word that is familiar to us through **yoga**, basically means breath. The Chinese *chi,* expressed through **Taoism**, relates mainly to the invisible circuitry of the life-sustaining flow. This form of energy is utilized in Oriental arts, such as *acupuncture, feng shui* and *tai chi*. The Japanese word to interpret this elusive essence of life is *ki*. While *ki, prana, chi* and *spirit* mean basically the same, they are interpreted, expressed and practiced in various ways.

Trees are sometimes considered synonymous with *ki* because the Japanese **Shinto** *Kami* gods are thought to reside in trees. In one English dictionary of foreign words, tree is the only definition for *ki*. This is misleading to someone new to the concept of *ki*.

I asked students in an English Conversation class that I taught in Japan, what *ki* meant to them. Each gave a different answer. Actually, *ki* is all-encompassing.

I worked part-time to earn *yen* (Japanese currency) and save my devalued dollars. When I applied for employment at a Japanese-English newspaper company, the American interviewer was confused about my studying *ki*. He had learned from a modern translation that *ki* refers to weather or atmospheric pressure. After World War II, the Japanese Ministry of Education simplified the *ki* symbol with an x-like cross, meaning to close off or seal inside. This distorted the original interpretation of *ki*. (*See* Illus. #10)

Revised KI Symbol

Illus. #10

The original cross symbolizes the four directions. The short lines complete the eight directions and represent rice, the earthly sustenance. The top lines indicate clouds and heaven. The angled line, in between, represents the uniting of heaven and earth. (*See* Illus. #11)

Original KI Symbol
Official Calligraphy by Kiochi Tohei

Illus. #11

The Use of Ki in Everyday Life

> *"The fact that the mind rules the body is, in spite of its neglect by biology and medicine, the most fundamental fact which we know about the process of life.*
> Franz Alexander, MD

My mission in Japan was to learn as much as I could about this elusive universal vital energy that I interpreted in Chapter One as spirit-energy and labeled **spirergy**. *Ki* used in cooperation with mind and body coordination, describes the word **tri-tuning,** also coined in Chapter One. Tri-tuning is *not* a substitute for the word *ki* alone. Tri-tuning is accomplished only when mind/body coordination is blended with *ki*. Spirit-energy or spirergy can be more closely defined as *ki* alone. (*See* Part II, TRI-TUNING.)

The art of using *ki* has been demonstrated in Oriental crafts such as calligraphy, *Ikebana* (flower arranging), and paintings—for hundreds, perhaps thousands of years. The idea of consciously utilizing *ki* has spread into Western arts. The Japanese improved upon the *ki* concept they borrowed from ancient China. This approach is slowly being introduced and adopted around the world.

In jest, I suggested to a class of English Conversation students I was teaching in Japan that, in the future, they might look to the Western world in search for the ancient philosophical secrets that they are fast discarding in favor of Western reasoning and technology. They smiled in their usual quiet way without comment.

In modern Japan, many regard the ancient practices as archaic, though these inherent traditions are still evident in their culture, their psyches and their mythology. Most Japanese respect the *martial arts* and regard their many ancient traditions as something to celebrate during their many holidays, but not to be taken seriously. This practice parallels Western traditions, such as those who celebrate Christmas but no longer believe in its Christian meaning.

Some Japanese can't understand why Westerners would want to study their ancient philosophies and practices. Now, the Japanese are racing to implement and enjoy Western technology.

During my brief tour of China in 1988, we were roused early one morning to witness the *tai chi* exercises at a park in Beijing. Morning exercises are a normal way to start the day in the Orient. The irony of this story is that farther along in the park, Chinese of all ages were practicing Western aerobics to disco music.

It was disappointing to learn that when the Japanese established businesses in the United States, the practice of morning exercise was discouraged by most American executives. They claimed that mandatory exercising would not be appreciated by Western workers.

Becoming one with a *ki* state-of-being is the basis for performance of phenomenal feats in the Eastern *martial arts*, healing arts and spiritual transformations. I know from experience that this state-of-being is an essential part of the mental state required for fire-walking.

An Eastern Orientation ▲ 37

I want to emphasize the fact that it is *not* the purpose of this book to: flaunt phenomenal feats, sensationalize the breaking of bricks, promote the performance of exotic physical contortions, or attain magical levels of consciousness. There are many books available for anyone who wishes to learn these practices.

Through *Ki Development* and **Ki Wellness** programs, we learn to use this same resource as expertise for performing simple everyday accomplishments in a gratifying manner. My purpose is to provide a means for using this same energy as a way to create personal happiness by replacing the fears that cause unnecessary chaos in our lives.

At the least, most participants who learn proper uses of *ki* also experience confidence, clarity of mind and an ease of living. It is an uplifting experience to a higher understanding of spiritual values and a more satisfying participation in life.

In Bill Moyers' TV documentary, *Healing and the Mind*, two *tai chi* masters demonstrated the use of *chi*. Ming Shi moved a line of men who tried to resist his attempt. Ma Yueh Liang, age 91, said it had taken him ten years to discover his *chi* and thirty years to learn how to use it.

At a *Ki Wellness* workshop I conducted shortly after that documentary aired, we discussed the TV program. After learning and practicing tri-tuning, a student asked why it had taken Ma Yueh Liang thirty years when she had just learned how to use *ki* in five minutes.

The rudiments of utilizing the synergy of mind, body and spirit are simple and natural. This foundation was demonstrated throughout Chapter One. Ma Yueh Liang was speaking of becoming a master of *chi* after practicing and gaining an in-depth personal understanding of *chi* (or *ki*) through his feeling nature. This mastery is a never-ending endeavor. He said, "When we persevere and learn the benefits of *chi*, we won't stop."

Easterners are willing to patiently practice until a skill becomes meshed with the very fibers of their being. Westerners depend mostly on logical thinking, thus discarding the benefits of rote learning.

Explaining *ki* or *chi* is more perplexing than using it. Scientists do not fully understand *life*, or exactly how and why it came into being on this planet. As yet, there is no complete explanation of how sleep restores this mysterious life-sustaining essence called *ki,* or how it functions in our self-healing bodies. Fortunately, we can sleep without understanding how it sustains us and get well without knowing why we were ill.

We use electricity in spite of the little we know about its source or its effects on the human body. We can drive automobiles without knowledge about the mechanics of how gasoline is changed to energy under the hood.

When I began teaching *Ki Development*, students often complained, "We have had several classes and you still haven't explained *ki*." Using the analogy of driving a car, I asked how many of them could explain how the energy from gasoline and the motor mechanics makes the car move. *Ki* can be better understood through personal experience than by speculative explanation.

We can benefit from *ki* without full knowledge of what it is, its source, its form or the evidence of its extent of existence in the universe. Its real value lies in our everyday awareness, practice and perseverance; the joy of living it and learning to reap its rewards.

An American *kiatsu* classmate in Japan, who had studied *aikido* for many years, admitted that he expected to learn the healing art of *kiatsu* much faster than those of us with very little *aikido* martial art experience. He found that, like the rest of us, he had to learn step by step to sufficiently apply *ki* in the practice of *kiatsu.* If mind/body coordination with *ki* is to be proficiently used, each way it is applied must be practiced until it becomes a skilled habit. By further perseverance each use can be developed into an art.

Contrary to this statement, all of us have heard about miraculous feats of physical strength in times of danger. There are confirmed reports of those who have lifted cars so that pinned victims can escape. Others have carried heavy objects from burning buildings that later they couldn't budge. We know that supra-normal actions are possible through extraordinary phenomena that still elude scientific explanation. These are examples of our natural potential ability that is available to us. How much we develop this possibility beyond the norm, through coordination of mind/body with *ki,* depends upon our willingness to simply practice routinely.

As in the saying that life is simple unless we complicate it, we restrict ourselves by our own limiting fears. *Tohei Sensei* often reminded us that life seems complex because of our limiting viewpoints, and added that the solutions for most problems are simple.

Tohei Sensei's Ki Development Training

> *"The Japanese use the word ki daily, but they to seem to know little about its real meaning or [how] to develop it."*
> Koichi Tohei, *Book of Ki*

The development of *ki* with mind and body coordinated, is *Tohei Sensei*'s passion and the main thrust of his training. The realization that "when the body moves the mind also moves," came to him during a Zen meditation class he attended. When one student was lightly pushed on the shoulder, he claimed that only his body moved—not his mind.

Tohei Sensei says that he developed *ki* testing to make it clear that when the body moves, the mind also has moved.

Branches of the *Ki Society* that *Tohei Sensei* formed to teach *Ki Development* now exist in more than seventy countries around the world. Without *Tohei Sensei*'s *Ki Development* program, those of us who wish to practice mind/body coordination with *ki* in our daily lives, excluding *aikido* training, would have no specific instructions. (*See* Part II, MIND-BODY COORDINATION.)

Tohei Sensei studied *aikido* and *ki* under *Ueshiba Sensei*, founder of the martial art, *aikido. Tohei*'s understanding of *ki* was refined by the teachings of Tempû Nakamura Sensei, a Japanese doctor who had studied *yoga* in India and had earned a medical degree from Columbia University in New York City. It was Nakamura Sensei's revelation: "the mind leads the body," that gave *Tohei Sensei* a deeper insight into the nature of *ki. Tohei Sensei* concluded that the body and mind must first be integrated to achieve union with *ki* and become one with the universe.

In *Ki, A Road Anyone Can Walk,* William Reed quotes the personal endorsement by Nakamura Sensei. "Mr. Tohei has realized that the essence of the *martial arts* is not technique, which is no more than a branch, but the mind itself…"

After teaching in Hawaii and the United States, beginning in 1953, *Tohei Sensei* blended Eastern and Western perspectives when teaching *aikido* and *Ki Development.* Traditionally, Japanese are instructed to observe, repeat and learn by doing—with a great deal of practice and very little questioning.

In the United States, *Tohei Sensei* was confronted with a different kind of student. Americans wanted to know what *ki* really was all about. They challenged him to give specific answers as to how and why it worked.

His logical answers often satisfied Westerners, but *Tohei Sensei* found that they were *not* so willing to practice. He combined the two approaches: a mental understanding of his *ki* principles and practice until mind/body coordination with *ki* extended becomes a subconscious habit.

Years later, an interview with Virginia Ki Society Chief Instructor *Sensei* George Simcox was quoted in *Aikido in America* by editors John Stone and Ron Meyer. "He [*Tohei Sensei*] would never have gone in the direction he did if it had not been for his experience in America from '53 on…. His whole teaching mechanism is built on dealing with the whys that he got here in the United States."

This is one example of how the blending of knowledge from East and West can create a synergism of ideas that becomes an asset to the whole world. The opposite use, dishonesty and envy between cultures, results when one side steals another side's ideas without giving credit to the originator. As Westerners, we must not forget that if Eastern philosophers had not maintained the *oneness* perspective of mind/body/spirit, we would have only obscure sources from which to learn its benefits. *Tohei Sensei* could not have come to his Western *logical* conclusions, had he not already been immersed in the ancient Eastern *feeling* traditions.

Here are the four basic principles which *Tohei Sensei* teaches his students so that they can grasp mind and body coordination with *ki*. Beginners learn by mentally reviewing the sequence:

Tohei Sensei's Four Basic Principles

1. Keep *one point*.
2. Relax completely.
3. Keep *weight underside* (release body weight to gravity).
4. Extend *ki*.

1. *One point* is the center of balance in the lower abdomen, where the body and mind join to create mind/body coordination. *One point*, known as the **hara** in Japanese and *dantein* in Chinese, is usually thought to be about two inches below the navel. Some, especially ancient *martial arts* masters, trained their students to harden the *hara* area with muscle strength.

Tohei Sensei teaches that the *hara*, or what he coined the *one point*, is not a stationary or physical spot to be stiffened. It is an invisible, non-physical point in the lower abdomen that, according to bodily position, moves to help us maintain balance.

In William Reed's *Ki, A Practical Guide for Westerners*, he defines *Tohei Sensei's* phrase *one point*, as "a dynamic point of mental focus."

2. Relax completely means being mind/body coordinated by keeping *one point*. *Sensei* Reed explains that tightening up is usually seen as strong and slackening is regarded as weak. Instead of shifting back and forth from strong to weak, "it is best to understand relaxation in terms of mind and body unification."

3. Keep *weight underside*. (Release shoulder tension. Let gravity hold you up.) "The weight of all objects naturally falls underside." *Tohei Sensei* states in his *Book of Ki: Coordinating Mind and Body in Daily Life*, "The only time the human body is any different is when it is tense. When you are calm, the weight of all parts of your body will be underside."

4. Extend *ki*. *Tohei Sensei* says that just as sound and light travel, so does *ki*. It flows in whatever manner the mind directs. In his book,

Ki in Daily life, he explains that "when we extend *ki*, a new supply of *ki* flows into our body.... If we keep one point, relax and keep weight underside, they are all the same state in which *ki* is extending."

Principles (1) and (4) relate to mental motivation; (2) and (3) relate to bodily action. The body is the visible part of the mind and mind is the invisible part of the body.

This four-step sequence of the four principles acts as a crutch while the beginner learns the *feel* of mind/body coordination when extending *ki*. When confronted physically or verbally, we don't have time to rehearse these four steps. We must practice to know how it *feels* to be mind/body unified with *ki*. When this feeling becomes recognizable, we can retrieve that state-of-being and react naturally at any moment.

Tohei Sensei teaches that if you use one of the four basic principles, you automatically get the other three. Yet, in practice he says we tend to go too far in a particular direction. By swinging back and forth, we can regain the balance of center. This centering can also be accomplished by mentally or verbally saying half-half-half as you bring your focus back to center.

It is absolutely necessary to practice mind/body coordination with extended *ki,* until the process becomes second nature. *Ki* practice trains and allows the mind to flow naturally, according to universal law. (*See* Part II, FLOW.)

New Aikido Organizations

> "It is now possible for someone to be exposed
> to the principles of aikido without even knowing its name
> or practicing one of its physical techniques."
> John Stone & Ron Meyer
> *Aikido in America*

Morihei Ueshiba, founder of the martial art *aikido*, taught *aikido* until he died in 1969, at age 86. His son, *Kisshomaru Ueshiba*, replaced him as head of the International Aikido Federation in Tokyo, Japan.

Over the next few years, *Tohei Sensei* and several other followers of Ueshiba Sensei formed separate *aikido* organizations. Each varied their programs somewhat from the original *aikido* practices. At present, there are many *aikido* organizations in Japan. Most have members in other countries. Some *martial arts* instructors, especially in Western countries, blend their own brand of *aikido* and explanations of *ki* into their training.

I asked a teen-aged student, who also was studying karate, what he had been taught about *ki*. He said it was mentioned a few times, but "we were told it was too difficult to understand until you are an advanced student." He added that he felt that karate would be easier to learn through *Ki Development* training.

While *ki* was an important part of *Morihei Ueshiba's aikido* martial art, he spent relatively little time defining what he thought about its meaning. Easterners learn by a sense-of-being, which is expected to be realized through the osmosis of repeated practice. They are not so prone to logical-type thinking or questioning as Westerners tend to be. Such concepts as *ki* tend to be left in the mystical or unexplained realm. The idea of *ki* (*chi* in Chinese) was borrowed from Chinese philosophy around the seventh century CE. To an extent, it was blended with their native Japanese *Shinto* religion.

Ki is something known to exist and is culturally used in Japan, but it is considered sacred and indefinable. When *Tohei Sensei* began to teach *Ki Development*, after returning to Japan from the United States, his program was considered a sacrilege by many Japanese *aikidoists*.

After forming his own organization, he was free to teach and research the unlimited possibilities of *ki*. To help students become aware of and use *ki, Tohei Sensei* uses various demonstrations of the kinetic, or muscle, testing that he calls *ki testing.* It is the simple muscle testing demonstrated in Chapter One to determine mind/body coordination by tri-tuning. (*See* Part II, KINESIOLOGY)

Kinetic Ki Testing

To Test:

1. **Sit in a chair**.
2. **Ask your partner to stand behind you and place his/her hands on your shoulders to prevent you from standing.**
3. **Your objective is to stand up but you will find it difficult, if not impossible, to stand.**

4. **Repeat the test.** (Your partner should remember that this is a test of comparable strength, not brute strength.)
5. **This time, (partner repeats as above) coordinate your mind and body, extend your *ki* (carry out your intention) and stand up.**

If you maintained *one point* or any of the four principles, you succeeded. If you allowed your mind to dwell on the *enemy* or obstacle (your partner's hands), you failed to stand.

Our fear of failing weakens us and we lose our *one point*—our body-centered focus. Now trade places with your partner, repeat the test and discuss the advantages of using *ki* awareness in your life.

This test is one of the hundreds of *ki* tests that *Tohei Sensei* and other *Ki Society* instructors have devised. The testing helps to teach *Ki Development* and *aikido* students how to practice by using mind/body coordination with *ki*.

Ki Exercises

> *"The most important principle of exercise is that it should enhance rather than diminish energy, strength and vitality."*
> Dr. Deepak Chopra
> *Perfect Digestion*

The testing of mind/body coordination with *ki* is also used as an essential part in performing several sets of special physical exercises. These are practiced as preparation for *Ki Development* and *ki-aikido* sessions. These exercises involve every muscle in the body with special emphasis on muscle movements that are seldom used. This helps strengthen and balance both the flexion and contraction of all our many body muscles.

The ending to one set of exercises involves shaking the entire body:

<u>**Whole-body Exercise with Ki**</u>

1. **While standing naturally (not normally), lift and lower your heels rhythmically up and down (heels not quite touching the floor).**

2. **Continue and, if necessary, place one hand over the lower abdomen just long enough to get yourself mind/body coordinated (focus on your *one point*).**
3. **Relax your shoulders so that your body weight stays underside.**
4. **The rhythmic bounce of your body will allow your arms and hands to move and shake naturally, without exertion on your part.** The faster you raise and lower your heels, the more vigorously your arms and hands will shake naturally.
5. **Slowly decrease your momentum until you are still.** You may be aware of a continued energy tingle in your hands or other parts of your body.

Originally this exercise was taught with an emphasis on shaking the hands. Shaking one part of the body at a time is often taught in speech classes as a means of relaxing before giving a talk. Practice both ways, first shaking the hands and then letting them shake naturally with the body rhythm. Compare the stress involved when merely shaking the hands, to the vibration and stability of the natural whole body involvement.

When used to end a series of exercises, this exercise adds another touch—the feeling of euphoria after the stimulation of action. This exercise can be done for fifteen seconds or so, any time you need to relax, invigorate your body or to increase blood circulation. (*See* Part II, EXERCISE.)

Ki Meditation

> *"Meditation...it is to understand the nature of our thoughts as thoughts and our relationship to them, so that they can be more at our service rather than the other way around."*
> Jon Kabat-Zinn
> *Wherever You Go, There You Are*

Tohei Sensei teaches meditation from a mind/body and *ki* perspective. In most methods of meditation, you are instructed to center your thinking at your forehead.

Mind-body Focusing for Meditation

1. **Have a partner *ki* test (placing his/her hand on your upper chest between neck and shoulder) while you focus on your forehead.** You probably lost your balance when tested.
2. **Now focus on your mind/body center (the *one-point* in your lower abdomen) while your partner tests again.** You should be more stable. If not, you were not in a state of *one point*.

Tohei Sensei emphasizes that *thinking* or meditating at the center of the abdomen does not mean that your brain is in your belly. His instruction to "keep *one point*" can be more closely associated with the phrase "gut feeling."

In one simple form of *ki* meditation, *Tohei Sensei* tells a story from the Persian Arabian Nights fables in which:

> A stranger enters the village with what he calls a magic pot. Villagers who examine the pot tell him that they don't see anything magical about an ordinary black kettle. The stranger directs the villagers to put all of their troubles into the pot. He tells them that their troubles will disappear if they leave them in the magic pot.
> It works only for those who leave their troubles in the pot.

Tohei Sensei uses this allegory as a meditation. Mentally imagine putting your troubles into the *one point* and sending them out into space where the universe, in its Infinite wisdom, will help solve them. If a problem returns to mind unresolved, simply re-evaluate what can be done about it and send the remainder of the situation again—out through the *one point* and into the universe.

A solution to your problems may come to mind when you least expect. It is that momentary insight that we call an "aha." Time and change might also erase the problem, especially when we rely on the universe for solutions. (*See* Part II, MEDITATION.)

Western Puritanism was preached as *repression* of our sufferings. The 1960s psychologists advocated *expression* of our troubles—getting them out, no matter who was hurt by our actions.

Rather than either of these extremes, sending our problems into the universe is a harmless way to acknowledge and *release* them into the arms of the *Infinite*. From a Western mind-set, this is "letting go and letting God." Instead of repression or expression—just release!

Kiatsu Healing Art

> *"Nature is a great medicine and man possesses that medicine within himself."*
> Philippus Aureolus Paracelsus

Young **Koichi Tohei**'s (later known as *Tohei Sensei*) *aikido* training was interrupted in 1944, when he was sent to China as an officer in charge of 80 men during World War II. There he faced the difference between practicing the *martial arts* and the reality of implementing the merits of his *aikido* training in the midst of battle. He experienced real fear and decided to deal with death by surrendering "…to the universe the decision of whether I will live or die."

He also discovered that when he or his fellow soldiers became ill or were injured, he could promote healing by combining the state of mind/body coordination with *ki* and the Japanese folk cure of healing through the hands. After the war, he continued to experiment with *ki* healing. Over the years, he developed a healing art system that he named *Kiatsu*, meaning treatment by *ki* pressure; a directed flow of *ki*. *Kiatsu* is not to be confused with *Shiatsu*, another Japanese healing art meaning finger pressure.

In 1980, *Tohei Sensei* established a two-year course to certify *kiatsu* practitioners. I attended and graduated from his seventh class in March, 1988.

Kiatsu is a treatment administered by *ki* transference. Using the analogy of jump-starting a weak battery from a well-charged battery, the *kiatsuist* acts as the jumper cable. It is not the practitioner's energy, but rather the universal energy that is employed. When properly mind/body coordinated, the therapist becomes a conduit through which cosmic energy is attracted and extended to the client. This action can also be used for self-healing.

Only specially certified instructors are allowed to train and certify new therapists. *Tohei Sensei* debated whether to require *kiatsu* students to have prior medical training. He concluded that the success of *kiatsu* practice depends more on the student's ability to extend *ki* effectively, with mind/body coordinated, than by medically assuming where the body needs *ki*. Our bodies, in their infinite wisdom, know better than we where to send and how to utilize healing energy.

All of us are self-healing entities. Our bodies heal themselves through various sources of energy or *ki*. Among them is the energy metabolized from the food we eat, water we drink, air we breathe, sleep and the tender loving care we give ourselves and each other. *Kiatsu* treatment is a compassionate supply of *ki* healing energy transference, given with mind and body coordinated.

Sampling of *Kiatsu* Healing Art

1. **Place your two middle fingers at the temple area on each side of your head.** Let the other fingers and thumbs rest comfortably against your head.
2. **Coordinate your mind and body at your one point and imagine the energy streaming up and out through your arms and middle fingers, into your head.**
3. **Tell your partner to test by grasping your wrists and gently trying to pull your arms away from your head.** If he/she succeeded, it was because you lost your one point.

4. **If necessary, continue the testing until you can maintain the flow of *ki* into your head and remain stable.**
5. **Exchange partners and repeat the instructions.** This particular *kiatsu* treatment is good for mental fatigue and eye strain.

Just as a beginning piano student can learn a simple piece of music in a short time, anyone can learn the rudiments of *kiatsu*. A few lessons do not qualify a pianist to play at Carnegie Hall or a swimmer to qualify for the Olympic Games. The lack of expertise does not prevent a beginner swimmer or pianist from enjoying what they have learned. Much training and practice is necessary to become deserving of *kiatsu* certification, but a novice can perform *kiatsu* for his or her self-healing and to aid others.

I recall the *ki* testing and the *sensei's* compliments during our first *kiatsu* class. I wondered what more I needed to learn that would take two years of study. When I experienced the difference in effectiveness between the *sensei's kiatsu* treatments and practice treatments by beginning classmates, I realized that there must be much more for us to learn. (*See* Part II, HEALING and HEALTH. Also *see Kiatsu* in Glossary.)

Whole-Body Breathing

> *"Every moment of every day your energy level is affected by the quality of your breathing, as well as the quality of the air you breathe."*
> Louise Taylor and Betty Bryant
> *Ki Energy for Everyone*

Tohei Sensei expressed the value of deep breathing over and over, not only to relieve stress but mainly as a source of healing. He developed what he called *whole-body breathing.*

Basic Whole-body Breathing Technique

1. **Sit, lie, stand or kneel with a straight, not rigid, back.**

2. **Breathe *out* slowly through the mouth.** Imagine your body as a vessel being emptied from the top of the head down to the toes.
3. **Allow your body to breathe *in* through the nose, slowly filling your body vessel from toes to the head *equally* as long as the out-breath.**

To reverse illness, continue breathing *out* and in, for at least 20 minutes each session, as many times each day as you wish.

Deep breathing can be practiced for any length of time, anywhere, especially to relax and relieve stress. In conspicuous places, like long check-out lines or during angry moments, breathe through the nose, out and in for equal lengths of time. (*See* Part II, BREATH.)

Practical Application of Ki

> "It [ki] is held to be 'Intrinsic Energy' or 'Inner Energy' and possessed by everyone although developed by only a few."
> A. Westbrook and O. Ratti
> *Aikido and the Dynamic Sphere*

Tohei Sensei's Ki Development program teaches how to use *ki*; particularly its value in our daily lives. Learning about *ki* while practicing *aikido* does not guarantee that a student understands or uses the concept of *ki* in everyday activities and in relationships with others.

When we develop a conscious self-awareness of how we relate to others as well as with ourselves, we will gain a different perception of our personal world and our relationship to it. Some of our latent fears can be diminished quickly, while our ingrained traits may prove to be a lengthy challenge of trial and error.

A favorite story told at the *dojo* in Japan was about a woman who had asked if she could kill someone with *aikido* techniques. The answer was yes, though it was not recommended.

> When the Japanese woman began *aikido* training she told the other students that her husband was mean and unfaithful. He had left the family. During practice she never smiled or made friends.

Eventually, she softened and began to smile. Later she admitted that she had realized through *aikido* training that her own disposition had caused the separation. She was happy that her husband had returned and was sorry she had wanted to kill him.

With an awareness of *ki,* each of us can explore new ways to enhance our lives. To what extent we coordinate mind and body with *ki* extended, depends upon our individual awareness, our desire for self-improvement and the patient practice required to fulfill that desire.

Tohei Sensei teaches that we must walk our own unique pathways; each different from everyone else. How we use *ki* greatly effects our daily life. *Ki* is a part of us whether or not we become aware and/or utilize it to our advantage.

Choose Your Perspective

> *"What good does it do if you can only coordinate mind and body in a quiet place? ...If you cannot be unified in the midst of your daily work, what good does it do you?"*
> Koichi Tohei

You have now experienced mind/body coordination with *ki*, or what I have termed tri-tuning, based on both Eastern and Western definitions and explanations. Choose the terms, and their usage, that are most appealing to your mind-set. Then apply them. We learn through association with what we already know; through the limited eyes of our own experience.

Buddhism teaches and encourages freedom of personal belief. *Guatama Siddharta* (the original **Buddha**) said:

> "Believe nothing, O monks, merely because you have been told it...or because it is traditional or because you yourselves have imagined it. Do not believe what your teacher tells you merely out of respect for the teacher. But whatsoever, after due examination and analysis, you find to be conducive to the good, the benefit, the welfare of all things— that doctrine believe and cling to, and take it as your guide."

It is customary in the East to show respect toward each instructor's techniques without criticism. Quite often an Eastern guest *sensei* will say to Western *ki-aikido* audiences, "You may not agree with my teaching, but please be willing to listen and practice the way I instruct, while I am teaching. Afterward, you can believe and practice as you wish."

Tohei Sensei assured us early in our course that we were free to hold whatever religious beliefs we chose. His philosophy is that each of us must walk his or her own path up the spiritual mountain of life. He says that as we climb higher, where we can see beyond the lower mountain peaks of doubt that obscure our understanding and trust, our spiritual vision will broaden. At the top, he believes, the universal view will mean the same to everyone.

Ki, by whatever name we call it and however it is interpreted, is a key to unlock the secrets of how to live life naturally—beyond fear.

Review of *Ki* Tests in Chapter Two:

1. *Tohei Sensei*'s Four Basic Principles, p. 41
2. Kinetic *Ki* Testing, p. 43
3. Whole-body Exercise with *Ki*, p. 44
4. Mind-body Focusing for Meditation, p. 46
5. Sampling of *Kiatsu* Healing Art, p. 48
6. Basic Whole-body Breathing Technique, p. 49

Chapter Three

The Paradox of Opposites

"What ills from beauty spring."
Samuel Johnson

East and West as Opposites

*"...at best [Japan] might achieve
the first real synthesis in history
between the essential values of East and West."*
Arthur Koester

AN ENGLISH CONVERSATION STUDENT in Japan asked me, "Why do you point to your head when you say, 'I think'?"

I was stunned. "I guess because that's where my thinking comes from." I had pointed to my head while pondering the answer to another student's question.

"When we think, we point to our heart," she added.

Orientals are primarily feeling and group-minded people, while we Occidentals are individualistic thinkers. This does not mean that Westerners don't have feelings or that Easterners don't think. Westerners relate feelings with emotions and Easterners tend to hide their emotions. What is referred to as an Eastern *feeling nature* is more closely associated with instinct and intuition. It is more in tune with what is meant when we remark, "He really has the *feel* for playing basketball." or "She just doesn't have the *feel* for that part in the play."

Usually, as Westerners, we tend to analyze from a logical, reasoning, left-brained viewpoint. Orientals are more introspective, using a creative, right-brained approach. Both East and West could benefit by fusing these opposite traits in a complementary way.

An Eastern feeling nature is more than emotions and the five senses; it is a sense of "knowingness" or "mindfulness." Although most Easterners are racing to become Western, some of the innate ancient Oriental sense-of-oneness—mind, body and spirit—prevails, in spite of the decaying spiritual roots that spawned it. *Feeling* from this perspective is quite different from merely allowing our five senses to dominate us.

In the West, we tend to limit our logic to the five senses, scientifically accepting only that which can be proven in a test tube. We are top-heavy with reasoning. This has served well for rational thought and technical progress, but it tends to prevent us from heeding the subtle pleas of our inner voices.

The Quakers called these nudges of inner spiritual wisdom "the wee, small voice." Dr. Deepak Chopra refers to the cliché, our "gut feelings," which he claims is literally true. He explains in many of his publications that scientists have proven that every cell in our bodies contains memory. In fact, some scientists now claim that every cell is a replica of the entire universe.

Tri-tuning helps us heed these nudges of wisdom. It gives balance to reasoning and intuition. It lends to a sense-of-flow. (*See* Part II, FLOW.)

Western *thinking* has given rise to great achievements in the material and technical worlds. In the process, however, we have neglected the calm *feeling* nature that could keep us in balance and our technical accomplishments more spiritual and humane. Modern Japanese are following the Western pattern of materialism which, blended with their inherent ancient wisdom, enhances the quality of their productivity. (*See* Part II, MATERIALISM.)

Third world countries are abandoning their ancient ways, either by choice or by force, in favor of modern technology. Much of their ancient philosophy has fallen by the wayside as they struggle to comply with more worldly cultures and become "Western."

The differences between Western thinking and Eastern feeling causes confusion between cultures. Each views the other from a different mind-set. Neither mind-set is complete in itself. There will always be inevitable pendulum swings. Nature uses change as a means to rebalance these extremes. Each culture could benefit from the other if we can learn to examine both sides with understanding. We can help Nature rebalance our world without extreme changes or the chaos of wars. (*See* Part II, CHANGE.)

In *Bridging Science and Spirit*, Norman Friedman equates the collective human consciousness to the left and right hemispheres of the brain. He compares the scientific view in the West to the left brain and the Eastern holistic approach to the right brain. Unlike the brain halves, which are connected by the fibers of the corpus callosum, he says that scientists have not yet bridged these differing orientations. He adds, "Reality cannot be satisfactorily explained by exclusively embracing either the Western or Eastern view."

Mr. Friedman says that in Western science we may have reached an impasse which might be solvable through the Eastern mystical suggestion: "creative use of the human mind." In conclusion, he feels that we are in need of something to surpass the limited methods and tools of Western science that cannot probe and examine the various states of consciousness now known to exist.

Teaching Ki Development to Westerners

> *"What we don't understand, we fear;*
> *what we fear, we come to hate."*
> Author unknown

Some students expect to learn Eastern philosophy through fearsome phenomenal magic and mysterious practices. When one of my *Ki Wellness* students brought members of her karate class to demonstrate the breaking of boards with their bare hands, my students were enthralled. One older student, in particular, lamented that she could not perform such feats to protect herself.

I pondered how to explain the depth of Eastern philosophy so she could understand that simple, everyday use of this so-called "magical" *ki* would bring her more enduring satisfaction than breaking boards with her bare hands. When we see beyond the human craving for sensationalism and strip away the fear-filled facade of mystery and magic, we can retain the wonder and utilize Eastern philosophy in practical ways. (*See* Part II, MAGNETISM.)

I concluded that to penetrate the Western mind-set with Eastern understanding, I needed new English words that would relate more closely to actual Eastern meanings. Every language lacks adequate words to express accurately the native wisdom of other cultures.

Even more confusing is the fact that within a language, people have differing connotations of a particular word. George Simcox, Chief Instructor of the Virginia Ki Society, experienced this *within* the English language. He was demonstrating *weight underside* to a new student. Each time he said, "*put* your arm out," and tested, her arm would go up. Finally, when he said, "*place* your arm out," she passed the *ki* test immediately. To her, *put* meant temporary, *place* was permanent.

When I began teaching *Ki Development* classes, I encouraged students to *feel* the experience of *ki* so that they could gain a better balance of thinking and feeling. (*See* Part II, BALANCE.)

Feeling, in this sense, was foreign to the students' perspectives. Eastern interpretation evoked questions about such phrases as "extend *ki*," "one point" and "relax completely." The word *ki* was strange and unknown, "one point" was odd and "relax completely" was interpreted to mean a limp, collapsed or lax body.

I adapted words connected with the latest Western "how to" programs so students could make the association between an Eastern and Western mind-set. While that didn't completely clear the confusion, it did lead to my coining the new words **tri-tuning, triality** and **spirergy.** (*See* Part II, TRI-TUNING, TRIALITY CONSCIENCE and SPIRERGY.)

Readers already familiar with Eastern terms may prefer to continue using them. By whatever terms you feel more comfortable, any translation is more easily understood through experience than explanation.

The teaching of *Ki Wellness* classes does not require a *martial arts dojo* with matted flooring where shoes are not permitted. Most of my students are middle-aged and senior females who find it difficult to spend much time, if any, sitting on the floor Japanese-style. A Western classroom setting and the more expressive coined words proved to be more appropriate.

The word tri-tuning evolved from my view that the first two *ki* test instructions (rigid and then collapsed) are opposites. The first, performed with rigid muscle power, creates stress. The second test, a collapsed relaxed body, causes a weak response. The third, or correct way, is accomplished by combining the first two and adding natural life flow; spirergy or *ki*. In trio, each complements the other two; total fusion of body, mind and spirit.

Our bodies and minds react with natural unconscious responses. We should be aware of the fact and thankful that we don't have to stop and instruct each muscle how it should move and join in correct movement with the next muscle in order to perform. Our thoughts and actions happen because of innate and learned habits. When we resort to muscular rigidity, we are trying to tell the body how to do that which, in its infinite wisdom, it already knows naturally. The "unbreakable circle" *ki* test, or skill, demonstrates this point.

The Unbreakable Circle

1. **Join the finger and thumb of your strongest hand.**
2. **Tighten the muscles in your arm and hand to resist a *ki* test.**
3. **Have a partner attempt to pull (not jerk) your thumb and finger apart.** You likely failed the test.
4. **Rejoin your finger and thumb without any resistance and ask to be tested again.** Your thumb and finger were easily pulled apart.
5. **For the third testing, unite mind and body by focusing at your center.** Release your body weight to gravity and extend your ki (spirergy) from your center, through your arm and into the circle formed by your thumb and finger.
6. **Ask your partner to test while you rely on this "gentle strength" to retain the unbroken circle.**
7. **Exchange roles and test your partner.** Analyze the three responses. Relate to how your muscles reacted naturally during the third testing when you were tri-tuned. This is the *ki* skill that Jane recalled when she panicked during her CT Scan. (*Refer* to Chapter One, Tri-tuning.)

Note: If you, or your partner, have carpal tunnel syndrome, this test may be injurious. Do not hesitate to decline participation in any of the *ki* tests or skills if you have health problems that could be aggravated.

When we accomplish tri-tuning as a habit or mind-set, we begin to develop a natural triality conscience. This helps us maintain or retrieve a sense of fairness and compassion, rather than lashing out—uncoordinated and defensively. A triality conscience enables us to react naturally and appropriately, rather than having to "think before we speak," or "count ten before we act."

The Mind of a Martial Artist

> *"The real way of the warrior is to prevent slaughter,*
> *It is the art of peace, the power of love."*
> Morihei Ueshiba

It was a life-saving necessity for samurai swordsmen to react correctly without having to stop and think what to do next during a battle. They practiced various techniques until their actions became second nature; habitual reactions coming from the subconscious mind.

Once the swords were drawn, one warrior lived and the other was killed. An honorable way of thinking was, "The only good sword is a sheathed sword."

An Oriental story of a warrior assigned to hunt down and kill a murderer, reveals one of the reasons why ethics are a very important part of *martial arts* training.

> When the villain was found, the warrior proceeded to draw his sword and complete his duty. Suddenly the murderer spat in the face of the warrior, who then replaced the sword and cursed the would-be victim.
>
> The murderer asked, "Now that you have found me, why don't you kill me?"
>
> The warrior answered, "Because now I would kill you out of anger."

If the warrior had killed the murderer out of anger, he would have brought bad *karma* upon himself. *Karma* includes both good or bad retribution; it simply means cause and effect or "as you sow, so shall you reap." A modern-day version: "What goes around, comes around."

According to Oriental beliefs in reincarnation, the warrior would in turn be killed, in this or a future life, if he had killed the murderer out of anger.

If the warrior had killed before the spitting, it would have been done out of duty to someone else's command. If he killed through assignment, he could perform the act with compassion for the dead man. Ideally, practice of the martial arts is a blend of compassion and survival. Basic philosophy of the *martial arts* centers on reconciling these two opposites.

Various *martial arts* evolved over the centuries, from sword fighting to weaponless combat, when weapons were forbidden by law. To a spectator who is not familiar with martial art objectives, martial art performances appear to be fierce fighting through competitive hatred. Westerners are often baffled over the claim that moral self-discipline is a substantial part of the training.

In martial art schools, like other organizations, occasional frailty of individual character does surface. In a few martial arts organizations, the main objective is to maim and kill. The "Karate Kid" movies depicted some of these treacherous motives.

While I lived in Japan, there was a newspaper report concerning two college students who were beaten because they neglected to launder the pajamas for their martial art superiors. One died and the other was hospitalized. This was an exceptional incident since, traditionally, character development and physical agility go hand in hand with martial art training.

Referring to the martial arts as self defense is a misnomer. When we are in a defensive state, we are weakened. We give our *ki* and our courage to the *enemy*. When our attention dwells on the enemy, we lack the courage and presence-of-mind to concentrate on a solution.

The word *warrior* implies—*one who is willing to courageously face his own fears*. When a warrior overcomes the ultimate fear, the fear of death, he is full of courage and composure. Ironically, history reveals that he is also less likely to be killed.

The real goal of the martial artist is to attain self-confidence; ability and stability—*to know oneself*. When we are not in tune with ourselves, a rephrasing of Pogo's famous comic strip is fitting. "I have met the enemy and it is me."

In Search of the Warrior Spirit, is Richard Strozzi Heckler's account of his experience as an *aikido* instructor and psychologist in a six-month experimental venture for the Department of Defense Special Forces program, The Trojan Warrior. *Aikido* and meditation, diet and physical training, psychological and family values were taught by fourteen experts, including a Tibetan monk and a Benedictine monk.

In an East West Magazine account (October 1990) *Sensei* Heckler reflected that some students questioned the value of *aikido* in direct combat, but one soldier saw the training as helpful to his skiing. Another admitted that he didn't hit his kids as much; he didn't react so quickly and his family liked that.

> *Sensei* Heckler concluded that: "what 'worked' was the discipline of harmony—the *aikido* principle of blending, centering, and *ki*.... We are in desperate need of a warrior who draws his or her power from an expanded awareness rather than from a stance of fear and aggression. This warrior could make the U.S. secure without making other countries feel insecure."

The editors of *Aikido in America*, John Stone and Ron Meyer, relate how disturbing World War II was to *aikido's* Japanese founder. *Morihei Ueshiba* was enlisted to teach *aikido* to important officials at the Japanese Military Police Academy, including Prime Minister General Hediki Tojo. During this period, *Ueshiba Sensei* concluded that the Japanese military was under the jurisdiction of reckless fools, devoid of statesmanship and religious ideals. He predicted that their slaughter of innocent citizens and destruction of everything in their path was contradictory to God's will and that their end would be a sorry one.

Ueshiba Sensei's spiritual mentor, Onisaburo Deguchi, leader of a native Japanese religious sect of *Shinto* called Omoto-Kyo, was imprisoned in 1942 because of his popular message for spiritual change in Japan. Discouraged and reflective, *Ueshiba Sensei* retired from martial arts instruction to re-evaluate *aikido* and his method of training.

After World War II, when the Allied Occupation's law forbidding the practice of the martial arts was lifted, he resumed teaching *aikido*.

He taught on the basis that there would be no more attack in *aikido*. He felt that by attack the spirit was lost and declared that *aikido* would be based on the "principle of absolute non-resistance."

Ueshiba Sensei emphasized what he called "*Aiki*;" the blend of harmony and unity that could be described as "create harmony." It is meant to be an attempt to bind the world in peace.

An Attitude of Holitude

> *"The greatest discovery of my generation is that a human being can alter his life by altering his attitude".*
> William James

As a beginning instructor, I often referred to "mind/body coordination with *ki*" as an *attitude*. This was confused with the saying, "He [She] sure has an attitude," meaning a bad disposition or character. An attitude can be good or bad.

Just as there is no English word that adequately expresses *ki*, there is no one appropriate word for the indescribable Eastern "feeling nature" often translated as oneness, meaning wholeness. To express this, I combined the words *holy* and *attitude* to form **holitude**.

The root word for *holy* is *one* or whole; *tude* means *ness*. Together they form a *Oneness* or wholeness. **Holitude** is an attitude of oneness, rather than dualistic competitiveness that leaves us fearful and defensive. When we coordinate mind and body, act with an attitude of wholeness and compassion, our conflicts will dissolve into harmony. By tri-tuning with a triality consciousness, we perceive the world with a sense of holitude that invites peace. (*See* Part II, PEACE.)

When we act through an attitude of holitude, many of the problems that we face correct themselves. We can appreciate the interdependence of all life and act as though we realize that humankind is not indispensable. Our continued existence depends upon harmony with our environment, rather than continuing our historical political and religious beliefs in dominance over and subduing of the earth. An attitude of gratitude and a feeling of custodianship—instead of dominance over Nature—will be a better guarantee of our survival as a species. (*See* Part II, HOLITUDE.)

Positive Thinking

> *"All things, whether good or bad, can teach you a lesson."*
> Koichi Tohei

The discipline of harmony and blending of the opposites is a never-ending personal challenge. Tri-tuning can effect and assist every aspect or phase of our lives, depending upon our awareness and habitual practice. It serves as an easy means of coordinating mind and body. By complementing the opposites, any escalation of fear is more likely to be reduced.

It is more difficult to reconcile tri-tuning with positive thinking. Actually, the two have the same objective—to improve the human condition. The intentions of positive thinking and a triality conscience are essentially the same. If the words correct and incorrect, just and unjust or fair and unfair were substituted for positive and negative, it would portray a more accurate picture of the real meaning of positive thinking. Some so-called positives can be very negative. Ambrose Bierce summarizes this point in *The Devil's Dictionary,* "To be positive: to be mistaken at the top of one's voice."

How we associate positive thinking with the opposites, and the difference between Western and Eastern perspectives, creates confusion. Songwriter Johnny Mercer's *Accentuate the Positive* reflects the Western mind-set. We strive to eliminate the negative and anything in-between.

Amid differing views among Eastern philosophies, the *Buddhist* "Middle Way" countered the *Hindu* extreme opposite means for reaching **nirvana**. Some *Hindu* sects believed that *nirvana* could be attained by seeking worldly, sacred and mundane rewards, while those with the opposite view relied upon detachment from all worldly events. In China, the Buddhist Middle Way of avoiding the opposites, somewhat contradicted the *Taoist yin/yang* which complements the opposites. (*See* Glossary, **Eastern philosophy**.)

A "positive thinking" perspective equates positive with good and negative with bad. From a linear, past-present-future viewpoint, this is valid. The emphasis on positive thinking was a step in the right direction that has lifted many from low self-esteem to rewarding success.

Many lives have been enhanced by "how to" programs since Dale Carnegie introduced them in 1938 through *How to Win Friends and Influence People*. Other inspirationalists followed, from Norman Vincent Peale's *The Power of Positive Thinking* to Anthony Robbins' *Awaken the Giant Within*—along with a host of other authors.

Positive thinking also creates a pendulum swing to the opposite extreme. Until the middle of the twentieth century, it was commonly thought that children should be seen and not heard. The male, father-figure generally was the dominant head of the household. At that time, severe or capital punishment was a commonly accepted means for preventing social disobedience.

Unfortunately, the pendulum of extreme opposites is a double-edged sword. It cuts at the extreme ends as well as during its thrust away from as well as its return to balance. The inevitable swipes from one extreme to another generates the chaos of change along with the necessary adaptation that each cutting swing creates.

Fortunately, now children are seen and heard, but too many lack the responsibility of respect and appreciation. The father-figure or the stern boss, regarded as positive and necessary in former generations, is now seen as a negative or abusive character. Many law-breakers take advantage of the present positive and compassionate leniency which leaves victims maimed and unprotected. Actions that are seen as positive in one era are sometimes regarded as negative in another.

Ironically, many positive thinkers who abhor war, unconsciously condone a fighting conscience which relegates the losers to a slave conscience. Fighting is considered positive more than we consciously realize. Count the number of times each day that we are advised to fight: fight cancer, battle alcoholism, stamp out drug smuggling, avenge sex abuse, revolt against authority, declare war on bugs. Instead, we could direct more appropriate attention toward: preventing and healing cancer, overcoming alcoholism, morally educating youth, preventing sex abuse, and negotiating with authority. We could use more of nature's remedies to discourage small creatures—without upsetting the eco-system. Many small creatures and microscopic life, sustain our lives in ways we fail to recognize. Our attempts to destroy such things as bacteria, sometimes prompts them to grow stronger or mutate.

When religious groups meet solely to declare spiritual warfare against the devil, the devil becomes the *enemy* they perpetuate. Anything or anyone with whom we disagree can be declared a demon. The enemy is any aspect of ourselves that is considered negative; a self-fulfilling prophecy.

The early Christians aimed at carrying out Jesus' teachings of nonviolence. Romans 12:21 reads, "Be not overcome by evil, but overcome evil with good."

The "Onward Christian Soldiers" fighting mentality began when, in 313 CE, the Roman Emperor Constantine put a cross on his battle flag and espoused Christianity. Most of the succeeding Roman Emperors accepted and ruled Christianity on their own terms, reflecting the Roman conquering spirit. (*See* Part II, WESTERN RELIGION.)

Today, well-meaning community leaders encourage a fighting conscience. Oddly enough, it happens when mothers get MADD (Mothers Against Drunk Drivers). Taking measures to prevent drunk driving is commendable, but to approach it with a *mad* attitude is more injurious to the mothers and victims than to the drunk drivers.

Aggressive video games overindulge children in shooting, destruction and eradication. This habit sometimes sets a subconscious mental pattern for physical response with anything from rocks, fists, knives, implements or guns. It is the psychological response of repeated and ingrained over-indulgences that causes the damage.

The child who is nurtured in a moral atmosphere of guidance and responsible adult examples, is not as likely to be ill-affected by fictional violence as an unguided child living amid violent circumstances. Predominate trendy disrespectful peer pressures that reflect a chaotic lifestyle, somehow seep into society in general and become accepted as normal behavior. Thankfully, many youngsters rise above chaotic or violent home environments and degrading peer pressure to become respected citizens.

There are skills to be learned through video and other games when they are played with a triality conscience. Hopefully, nature's balancing act will create a more complementary mind-set concerning future competition of any form. We can only hope that, in the near future, there will be an inevitable swing from the present overdose of violence. A new perspective could whet the appetites of children and adults to seek video activities that are more palatable to the innate human sense of moral values.

When we dwell on fighting, we send defensive messages to the subconscious mind. Psychologists claim that only the conscious mind makes judgments about whether a thought or action is good or bad, real or imagined. When we react impulsively or by habit, we respond from our subconscious minds. If we choose to be bombarded with constant fighting and destructive thoughts, such as the violence on TV and other entertainment, our thoughts will reflect "garbage in and garbage out." (*See* Part II, THOUGHTS.)

If our moral values are based on a fighting or slave conscience, we will fight back or slink away, making matters worse. When our conscious judgmental minds and our subconscious habitual minds disagree with each other, we have to think twice before we speak or act, to avoid regrettable outbursts. (*See* Part II, FIGHTING and SLAVE CONSCIENCE.)

Tibetan meditation master Chogyam Trungpa remarked, "Americans try so violently to be non-violent."

War is just a collective action. It is an extreme example of our normal reactions to everyday fears. Governments are responsible for keeping their citizens safe, just as fathers and mothers feel compelled to protect the family from harm.

Everything has its opposite and every change creates a new set of opposites. The invention of the automobile added faster transportation, new jobs, speed, comfort and made possible a host of convenient by-products. Conversely, cars caused more accidents, put blacksmiths and other pre-industrial craftsmen out of work, created pollution problems and caused asphyxiation. Imagine the size of our national debt if skilled laborers such as blacksmiths and their families had been subsidized because their jobs were caught up in the wheel of change. (*See* Part II, CHANGE.)

New positive ideas are soon countered by the exposure of their negative side. A new prescription drug or herbal medicine recommendation is heralded as a miracle cure until its harmful side effects or misuse are exposed. Each extreme sows the seeds of its opposite in accordance with Nature's law of balance.

What is perceived as positive or negative by those who are most influentially powerful, becomes the norm. Shakespeare said, "There is nothing either good or bad, but thinking makes it so."

Whether the results of any action are considered beneficial or detrimental depends more on the attitude and consensus of what is considered normal, than on what is best. Positive and negative are considered either good or bad, depending on whose values are used as a measuring stick. In its literal sense of fighting the opposites, positive thinking has its flaws as well as its good intentions.

What is considered good to one person or culture might be declared evil by another. Joseph Campbell, author of *The Power of Myth* said, "Everything is evil to someone."

Life is a paradox. Anything can be seen as positive or negative, depending on how it is perceived. There are those who claim it is detrimental to be involved in any so-called negativity. They go to such extremes as not owning a TV or reading the news. They avoid people considered negative in any manner and consider themselves as being positive. We can become so engrossed in eliminating the negative that we become positive in a negative sort of way. Our determination to be positive creates habitual fear. (*See* Part II, HABITS.)

Some fearful people advise visualizing a form of protection around ourselves, such as angels or white light. There are stories, such as one about putting a mental protective shield twelve inches around an automobile. When a near accident ended, the two cars had stopped exactly one foot apart.

From a triality point of view, why not share the white light of protection to include everyone's car and expand the light to virtually protect the entire universe? This approach turns fear into caring and eliminates the "enemy."

Instead of avoiding anything we consider negative, we can send comforting thoughts to assist in soothing those involved in the bad news on TV, or the troubling events we read and hear about. Our cares can be sent in the form of prayer, meditation or a simple phrase that demonstrates wishing them well.

Contemplate, for instance, the affect if even a majority of the earth's human inhabitants prayed or sent wishes that each hurricane or typhoon would turn and stay away from land. It would be interesting to observe the results.

When we are aware of a dangerous situation, but cannot or should not intervene, we can mentally say, "God Bless," "good luck," "all the best," "best wishes" or whatever fits our sincere compassion. When we watch disturbing news on TV, hear the wailing of police car and fire engine sirens or find ourselves in the middle of any controversy, this state of tri-tuning can be used to help others. Sending compassionate thoughts and prayers to others will reduce our own fears as well.

Substituting the words "appropriate" and "inappropriate," or "apt" and "inept," can take positive thinking out of the realm of positive or negative. Decisions based on fairness offer more flexible and timely decisions, from a wider scope of choice. Tri-tuning influences us to act according to circumstances and helps us overcome fear. It brings forth our best response. Whatever term is used: "positive," "appropriate," "apt," or "just," is not so important as basing the decision on a triality conscience.

By tri-tuning with a triality conscience, we can help others to lift themselves when they are down. We can help each other turn fear into care. (*See* Part II, TRIALITY CONSCIENCE.)

Unity of Calm and Action

> *"Center is a place where stillness and movement become as one."*
> Joseph Campbell
> *The Power of Myth*

Tohei Sensei strongly recommends a positive outlook, referring to the opposites as plus and minus *ki*. He encourages positive thought, words and actions to create what he calls plus mind or plus life. He also refers to the Eastern value put on combining calm and action.

In *Ki, A Road Anyone Can Walk*, William Reed quotes *Tohei*, "The universe itself is beyond opposites; but the world we live in is a relative world of opposing forces, plus and minus, *yin* and *yang*. Every light casts a shadow. Reality is a mixture of good and bad elements."

He says that *Tohei Sensei*'s coined phrase "extend *ki*" means having a positive mind. *Sensei* Reed adds, "This is not just a wishful mind, without mind and body unified.... The power of positive thinking is not a new idea, however, most people misunderstand what kind of power this is and how to attain it."

Tohei Sensei explains that many people consider the use of diametric opposites, calm and action, as strange. In his book, *Ki in Daily Life*, he uses the analogy of a child's spinning toy to illustrate how the top gains calm stability the faster it spins. Though calm and action are thought to be opposites, they ultimately unite. "The strength of action is born from inner calm.... Whether you are active or still, if you keep your mind and body unified, you will have mastered the secret of the unity of calm and action." We can instantly move with greater speed when we are calm. By the same token, he teaches that mind and body are essentially one. To equate *ki* as spirit and the body as matter is to separate mind and body.

Normally in the West, the mind and body are regarded as opposites. Some religions combine the spirit/mind and separate them from the body. Usually, mind or intelligence and spirit or soul are also considered separate. All of these reasonings create a sense of separation instead of unity.

We not only separate ourselves outwardly from others, we are tormented by the inner mental and emotional battles we fight. These separations result from contradictions among the opposing voices in our heads and the emotional appetites of our bodies. A fighting or slave conscience leaves us with two options, either to fight or flee from the situation. Both tend to separate us within ourselves and from each other, without a third option to complement both sides of our dilemmas.

The Western Biblical Genesis version of the creation story has influenced us to believe in separation between God and ourselves. We look at the world from our usual linear perception of past regrets—and fear of the future.

In the 1960s, the slogan "be in the now" became popular. It emphasized the value of present moment concentration, instead of dwelling on the past or what might happen in the future. Metaphorically speaking, when we are in the present, we are in the Presence; in tune with the *All.*

Being in the present can be a paradox. Experienced through tri-tuning, the past, present and future are combined. Being in the *now* can also be construed as an attitude of living for the present moment, without regard for the lessons of the past or responsibility toward the future. Our attitude determines which of these two opposite reflections, "the great me" or "all for one and one for all," will be created. The person who submits to momentary pleasures or abuse, without regard to self-esteem, self-respect or social responsibility, does not gain by being in the present moment.

When mind and body are coordinated, the third dimension of tri-tuning; the proper use of *ki* or spirergy, comes into play. A state of tri-tuning provides clarity to choose an appropriate response. It also provides the serenity of "mindfulness" or "sense-of-knowing" that our best path has been chosen. We are in the Presence when we are melded into the triad of past, present and future that propels us toward the ultimate level of all-knowing. It is a step over the threshold into what we inevitably seek—the peace that passes understanding—from whatever spiritual source we feel it can be received. (*See* Part II, SPIRERGY.)

In Eastern enlightenment or **nirvana**, there are levels of attainment. A deeper sense of awakening can be realized over and over again. There are stages of understanding in all religions. Evangelist Billy Graham says that to be reborn, the decision to give oneself over to God, is only the first step. Then the work begins. This is the experience in the Eastern path to *nirvana* or *satori* as well.

We use *ki* all the time. Normally, when we are not tri-tuned, it is either positive or negative *ki*. Whatever we do and however we do it, we are using *ki*. A con artist is an expert at using *ki*—inappropriately. A murderer uses *ki*. Any force that injures or sustains is *ki*. Our *intentions* determine how we use *ki*. In this same vein, Sir Walter Scott said, "Oh, what tangled webs we weave when first we practice to deceive."

When we use *ki* in conjunction with mind/body coordination, we are naturally more inclined to be compassionate with others, as well as toward ourselves. We are more confident and less fearful. Without mind/body unified, we become apprehensive. We are more likely to use force or manipulation because we are reacting through fear.

The Jewish practice of bodily movement (swaying back and forth) during prayer, serves as a reminder of the existence of the body as well as the mind. This compassionate thinking and feeling creates a natural triality conscience.

From Ming Shi's *Mind over Matter*, Thomas Cleary translates in detail how to attain "a coordination of stillness and movement in consciousness, energy and spirit." He explains how "'thought' activates 'intent' to process vitality, energy and spirit." When done correctly, this melding gives rise to change, which elevates the level of consciousness. This enhancement incites an interaction between vitality-energy-spirit and thought which allows direct action on consciousness without the mediation of intent. "Thought and consciousness interact, thought and intent interact, intent and consciousness interact…three levels of using consciousness to refine consciousness so that consciousness refines consciousness."

This is the sequence of unfolding for higher levels of consciousness to be attained. These levels go beyond the experience of average perception and beyond our normal thinking. (*See* Part II, CONSCIOUSNESS.)

Yin/Yang

> "Contrast always indicates a unity
> and the basis of every pair of opposites."
> Ernest Wood, *Zen Dictionary*

The Chinese *Taoist* philosophy of **yin/yang** can be very misleading when interpreted from the Western view of positive meaning good and negative as bad. The winner in a Western national speech contest based her talk on the advantages of being yang over being yin. Also, when I asked a waitress the meaning of the *yin/yang* emblem she was

The Paradox of Opposites ▲ 71

wearing, she said her necklace was a Chinese magic charm to bring her good luck.

With these incorrect interpretations of yin and yang, it's little wonder that *Eastern philosophy* is so misunderstood or labeled "occult" and mystical.

The *yin/yang* symbol (*See* Illus. #12.) depicts the *Taoist* idea of positive and negative forces with their compatible and complementary relationship to each other. The two equal, intersecting droplets are encased within a circle. Each of the two curved droplets is centered with a dot of the opposite color (usually black and white).

YIN / YANG Symbol

Illus. #12

This configuration indicates that within every negative there is a seed of the positive, and vice versa. The tail of one side merges into the head of the other. This indicates how the extreme of one opposite becomes the beginning of the opposite extreme. Merging of the opposites creates a balanced symbol.

From a *yin/yang, Taoist* philosophy point of view, the opposites complement one another. When positive, active, male, creative, light, sun, day, heat and sweet are listed as yang qualities, it doesn't mean that the yin list of negative, passive, female, receptive, dark, shadow, night, cold and sour are bad or inferior. It indicates that each serves to complement and reinforce the other.

When electrical components are referred to as male and female sockets, there is no intention of demeaning or exalting either gender. The ideal for a successful marriage or any kind of partnership would more likely be realized if the teamwork of complementing their opposite traits were brought into play.

The *yin/yang* perspective of positive and negative, that dates back to the third century BCE, elevates us to a more harmonious outlook on the opposites. Our Western view of duality toward the opposites creates unnecessary chaos. We strive to eliminate everything that is considered to be negative. Merging the supposed opposites, mind and body, creates a synergy of restful alertness that transforms us beyond the normal fears that keep us unbalanced. (*See* Part II, OPPOSITES.)

As author of the ancient Chinese *Tao Te Ching*, Lao Tzu explains,

> "Out of *Tao* [the spiritual path or truth] comes two, from two comes three; from the three all things come. The shade *yin* is on the back of everything; the light of *yang* is on the face of everything. From their blending together balance exists in the world...."

We cannot create light by stamping out darkness. When we turn on or accept the light, darkness disappears from view. It still exists as the counter-part of light.

Our fighting or slave consciences create a win/lose attitude that keeps us in a chronically fearful state of losing. A triality conscience creates a natural win-win balance of oneness and harmony. (*See* Part II, WIN-WIN and HARMONY.)

Western Dualism

> *"A religion contradicting science and a science contradicting religion are equally false."*
> P. D. Ouspensky

The concept of yin/yang is difficult for Westerners to comprehend because we have been indoctrinated with dualistic theories since recorded history. Basically the word *dual* means two, double or couple. This meaning became twisted by the Western philosophy of dualism as opposed to monism, which means one. In philosophy, according to Webster's *New Universal Unabridged Dictionary*:

> "Monism is the doctrine that there is only one ultimate substance or principle, whether mind (idealism), matter (materialism), or some third thing that is the basis of both; the doctrine that reality is an organic whole without independent parts."

That third thing is what we are calling spirergy. Mind and matter are the same as mind and body or spirit and matter.

Western theology designates dualism as representing two radically different principles, one good and the other bad. This doctrine claims that man has two natures, one spiritual and the other physical. (*See* Part II, DUALISM.)

The Paradox of Opposites ▲ 73

Zoroastrianism appears to be the historical source of Western dualism. The principles of good and evil are portrayed as a Heavenly God with his band of angels, promoting the forces of life against the demon supporters of death and evil. There is evidence that the teachings of Persian prophet, *Zoroaster* (c.630-555 BC) influenced Judeo-Christian beliefs in demons, angels and the hereafter. (*See* Part II, DEATH.)

In the *Tao of Physics*, Fritjof Capra relates that until the fifth century BC, the Greeks saw no distinction between spirit and matter; the animate or inanimate. The split came from the disagreements between Greek philosophers Heraclitus and Parmenides. Heraclitus taught that changes in the world arose from a cyclic interplay of the opposites. It was this action that formed the unity of ever-changing, or Becoming, which transcended all opposing forces.

Parmenides' belief in an unchangeable Being or intelligent God, who directs the world, led to the separation of spirit and matter. This belief shaped the fundamental concepts of dualism in Western philosophy and religions. The Greek philosophers Socrates, Plato and Aristotle echoed the sentiments of *Zoroaster* and Parmenides to some extent. They considered the body to be a material hindrance to the freedom of the mind.

Modern scientists in the 1600's, led by Rene Descartes, emphasized the separation of mind and body to help them escape dogmatic church restriction and persecution. They surrendered the mind to the clergy and took command of the body themselves. Although Descartes was a religious man, he sought freedom from Papal authority to experiment with new scientific ideas. Westerners, scientists and theologians alike, have looked upon the mind and body as separate entities since that time. Scientific evidence, particularly through advancement in physics, has prompted a re-evaluation of Western and Eastern mysticism and the mind/body/spirit connection.

Opposite Extremes

> *"In a mad world, only the mad are sane."*
> Akira Kurosawa

In the whole world, throughout history, it has been an apparently normal reaction among humans to take sides and fight to the finish of win or lose over everything from ideals to possessions. This ingrained habit includes every type of conflict from innocent games to all-out warfare. With varying degrees between fair play and cruelty, humankind has settled disputes by a winner-take-all philosophy. Few other creatures on earth take competition to such massive warring extremes. (*See* Part II, POWER.)

The late anthropologist, Margaret Mead, told of two tribes who set aside one day each year to war on each other. The fighting ended with a feast enjoyed together by both tribes, after burying the dead. When asked why they performed this deadly ritual, no one knew. It had been a tribal tradition handed down from generation to generation.

Before we excuse this custom as typical of ignorant savages, we should examine our so-called *civilized* traditions. Some aspects of war between nations resemble this tribal tradition. In the original Olympic Games some types of competition were a fight to the finish. The losing contender could bow out at any time, but most chose the honor of death rather than the humiliation that staying alive would bring upon them.

Jiddu Krishnamurti said, "War is just a spectacular expression of everyday life." The chronic conflicts in our lives are unending mini-wars that collectively do just as much, if not more, damage than major warfare. They simply occur on a smaller, more subtle scale.

Early European explorers killed thousands of natives wherever they settled if they did not accept Christianity. Explorers and missionaries destroyed sacred spiritual relics and records as well. Over the centuries, millions of people in Europe and elsewhere were subjected to slavery or death in both primitive and modern cultures. During the Reformation period, thousands of Europeans were killed because they wouldn't submit to whatever Christian sect their ever-changing rulers chose to follow.

American religious freedom was born out of the horrible religious persecution by European rulers and rival Christian groups, especially from the fifteen through the seventeen hundreds. American democracy, that is now so taken for granted, was a quantum leap from the tyrannical kings, lords and magistrates who dominated European jurisdictions. (*See* Part II, FREEDOM.)

Why do we humans, with all of our logical knowledge and claim of superiority within the animal kingdom, continue to persecute each other? Can it be that the killings are Nature's way of countering our irresponsible over-population problems?

Animals instinctively reproduce according to the adequacy of sustenance available. They live in balance with Nature, whether it means meeting their personal demise or not. What is often called "the law of the jungle" could better be described as "one for all and all for one." Humans could live by an attitude of oneness, if we would learn to complement Nature's laws. (*See* Part II, NATURE.)

How do we view our continuing over-population of the planet Earth? From a fighting conscience view it means siding with either pro-life or pro-choice. Killing and maiming have been used by each extreme side to prove its righteousness. Both sides have valid and illogical or humane and inhumane points of view. If viewed from a triality conscience, each would consider the merits of the other's rationale and negotiate rather than retaliate. (*See* Part II, FAIR-MINDEDNESS.)

Deserts and land depletion are partly caused by human misuse of the earth and irresponsibility toward over-population. The opposite view would bring about strict laws concerning childbirth and land usage. Paradoxically—if wars, violence and disease were substantially curtailed, the opposite swing would be a population explosion that would completely imbalance the limited provisions necessary to sustain all human life.

The extreme of public opinion that once limited the female to the role of a housewife, has swung to such an extreme that those who choose to be exclusively homemakers are often humiliated. The former strict rules and maximum-production expectations enforced by employers, have been replaced by laws prohibiting the firing of irresponsible workers, even if their poor work performance endangers the lives of innocent people.

There are extremist groups on opposing sides of everything from insects and owls, to gun laws and drugs. Ironically, some of the same people who march against deforesting, soil erosion or nuclear plants are the first to complain about rising costs of wood products, foodstuffs and energy supplies. Some environmental protesters who know little or nothing about an issue join the protest, consciously or unconsciously, just for the enjoyment of a fight. There are those who are on the side of pro-choice for humans, yet vehemently protest the killing of an animal.

So much human energy and valuable time is wasted fighting each other or fighting for one side of an issue. Through a collective consciousness of holitude, the time and energy that is now being destroyed could be saved and used wisely. If those involved would tri-tune the situation, each group would consider that the other side has valid reasoning to contribute. Neither side would rally with a fighting conscience of winner-takes-all. Both sides could present their grievances and solutions without provoking retaliation or cunning connivance. (*See* Part II, TIME.)

Humans have the mental capacity to recognize and understand Nature's universal laws and the changes they bring about. Instead of using this ability, too often our lack of concern, careless stupidity and greed cause unwarranted devastation and destruction.

The pendulum swing of extremes is Nature's balancing act for change and recycling. We do not need to get rid of the safety valves of extremes. It is the needless fighting and slave conscience that provokes the extremes which many times are mishandled, causing even more unwarranted devastation. Legalized slavery has been abolished all over the world. The remaining human fighting and slave conscience is more dangerous than the natural disasters, dangerous animals and invisible microbes—all combined.

The Ball of Knowledge and Awareness

> *"There are no experts;
> only varying degrees of ignorance."*
> Author unknown

What we know and don't know about a given subject, issue, event, theory or idea can be visualized as balls of knowledge. Each ball contains the visible surface facts of all sides as well as the unexposed knowledge inside. There is a portion of each ball or situation that we are aware of at the moment, and the side or sides that are invisible or unknown to us. Someone viewing from another side of the situation sees only the opposite surface information. Everyone views the situation from his or her point of view. Parts of the interior of the ball are comprehended only by those who are more intuitively aware.

Each of us looks at any given situation or the *ball of knowledge* through the limited eyes of our own experiences.

> Deception of our normal perception is demonstrated in the story of a horseman whose hat was made of red material on one side and blue on the other. Onlookers were lined up on both sides of the racer's path. He rode the length of the track, then secretly turned the hat around so that each side would see the same color, as he returned, that they had seen before.
>
> After the race, viewers on one side insisted that his hat was blue, while those on the other side argued that it was red. The verbal and physical fights that ensued left a formerly friendly crowd—angry, injured or dead.

How often this scenario is repeated in our lives through everyday simple and complex misunderstandings. There are potentially endless balls of knowledge on given subjects and their contents change with time. The lack of sufficient awareness often prevents recognition of the knowledge hidden within a given ball. Consequently, what is humanly known about any subject or situation is not the whole truth.

We cannot know absolute truth unless we are all-knowing. No one person or group knows everything possible about any subject or situation. The way we interpret what we see depends upon what we perceive as correct or incorrect, just or unjust. Our personal perspectives hinge on the sum total of our genetic inheritance and our life's experiences.

When most of us look at a rock, we see a rock. A geologist can look at a rock and record pre-history. Still, those facts are based on limited scientific knowledge and are subject to scrutiny. According to Arthur C. Clark, noted author and scientist, "Not only is our world more mysterious than we imagine; it is more mysterious than we *can* imagine."

Each ball represents an individual's knowledge, a group's consensus or the total information knowable about a given subject or incident. Even that perception is constantly influenced by the interference of other ever-changing balls of knowledge. Formerly hidden knowledge may become known. (*See* Part II, TRUTH.)

A pebble thrown into a calm lake produces circular ripples. When another pebble is thrown nearby, the ripples intersect. In quantum physics this is known as interference. The results influence the possibilities of change in the innumerable patterns of organic reality. Likewise, the intelligence within the various balls of knowledge effect one another. Each of our personal balls of knowledge influence each other's *balls of knowledge,* as well as the ever-changing conclusions through group consciousness.

So far, the human mind has not fathomed the Universal *ball of knowledge* containing all truth; the ultimate of potential knowledge. It is calculated that humans, including Albert Einstein, understand or are aware of less than 10% of our potential mental capacity and how the brain functions. Throughout history, humans have created gods who supposedly represented the full 100% of potential universal thought that in some unknown capacity is at our mental disposal.

We can increase our understanding by a willingness to compare both sides of our personal balls of knowledge concerning each particular subject or action. What is hidden inside each *ball of knowledge* requires *intuition*. When we complement the opposite sides of a situation, what is hidden inside the ball will more readily reveal itself intuitively into our conscious minds.

The challenge of becoming aware of our balls of knowledge is reminiscent of the words in Robert Burns' poem. "If we could see ourselves as others see us...," we would be lifted from the self-image about some misgivings that our low self-esteem has tricked us into believing, but deflated concerning our ego masks of false protection. Tri-tuning with a triality conscience can help us examine our real selves, face our frailties and promote our potential without self-guilt or punishment.

Through consideration for the opposite side of each ball, we can research and debate information that is not already known to us about a particular subject. It is said that with a view of one side only, we can never come close to *truth*. (*See* Part II, TRUTH.)

Woodrow Wilson said that "the act of compromise is the art of government." In his university courses, Newt Gingrich tells his university students that it is all right to be strong-minded, so long as we are willing to walk around the tree (the issue being debated) and consider the opposite view.

Looking at opposing issues is the first step. The second step is acting with honest intent. We can make integral decisions only when we understand both sides of an issue. We may not all come to the same conclusions, but each will come from an informed and unselfish approach.

What is contained inside each *ball of knowledge* can be learned by developing our innate intuitive potential. The more we tri-tune, the more intuit we become, because we are looking at both sides with integrity. This simultaneous thinking and feeling induces intuitive revelation. (*See* Part II, INTUITION.)

Stories such as *Babe, The Little Prince, Johnathan Livingston Seagull, E.T. the Extra Terrestrial,* Grail stories and myths speak subliminally to the deep-seated awareness of our subconscious values and penetrate the heart of our desire to experience harmonious understanding. They take us beneath the crust of what we think of as reality and allow us a momentary glimpse into the innermost esoteric core of the balls of knowledge that we seek to fathom.

Those with the gift of clairvoyance, or other extra-sensory abilities, can project further into the invisible center of a *ball of knowledge*. Each of us has the potential to increase our capacity for peering intuitively into our own crystal balls of knowledge. We can learn to see more of what normally remains hidden. We create our own imbalance by either over-indulging in logical, left-brain thinking or by frivolous right-brained irresponsible emotions.

Instead of encouraging our potential awareness or intuitive ability, the peer pressure to conform with political and social correctness leads us to believe that whatever is determined as "truth" at a given time or place is absolutely correct. The same can be said about religious beliefs, forms of education or any other facet of life. We fail to realize that interpretations of these beliefs and supposed truths will invariably change with time.

One cliché from the 1930's, "Don't talk to yourself," was usually followed by, "Above all, don't answer yourself." This influence discouraged self-communication and inner exploration; examining or knowing ourselves. To "know ourselves," we need to communicate with our innermost selves and listen to the answers we get through our "aha's", "gut feelings", and the "wee small voice" within. Those are the intuitions coming from within our crystal balls of knowledge that are all too often ignored.

Throughout history, accepted facts have been fought over and changed. We live in a world of variables. We are influenced to act as though at any given time our world is at the point of all-knowing "correctness." Our eyes are closed to the fact that other individuals and groups have their own ideas about what is correct. We continually fight over, rather than collaborating, what is best for the common good.

Through a triality conscience we can better understand any issue with a sense of awareness that we do not know everything. We also need to face the fact that many times momentary decisions must be made on the basis of our limited information. Anthropologist, Margaret Mead, said, "In this world, you cannot complete an education."

Yet, we make choices and act as though we know all that can possibly be known about a given situation. Truth is as relative as anything else in the universe. When we see the universe through the spectrum of our limited balls of knowledge, we can respect each other's views with more tolerance. Living beyond fear diminishes our need for a fighting conscience and encourages a triality conscience.

All balls of knowledge, including our own, change with time and experience. Normally we only comprehend our own perspective of the visible side of our personal balls of knowledge. The invisible side hides the unknown from us, unless we are willing to walk around and examine the other sides. Sometimes we don't know—that we don't know—what we think we know. We can feel certain of the truth about a situation and be entirely incorrect. It is a matter of not knowing that we don't know. Although we can search deeper into our balls of hidden knowledge, we cannot be completely cognizant of every bit of knowledge at any given time. As Will Rogers said, "Everybody's ignorant, only on different subjects."

Some scientists and clergy now believe that we have within ourselves the potential of "all-knowing;" that every body cell is a microcosm of the holographic macrocosmic universe.

Through awareness we can seek our holy grails of universal knowledge contained within our balls of knowledge. When we learn to coordinate our instincts and our conscious minds, we can tune into our spiritual and subconscious minds. We can become aware of the possibility of becoming one with the all-knowing cosmic consciousness present in the Universal *Ball of Knowledge;* through whatever we perceive concerning the universal term—*God*.

Beyond the Opposites of Positive and Negative

> *"I assure you that you will accomplish*
> *all you set out to do or need to do*
> *with much more ease, efficiency, pleasure and satisfaction*
> *when you merge mind, body and spirit with the task at hand—*
> *and you will experience serenity."*
> Carl Jung

Tri-tuning is not a matter of disregarding positive thinking. It is positive thinking from a different level. In the manner that it is intended, positive thinking is a necessary cultural ingredient. We must make decisions as to what is correct or incorrect, just and unjust, every moment of the day. Tri-tuning is putting the negative in perspective from a broad spectrum of insight by using both of the opposites aptly—with an appropriate sense of fairness. (*See* Part II, FAIR-MINDEDNESS.)

The biggest problem with changing from a predominantly "positive thinking" mind-set to a triality conscience is letting go of fighting the opposites. That is—do not think that by choosing one side, its opposite must be completely destroyed. Some examples are: fad diets, political and religious beliefs or any extreme opposite thinking. When "reduced fat" became an issue, dieters and advertisers swung to an anti-fat craze. Much damage was done by the time opposing facts came to light showing that too little fat is also injurious to human health.

Another extreme example: when a new love affair or marriage replaces a former one. Even counselors will sometimes advise their clients to get rid of all material reminders of bad memories. The knowledge of our happy and unhappy past experiences are a part of us that may very well help guide us to make better decisions in the future. All memories represent a part of our learning experience and sad memories cannot be tossed out without ill-effecting the happy ones. (*See* Part II, HAPPINESS.)

From a scientific perspective, physicists now speak in terms of chaos within order through such realizations as Heisenberg's uncertainty principle. In the relationship between matter and anti-matter each has its positive and negative aspects. Matter is condensed energy. Motion is unformed energy. When combined, matter and anti-matter are found to be *pure energy*. Experiencing pure energy is the indescribable epitome of ultimate hope. This is the experience that we subconsciously seek to know and enjoy.

Through a triality conscience, we can recognize that the oneness of the universe includes both the light and shadow sides of everything. Dealing with life through an attitude of "just be" takes us beyond positive and negative; toward balance within imbalance. It elevates us above the mundane mishmash that keeps us swamped in the murky waters of needless conflict and fear. (*See* Part II, FEAR.)

Sheldon Kopp, author of *Mirror, Mask and Shadow, The Risks and Rewards of Self-Acceptance*, ended his book with the following paragraph:

> "The only creative act necessary to the continuing development of my self is willingness to peer more deeply into the shadows so that I

may see more clearly. But these transformations cannot be gained without cost. They require my learning to live the rest of my days in the ambiguity of knowing that *of all that I am, I am also the opposite.* I cannot rid myself of my demons without risking that my angels will flee along with them."

A Magic Wand

> *"The Wizard is beyond opposites of light and dark, good and evil, pleasure and pain.*
> Dr. Deepak Chopra
> *The Way of the Wizard*

Tri-tuning is not a magic wand in the sense that with one lesson, one course or that by years of practice we are likely to become our anticipated ideal of a super happy individual. It *is*, however, a magic wand for helping us realize many of our desires for personal improvement and happier relationships. Tri-tuning elicits the kind of happiness that is quoted to be "like a butterfly that settles upon you when you least expect."

Tri-tuning is a tool to aid any self-help program. When attending "how to" workshops and seminars, the suggested program can be carried out with less effort by tri-tuning. The instructions will be more easily learned and they will be much more effective.

Richard Heckler said of the soldiers in the Trojan Warrior Project, "A few of them have an inflated view of graduating six months later with super-human powers."

So many newcomers to the transpersonal (mind/body/spirit) world expect immediate transformation with minimal effort on their part. To others, the supposed magic of it all is frightening and misleading.

I am forever grateful for the advice given by a seasoned paranormal advocate. Twenty-five years ago, when I was about to launch into the metaphysical and holistic worlds, I expressed my fears. Her advice, which I pass along to apprehensive readers, was to avoid being hastily persuaded into a particular "cure-all" or "quick-fix." Also, avoid following any religion or persuasion that takes control over you and forbids your personal freedom of choice in the matter. Be cautious of those who demand your complete allegiance or ask you to surrender yourself to doctrines presented as absolute; the only truth. (*See* Part II, TRUTH.)

As humans, we tend either to be lured by utopian promises or to blindly reject new knowledge because of our fearful resistance toward change. As I advised at the end of Chapter One, practice the three A's—awareness, analysis and application of what is personally acceptable to you. Choose what you accept through your own personal *knowingness*—your wee small voice—and apply it.

By this cautious advice, I do not mean to discourage the possibility of instant knowing or healing. Anything is possible, although immediate changes are not probable. However, this is mainly because of the limitations we humans put upon ourselves because of our misunderstood fears.

Tri-tuning is not based on any particular theory, power or control system. It is simply a tool to enhance everyday life in whatever manner it can help promote personal growth. It is a matter of how each person chooses to apply tri-tuning through the holitude of a triality conscience. Others can assist us but as adults no one should make, or have to make, demands of us. It is both our privilege and responsibility to make fair-minded reliable choices concerning our rights while remembering to respect the rights of others.

Theologians, scientists, politicians and ordinary citizens of the world can put an emphasis on faith, hope and love. With these in mind, instead of control and the provocation of fear, we will more easily relate to having "the faith of a mustard seed" (Matt. 13: 31-32).

A tiny seemingly insignificant mustard seed, as referred to by Jesus, allows itself to become what it is to be, without fear. We can surrender to "just be," through a personal "knowingness" about our unlimited possibilities. In Jesus' words, "If you say unto this mountain, be removed and fall into the sea, it shall be done" (Matt 17:20). These possibilities can be more easily understood through tri-tuning, triality and an attitude of holitude.

Humankind chose the route of matter; a materialistic and technical means of utility, locomotion and speed. The mystics would say that the same and even more could have been accomplished through mind and thought, without fear. We cannot blame science or technology for our troubles. Only what we are willing to utilize and consume is continually produced. What each of us chooses and how we use it will determine whether the human specie survives.

Through the advantages of technology, scientists are uncovering evidence that projects new light on theology and spirit. We do not have to choose between matter and mind. Technology and the information age may yet lead us full circle to a better understanding of what mystics and masters, throughout the centuries, have attempted to convey. (*See* Part II, SPIRIT.)

So long as humanity duels the opposites by either a fighting or a slave conscience of win vs lose, lord vs slave, good vs evil—conflict will reign over caring. Complementing the opposites will turn the world upside down. Evil, spelled backward, will allow us to l-i-v-e. Whether you espouse the words tri-tuning, triality, spirergy and holitude or feel more comfortable with other virtuous or spiritual words, the real significance lies in the ideal and virtuous ways they are carried out.

Review of Tri-tuning Skills in Chapter Three:

1. The Unbreakable Circle, p. 57

86 ▲ Tri-Tuning

Chapter Four

Gleaning the Best from East and West

> *"There is an essential harmony between the spirit of Eastern wisdom and Western science."*
> Fritjof Capra

My Introduction to Ki Society International

> *"There is no coincidence in the universe—only a grand design; an incredible 'snowflake.'*
> Neale Donald Walsch
> *Conversations With God, Book 1*

THE THEMES OF MANY PUBLICATIONS, such as *The Celestine Prophecy* and *Conversations with God,* leave us wondering whether there really are no coincidences or to what extent our lives are happenstance. My first encounter with *Ki Development* practice came in 1983 when I *just happened* to arrive on vacation in the Washington, D.C. metropolitan area the same weekend that Koretoshi Maruyama from Japan was conducting an *aikido* seminar for the Virginia and Maryland Ki Societies. During the previous year, I had read *Koichi Tohei's* books, *Ki in Daily Life* and *Book of Ki*: *Co-ordinating Mind and Body in Daily Life,* but I had never practiced any form of martial art.

As I joined the group on the mat (a covering on the floor of the *dojo*), the bowing began. Immediately, I was torn between my enthusiasm about the philosophy of *ki* and the fact that I didn't want any part of Japanese subservience. At that time, I considered the act of bowing synonymous with "bowing and scraping."

When I learned the Oriental significance of bowing, I was humbled. In *Ki-aikido* practice, the *sensei* and students bow to the *ki* symbol (representing the universe) with gratitude for what the Universe can teach us. The *sensei* then turns and bows to the students with thankfulness. Without students, there would be no one to teach. The students return the bow with respect for the instructor. Without a teacher, we would have difficulty learning. In general, the bow symbolizes recognition, respect, honor, appreciation, gratitude and thankfulness. (*See* Part II, THANKS.)

Three years later, in an English Conversation class I was teaching in Japan, a student asked if everyone in the United States carries guns. I said it was easy to see how they could get that impression from western and gangster movies. I added that we get the idea from Japanese samurai movies that bowing is subservient.

The students were appalled that we would interpret the bow as subservient. They reminded me that bowing is always reciprocated.

Subconscious Fears

> *"In this life there are no guarantees; only choices."*
> The Golden Girls TV Show

Minor, unsuspecting impressions can sink deep into the unconscious mind as lasting memories. In Japan, I was baffled by my own reaction to workmen dressed in the jodhpurs-type breeches that Japanese soldiers wore during World War II. As a teenager during the war, my only association with that attire was through war movies and newspaper photos. Yet, until I became accustomed to them, if I rounded a corner and suddenly encountered Japanese workers wearing those breeches, my latent fears were re-enacted through goose pimples and momentary panic.

It was puzzling to me why movies and the hate we had held toward the Japanese, who were then scornfully known as "Japs," could still have such a subconscious effect on me. I wondered what it must be like for military war veterans, and other victims of the war, to overcome their fears and hatreds. By reasoning with myself that there was no longer a need for fear, I replaced this unnecessary subconscious habit. The replacement was made easier by my ever-growing respect for and camaraderie with the Japanese people.

As adults we often continue to harbor old fears and resentments, consciously or unconsciously, that date back to childhood. Cultural impressions, retained into adulthood, can outlive their threat to our welfare. Even a simple remark, well intended, but presumed to be a personal insult or ethnic slur, can fester into unresolved hate. The conscious or subconscious memory of these events can make us quick to retaliate when we feel threatened.

Family conflicts often stem from the mistaken childhood impressions that some adult children subconsciously hang on to concerning their parents. Parents tend to think of their adult offspring as children, and adult children continue to relate to their parents through childish eyes. The value of gaining adult maturity is reflected in St. Paul's admonishment in I Corinthians 13:11: "When I was a child, I spake as a child, I understood as a child, I thought as a child; but when I became a man, I put away childish things." Occasionally we need to do a spring cleaning of the dusty, out-grown relics in our mental attics.

Warranted fears that remain a personal threat into adulthood can be dealt with through tri-tuning rather than hate and vengeance. With a better understanding of family and cultural habits, we can more easily detect actual ill-meant or subversive threats. Whether the source of cultural fear is foreign or domestic, our value systems will benefit from periodic updates. By evaluating and replacing outdated habits, we can tame our dragons of misgiving that should no longer control us.

During Bill Moyers' TV interview for *Wisdom of Faith*, Houston Smith said, "Psychologists have found that humankind's greatest yearning is to be lovingly related to [by] others." Members of all cultures have a potential for compassion, which is the core of spirituality. Still, civilizations have been stymied by prejudice and the fear-filled grasping for control.

Sometimes we are blind to the well-intended concerns of other people. A parent's valid motive for discipline can be interpreted quite differently by a child. At all ages, we create imagined *enemies* that result from our fabricated fears; our misconceptions. Inappropriate actions can sometimes be committed with good intentions. When triggered by irresponsible, abusive parents, quarreling siblings, disrespectful children or by stormy relationships, these actions stem from a subconscious fear of rejection.

Unresolved fears, whether real or imagined, can lead to phobias and panic attacks, depression and inappropriate behavior. When reviewed through a triality conscience, we can minimize and eliminate the detrimental effects of the unwarranted fears in our lives. We will see them in a different light and cast off the habitual memories that we have allowed to smother both personal and global happiness. By evaluating our anger, jealousy, prejudices and other traits anchored in fear, we can help overcome the anxieties born out of our fears. (*See* Part II, ANGER.)

Intercultural and Universal Understanding

"When one helps another, both are strong."
German Proverb

The Golden Rule, "Do unto others as you would have them do unto you," is a universal altruism expressed in most cultures. The world would be a safer place if humanity would do more than pay lip service toward fulfilling this natural law. After each war, meaningful quotes are uttered about how the peace was won. Then a post script of regret is added; that humankind has yet to learn how to live harmoniously, in such a manner that war would be deemed unnecessary.

The technical advancements of world transportation and communication are propelling us into a strange new world much faster than we are coming to understand and tolerate each other's customs. The volume of new information doubled and redoubled during the twentieth century. At that pace, imagine how much more will come to light by the end of the twenty-first century.

The information age is providing data that, through a concerted effort to understand each other, can help promote intelligent decisions in foreign affairs and personal encounters. The down-side of mass information is that we must sift through controversial facts that may or may not be accurate. At best, broader knowledge provides the seeds from which mutual trust can grow. At the least, issues can be honestly spelled out with a firm insistence on fair dealings.

Misunderstandings breed mistrust toward the motives of nations and individuals. Mistrust is transformed into prejudice. Prejudice promotes hate. Hate produces dissension, territorial disputes and the tragedies of war. When we don't practice knowledgeable, honest evaluation and tolerance, we repeat the scenario of fear, greed, hate and war—generation after generation, century after century.

The accessibility to past and newly acquired knowledge incites us to reevaluate our microcosmic and macrocosmic worlds. Where did we come from? Why are we here? Where are we going? These age-old philosophical questions are still being pondered. Some scientists, particularly physicists, and some theologians are beginning to openly examine the obscure insight that both Eastern and Western mystics have kept alive for centuries. With the diminishing of totalitarian governments and doctrines, we are free to glimpse the light that has been eclipsed by suppression and control. A re-examination of the interaction between body, mind and spirit (soul)—our material, mind (thought) and ethereal worlds—is allowing us to develop our own perspective through the aid of various perceptions.

Whether or not the near-death experiences that have been recounted in recent years are actual, their messages are worth our contemplation. One part of Betty Eadie's *Embraced by the Light* was centered on the "ripple effect" that resulted from her every action, whether a simple act of kindness or a misdeed. The advice she envisioned changed her outlook on life's trials and oppositions.

> Her heavenly advisors said, "You needed the negative as well as the positive, especially on earth. Before you can feel joy, you must know sorrow."
>
> As she reviewed her life through a state of transformation, all of her actions in life took on new meaning. She realized that rather than a mistake, each experience was a tool for her personal growth. When she learned to avoid harmful actions, they helped her understand herself. She saw herself as growing in her ability to help others. She was astounded that many of both her sad and joyful experiences had been orchestrated by the guardian angels around her. Each was calculated to take her to higher levels of knowledge. She recognized that mistakes and harmful actions were repeated until she learned the lesson. She saw that once she learned, doors of opportunity were literally opened

to her. Things she thought she had done on her own had been influenced by divine help.

Her new perspective revealed her sins and shortcomings as multi-dimensional light. They grieved her, but proved to be tools to learn by—"to correct my thinking and behavior." She saw forgiven sins as blotted out, overlaid with new understanding and a new direction that led her to naturally abandon the sin. Only the education about the sin remained, which helped to increase her ability to help others. She understood her need to "truly forgive myself." If not, it would be impossible for her to do what she must do; "forgive others."

She realized that what she criticized most in others and forgave least "was almost always a behavior I myself possessed or feared having." What she gave out she received back. They were examples of her own weaknesses.

"All growth appears spiritually—most important—love others as myself. I had to search within myself to find it as well."

Betty Eadie's account is similar to other personal accounts of spiritual experiences. Actual or not, these accounts parallel the dilemma we create by our dueling of the opposites. They are examples of why and how an attitude of holitude, with a triality conscience, can enhance our everyday relationships with each other. They convey a way and a reason for us to reduce our fears.

Aikido Tenkan Technique

> *"When true serenity is gained,*
> *To bow and to bend we will not be ashamed.*
> *To turn and to turn then will be our delight,*
> *Till by turning, turning, we come 'round right.'"*
> A Shaker Hymn

In an *aikido* technique called **tenkan** (pronounced tin-con; a pivoting and turning movement) the *aikido*ist or *nage* (nau-gay), who is being attacked, offers his/her left hand to the extended right hand of the attacker or *uke* (uuh-kay). When *uke* grabs (from underneath) the nage's wrist, *nage* has three choices. He/she can either (1) counter attack; (2) weaken and try to flee; or (3) blend and flow. By using the third reaction, the *nage* can use the uke's own *ki* or momentum to subdue him/her. Harmony will be restored or the attacker will be subdued.

(1) If the attackee (*nage*) defends him/her self with brute strength, the attacker (*uke*) gains the most power. (*See* Illus. #13.)

(2) If the attackee weakens and tries to withdraw, the attacker has all of the power. (*See* Illus. #14.)

(3) If the attackee extends his/her *ki* through his/her captured hand, steps forward and pivots clockwise, ending next to and parallel with the attacker, he/she is no longer on the defensive. He/she has directed his/her *ki* to blend with the opponent's *ki* to dissuade further attack. The attacker will feel powerless and may give up, allowing harmony to be restored. If not, the attackee continues to follow through the *aikido* technique, turning himself and the attacker until he/she is completely off-balanced or subdued; but without injury. (*See* Illus. #15.)

Illus. #13

Illus. #14

Illus. #15

Virginia *Ki Society* Chief Instructor, George Simcox, instructs that if the attacker indicates a willingness to call off the attack and the *aikido*ist continues to subdue unnecessarily, the act becomes punishment rather than defense. An *aikido*ist has no right to punish; his or her responsibility is to do only what is necessary for protection and to deflate or defuse the aggression. To get the *feel* of the vibes between partners during this exercise, practice these instructions.

Tohei Sensei advises that living by universal principles creates harmony and that living against them causes pain and conflict. He calls this the "principle of harmony and conflict."

Verbal Conflict

> *"To ease another's heartache is to forget one's own."*
> Abraham Lincoln

As a student of *Kiatsu* Therapy and *Ki Development* at *Ki Society International,* plus a part-time teacher of English Conversation in Japan, I had very little time or energy left to practice the martial art *aikido*. As a member of the senior age category, I placed the prowess of *aikido* practice low on my priority list. However, I did practice enough *aikido* in Japan and Virginia to experience the exhilaration, satisfaction and pure enjoyment that keeps *aikido*ists practicing to improve their skill and to reach goals of excellence.

Although I am not qualified as an *aikido* instructor, I demonstrate the previously illustrated *tenkan* technique as an analogy. It depicts the similarity between using mind, body and *ki* in physical prowess, as well as tuning-in (tri-tuning) with the same mental response to verbal attack.

Visualize using the *tenkan* technique as a verbal response. When we face a verbal attacker, our goal should be to neutralize the threat. If we react defensively, our response will be verbal retaliation. Compare this mental reaction to the brute strength demonstrated in the physical *tenkan* reaction of Illus. #13 in the prior list of instructions.

By choosing Illus. #14, we will weaken or try to flee. Verbally, we will express sorrow for ourselves and/or put the blame on the attacker.

The best reaction, Illus. #15, is an attempt to restore harmony by visualizing ourselves standing parallel with the attacker. Mentally, we visualize the situation from our attacker's viewpoint as well as our own; seeing both sides of the situation. From this vantage point, there is a chance for negotiation and understanding.

It is unusual to defend ourselves by getting closer to an attacker either physically or mentally. However, when we are tri-tuned with an attitude of holitude, the sincerity reflected through our subtle energy (spirergy) can be sensed by the attacker as non-aggressive. It will serve as a gentle persuasion for the attacker to withdraw his or her aggression. We can help the opponent "save face" in Oriental tradition.

The founder of *aikido*, **Morihei Ueshiba**, said,

> "The mistake is to begin to think that *budo* [stop the spear] means to have an opponent or enemy; someone you want to be stronger than, someone you want to throw down. In true *budo*, there is no enemy or opponent."

Remember, an attack is a response to some level of fear, whether it comes from the attacker's conscious or subconscious mind. An enemy has been envisioned for some reason. Even when we are attacked verbally by someone who has simply "gotten up on the wrong side of the bed," we are dubbed the *enemy* just because we are there at the time. When we allow our egos to run wild, we respond senselessly. (*See* Part II, EGO.)

When we tri-tune, we not only put ourselves into a naturally compassionate state, we help the opponent recover from his or her state of fear. He or she subconsciously feels the vibrations of our tri-tuning and will be more inclined to forget the hostility. *Ki* is free; it will manifest according to the intent we give it.

Historically, the Western military also has held certain chivalrous codes of ethics. In the movie version of *Ivanhoe*, a bit of compassionate advice was given, "You must defeat him by forgiving him."

Relationships and Family Conflict

> *"Whatever relationships you have attracted*
> *in your life at this moment*
> *are precisely the ones you need..."*
> Dr. Deepak Chopra
> *The Seven Laws of Success*

Although criminal assault is a possible threat to our lives, we are more likely to encounter verbal abuse in our daily lives than physical attack. When confronted, we either (1) return verbal abuse; (2) submit as the victim, or (3) attempt to resolve the problem.

(1) A counter attack of verbal abuse can actually strengthen the opponent. We give our energy (spirergy) to the attacker. This is an aggressive response. (*See* Part II, DEFENSE.)

(2) If we withdraw or show weakness, we empower the opponent with our *ki*. This is passive reaction.
(3) When we look at the situation through a triality conscience and recognize fear as the source of the problem, we are more likely to resolve the situation and help the assailant curb his or her aggression. This is a neutralizing solution to the problem.

Example: The husband arrives home, sees no evidence of dinner and yells, "I told you to have dinner ready early so I can get to my meeting on time!"

(1) The *aggressive* wife knows that everything is under control, but the remark angers her and triggers an abusive response. "I have other things to do besides being your slave." This irritates the husband even more, causing the verbal dialogue to escalate and the possibility of restoring harmony remote. Couples allow this type of conflict to become a chronic habit, creating endless family disputes.
(2) The *victim* wife retorts, "I can't do anything to please you!" She resorts to tears or walks away in silence. Either of these responses exasperates and angers the husband further. Again, she has given him her *ki* (her energy). She did not tri-tune the situation.
(3) The *peace-maker* wife senses the pressure he is experiencing, calmly tells him that dinner is in the oven and will be ready as soon as the table is set. She quickly explains the delay and suggests their having a leisurely dessert together after the meeting.

By neutralizing his negative *ki,* that would have been wasted by a confrontation, she complemented the opposites; aggression and passiveness. Which of these three responses would be most likely to receive accolades of gratitude; (1), (2), or (3)?

The husband was allowed to release his hurried frustration by blowing off steam without repercussion or additional conflict. The wife turned conflict into harmony by tri-tuning the situation. She looked at the problem from a triality or solution perspective with an attitude of holitude. (*See* Part II, DUALISM.)

All of us have been confronted with similar situations. It's easy to see why we tend to lash out abusively and receive abuse in return, especially when we're stressed or tired—and not tri-tuned. If we arrive home mentally tied up in our worries, it is so tempting to release our frustrations or to be drawn into any imagined or real family conflict that confronts us.

Inappropriate actions usually agitate otherwise happy family members into conflict. In a few seconds, everyone blows off steam and the whole evening is wrecked. Unless we can rescue each other by someone taking the initiative to turn conflict into care, the scenario becomes a crippling family habit.

Tri-tuning by just one family member can help everyone. A humorous remark can release stress and turn conflict into harmony. Sometimes the instinctive action of a pet can help dissolve family discord and restore *caring* for each other. Any means that will help us, or someone else, regain dignity after losing self-esteem is better than having everyone remain in the agony of conflict. (See Part II, HAPPINESS.)

All too often these habits set a pattern of inherited tendencies, repeated generation after generation. Depending upon many factors, sometimes experiences of abuse in dysfunctional families, fortunately, can influence offspring to use their childhood stumbling blocks as stepping stones into self-reliant adulthood. It may take determined practice for years, or generations of patient persistence on the part of adults, but the development of a triality conscience will eventually lighten family burdens.

To respond in a manner that helps restore harmony does not come easily for most of us. The norm of either a fighting or slave conscience is a challenging burden for most of us to overcome.

Mental worries reveal themselves through body language; poor posture, raised shoulders and stiff body motions. Western medical professionals are beginning to agree that mental rigidity also manifests in our bodies as physical ailments, especially arthritic and rheumatoid diseases. How we relate to others affects not only their physical, mental and spiritual health, but our own as well. (*See Part II,* POSTURE.)

Suggestion: Think about your posture and your physical ailments from this prospective. Without blaming or shaming yourself, begin to replace habits that may be causing these problems.

Blend and Mend

> *"On this day: mend a quarrel; search out a forgotten friend; dismiss a false suspicion and replace it with trust."*
> Author unknown

In one of his classes, Dan DeProspero, an American *aikido sen*sei in Japan, used "blend and mend" as a metaphor for the tenkan technique. By blending with an opponent, we can visualize the situation from his or her perspective. We can see where he or she is coming from and how we can help him or her through the conflict. This helps to turn conflict into harmony; another phrase that expresses the meaning of *aikido*.

When confronted in any manner, remember that an assailant is consciously or subconsciously in a state of fear. If we probe deep enough into the human psyche, we find that any kind of attack is caused by some momentary or latent form of fear.

Normally we think of fear as a tool for protection. Fear is simply our alarm system. If we allow fear to overwhelm us, instead of merely serving as a first warning, it will boomerang in ways we least expect. When we dwell too long upon our regrets from the past, we remain mired in subtle fear.

Gerald Jampolsky, M.D., in his book, *Love is Letting Go of Fear*, based on *A Course in Miracles,* explains that:

> "In order to experience peace instead of conflict, it is necessary to shift our perception. Instead of seeing others as attacking us, we can see them as fearful. We are always expressing either Love or fear. Fear is really a call for help, and therefore a request for Love. It is apparent, then, that to experience peace, we must recognize that we do have a choice in determining what we perceive."

Our egotistic needs for retaliation are triggered by jealousy, insecurity, anger, etc. They manifest as basic fears that overshadow love. Most are habits that have been practiced for years without an awareness of why or an effort to recognize the source of their origins. (*See* Part II, LOVE.)

When we remember that we are being attacked through fear, it will be easier to stay tri-tuned. We can use our energy for conflict resolution instead of wasting precious time and energy, judging and condemning our attacker. When the attacker senses our compassion, this recognition may ease his or her fear that provoked the attack. Fear can be something as simple as what is labeled a "bad hair day." Stress and chaos result from fears that we allow to creep into our daily routines. (*See* Part II, FEAR.)

The usual question is, "How can the mental process of tri-tuning be useful in situations of physical and weapon violence?" In some cases, it can be even more valuable than physical retaliation. A weaker person, unless specially trained in methods of defense, has slim chance against a strong attacker. Even a strong victim of attack by someone with a deadly weapon has little defense. The attacker with a weapon and under the influence of drugs, is the least predictable of all. Usually something more than physical or mental prowess is needed.

> A shop owner who experienced a hold-up was commanded to empty his cash register. Keeping his hands up, he looked the villain in the eye and asked, "How can I help you? Why do you need the money?"
>
> The attacker was gruff, with an answer that it was none of his business and to hurry up if he didn't want to be killed. The shopkeeper calmly tried again. In a soft, even voice, he reminded the hold-up man of the consequences of his act and once more offered help.
>
> The attacker's hands began to shake with fear and indecision. He began to sob, confessing that he was out of work, his family had no food and he was fed up with trying to make an honest living.
>
> The owner assured him that if he would put the gun down, he personally would supply food and help him find a job. The gunman submitted and the story had a happy ending for both parties.

If the attacker had been a hardened criminal or under the influence of drugs, the shopkeeper's method may or may not have been successful. He had tri-tuned naturally, most likely without ever having heard the terms mind/body coordination with *ki* or spirergy. Tri-tuning is a natural reaction when we *live beyond fear*. Many people have learned to live beyond fear through their upbringing, spiritual practices or cultural influence.

Whatever the source, when dire circumstances arise, how we respond can determine whether we live or die.

> A young woman, being raped by a psychotic neighbor, endured hours of torment by reminding herself that she must remain focused. Her attacker played the aggressor role for a while, during which he held a knife to her throat, threatening to kill her—while raping her. Then he would revert to sobs, telling her about his life of abuse.
>
> Or, he would play a perfectly rational role for a while, only to swing again into a violent rage. All the time she knew that if she didn't keep her composure, she would be killed. She talked, encouraged, soothed, touched, rationalized and even kissed him. (If she had succumbed to either the fight or flight mode, she would have given him her *ki*.)
>
> She remained calm throughout the ordeal. Finally, near daybreak, she persuaded him that the neighbors might see him in the daylight. He left. Later, he stood trial and was prosecuted for his crime.

She and the shopkeeper experienced the challenge of an Oriental saying that *Tohei Sensei* often quoted: "Look into the eyes of your enemy with so much love that he dare not attack you." In these cases, *kill you*.

The ideal behind the *tenkan* analogy of blend and mend is not exclusively Eastern. Many biblical passages parallel this solution. Jesus' words were "Agree with thine adversary quickly" (Matt. 5:25), meaning not to escalate the disagreement to the point where legal settlement is needed.

Blending with the intent to help mend, is more likely to end the conflict quickly. Somehow, by compassion and blending, we receive back the good intentions we have given. What we give through holitude is returned to us in some manner. It is a universal law; giving is receiving.

In *Dr. Dean Ornish's Program for Reversing Heart Disease*, he advises, "Acknowledge what the other person is saying." When we repeat what is said to us, especially in question form with a tone of concern, both parties know that the other is listening.

An example of this remedy could be:
"You drive me crazy when you do that!"
Answer: "I make you angry? I'm sorry. I meant…"

The person being confronted blends to start the mending process. In a sense, he or she agrees with the adversary quickly. When the victim acknowledges that the adversary has a point of view, the opponent is more willing to listen to the other side.

Above all, the victim has resisted the normal temptation to become defensive. Usually we are busy thinking of what we are going to say or do in retaliation. We don't really hear what the other person is saying, much less sense his or her real motives.

I was introduced to Dr. Ornish's book through a *Ki Wellness* student who was recovering from a heart attack. Several times he mentioned that what I was teaching reminded him of a book recommended by his physical therapist. Not only does Dr. Ornish give physical and mental recommendations to prevent and cure heart disease, he emphasizes how mental turmoil affects our physical health. (*See* Part II, ANGER.)

Jesus advised, "turn the other cheek." (Luke 6:29) Some biblical scholars have interpreted this verse as an idiom of that region which meant "look at the other side of the situation." This is a different, but more logical, view than the usual literal interpretations that allow others to take advantage of us or increase our fears.

> A Jewish couple in Colorado were being harassed by threatening phone calls. At first they reacted with fear and humiliation when the same man continually called to insult, accuse and threaten them. Then they decided to pray and to speak kindly to him, hoping to learn the motives behind his actions. Little by little they penetrated his fears. They learned that he was a lonely quadriplegic who had been convinced by a hate group that Jews were his enemies. Through the couple's encouragement, the three met and became friends.

In one parable Jesus quoted a King, "What you do for the least of these my brethren, you do also unto me" (Matt 25:40). From a sense of *Oneness*, what we do for anyone, including ourselves, we do for everyone. Likewise, what we do against others, or against our intuitive better judgment, directly or indirectly affects everyone and everything.

Sometimes we make heroes of those who help others but so many unsolicited acts of kindness are overlooked. The simple acts of bravery in everyday life are seldom broadcast on the nightly news. Accounts about these unsung heroes could inspire younger people beyond their fearful, sometimes resentful, skepticism about the world into which they were born.

A retired friend tells how, in the 1960s, her ventures into the metaphysical world of studies, including the Edgar Cayce ARE (Association for Research and Enlightenment, Inc.), changed her outlook on life.

> One day while walking home in New York City, she came upon a crowd of fifteen to twenty people. An elderly man and a young man were having an argument in the street, which had resulted in a standoff. Neither would give in and the crowd feared that the old man would be injured. She heard the young man threaten, "If you hit me with that chain, I'll kill you."
>
> Jean says that she doesn't know what made her do it, but she wound her way through the crowd, took the old man's hand and whispered for him to come with her. She led him away to his car and went on her way. The crowd dispersed and the conflict was neutralized by one unlikely person's courage. Jean acted as her brother's keeper through a third-person approach to blending and mending.

These stories are a few examples among the numerous acts of kindness throughout the world that reflect what *Tohei Sensei* calls the "principle of non-dissension." He defines it as the basic spirit or true form of the universe that we have forgotten. He disputes the belief that fighting is a natural jungle law. Animals live and die through an instinctive conformity to Nature's laws of *Oneness*. (*See* Part II, INTUITION.)

Non-dissension doesn't mean that we give in and allow others to run over us. *Tohei Sensei* describes it as a means of striving to live peacefully, avoiding arousal of the battles in our hearts. In *Ki in Daily Life*, he says:

> "Locking up the speech and actions of your opponent in your heart is not real non-dissension; it is endurance....This, too, is a sort of battle. The non-dissension we are speaking of arises when we do not harbor feelings against our opponent...to overcome discord without spiritual

pain, to laugh off any slander, and to lead astray any attack, without yourself receiving the blow."

Some *ki* experiences are impossible to explain unless we keep in mind that "thoughts are things." *Ki* is mentally, as well as verbally and physically, effective. We underestimate the energy of *thought*, which is a scientific-frontier subject with secrets yet to be explored and comprehended. (*See* Part II, THOUGHTS.)

When we are confronted with unusual and dangerous encounters, the knowledge and practice of *ki* awareness in everyday life can prepare us to react beyond our fears. A beginning *aikido* student, but advanced in karate, was walking home late at night. A hulking man and a young boy, crossed the street and headed toward her. Since her karate kicks and the few *aikido* techniques she had learned might not be adequate, she decided to "extend *ki*."

Later, she would relate that:

> "For some unknown reason, I began building a ball of light in my right hand. I visualized it as bright and glowing, grew it until it was the size of my favorite kind of ball, a volleyball. As the big fellow closed in for the kill, I mentally—with no physical motion other than continuing to walk—threw it in his face while sending along the thought, 'Don't even think it!' while glaring my disapproval of what he knew he shouldn't be doing.
>
> "He stopped dead in his tracks. His head jerked back, his jaw dropped, and he shook his head from side to side, looking at me stunned and blinking.
>
> What was still more remarkable was that his young companion then grabbed him by the arm and pulled him away. They both went back the way they had come, looking back at me in gape-mouthed astonishment as I just kept walking home."

She admits that a mundane explanation would be that he expected a small woman to show fear and hysteria. Another possibility is that on some level he was aware that she was throwing fire balls at him. Neither explains the actions of his young companion. "Either way," she added, "he did not get his knee caps kicked in and I did not get beaten up."

Three-dimensional Programs

> *"There are three sides to everything;*
> *your side, my side and the truth."*
> Author unknown

Like *Ki Wellness*, there are other programs in which three-dimensional approaches are used as a means of conveying appropriate thoughts and actions. Visualize each of these as a triangle of tri-tuning.

In *Martial Arts, The spiritual dimension,* Peter Payne equates his Head and Belly principles to the opposites, and the Heart principle as the integrating balance. He describes this new kind of energy as "the emergence of a new dimension...which is a generating force in itself." He uses such examples as scientific, hard and external for the Head; artistic, soft and internal as Belly; spiritual, resilient and relationship to represent the Heart factor. He points out that Western dualism gives value to the Head while devaluing the Belly as a dangerous imbalance that deprives both of their natural character. He sees this as the cause of heartless violence and rigid spirituality as well as the resistant or uncontrolled hysteria in need of a symmetrical balancing Heart Centre.

Rhoda McFarlane demonstrates a three-way choice in her book, *Coping through Assertiveness*. It is geared to help teenagers but can be beneficial for any age. She labels the three choices: aggressive, passive or assertive reactions. Her descriptive names and terms describe the mental *Voices* of conflict that debate between themselves within our brains. She shows how our "judgmental self" determines our behavior, feelings and self-esteem. "It is not what happens; it is what you tell yourself about it that determines the significance."

In one of her illustrations, a skier passes under a ski lift. When a friend on the lift shouts and waves to her, she skis on without response. The aggressive *Voice* of the person on the lift might say, "She's stuck up and I don't care because I don't need friends like her." The passive *Voice* might conclude that the skier is mad and doesn't want to be friends anymore. An assertive *Voice* would assume that the friend didn't hear or see her and that they will meet later.

Author McFarland's three-choice method parallels the fight, flight or flow of tri-tuning. When we flow (the assertive *Voice*) rather than responding with either fight or flight (aggressive or passive voices) we don't get caught up in false assumptions that trigger unnecessary conflict in our lives. If the aggressive or passive *Voice* should turn out to be true, they can be dealt with by tri-tuning also.

Another similarity to tri-tuning is Eric Berne's 1960's formula of Transactional Analysis. It became popularized as TA through his *Games People Play* and *I'm OK, You're OK* by Thomas A. Harris. The analogy of Parent, Adult and Child (PAC) response buttons that we push can be seen as a complementary triad.

Parent, Adult and Child are not terms of age; they represent states-of-maturity. Our Parent self is responsible, rational and in command. The innocent Child is free, playful and creative. The practical and reliable Adult balances the giving and receiving of "strokes" that help each of us play out and improve upon our "scripts" (our unconscious life-plans).

In *The TA Primer, Transactional Analysis in Everyday Life* by Adelaide Bry, she points out that, "All parents are heavy sometimes; parents need to be bossy sometimes, to tell you what to do, to keep you out of danger. But some parents are more opinionated than is necessary; some parents even take away your fun feelings if they are too heavy too often."

The same is true of tri-tuning. There are times to be commanding, times for submission and times that we can arbitrate to set fair-minded standards. With an attitude of holitude and a triality conscience, we are more likely to choose the most appropriate reaction. In fact, we can be commanding or submissive with a triality conscience when the need arises. We don't have to be young—to be young at heart, and we don't have to be grown up to have adult, responsible outlooks. (*See* Part II, OPPOSITES.)

Author Bry further states,

> "The best way you can feel is I'm OK, you're OK. This means you like yourself and other people, too. This means you use your happy feelings to love others, to get your work done, to have a good time. It doesn't mean you think the world is rosy or perfect; you know there are a lot of problems—every day—but you still enjoy living."

The popular "inner child" therapy is based on the Child aspect of Transactional Analysis. John Bradshaw, in *Home Coming, Reclaiming and Championing Your Inner Child,* referred to the celebrated painter, Georgia O'Keefe's autobiography, "Childhood seems to be a time when the inner quest is laid for many great creators."

He explains her comment:

> "Creative regeneration is the essence of life itself. Finding old memories, trusting your hunches and intuitions, and following your new energies may motivate you to risk new bursts of creativity."

There are theories that the DNA, the heredity with which we are born and have experiences from childhood, together, form the challenges that as adults we need to reconcile. My late, black friend and confidant, Blanche, often quoted Shakespeare:

> "All the world's a stage,
> And all men and women merely players:
> They have their exits and their entrances;
> And one man in his time plays many parts."

Blanche would add compassionately, " I think our purpose on earth is to help each other through our parts."

From this perspective, we don't have to waste our energy blaming parents and other relationships for our problems. According to some theories, what they did was their predestined designated roles to help set the stage for our learning experiences in life. Possibly their actions were intended to implant the challenges we needed to overcome and for building up the courage to rise above our childhood fears.

It is said that we cannot feel or express love and appreciation for others until we can feel good about ourselves. This includes forgiving ourselves as well. Reversing the Golden Rule, we can, "Do unto ourselves as we wish others to do unto us."

If we are kind to ourselves, the satisfaction of success will offset our disappointments when we do not live up to our own expectations. When we personally walk with the awareness of *ki*, spirergy, God, Higher Self or however we relate to the existence of Spirit, the unexpected and interesting events we experience will be worth the journey.

In *Recognition, Themes on Inner Perception,* Eden Gray refers to the "the point of stillness" at the top of a pendulum that Cabalists call the Limitless Light of the Unmanifest. In the diagram that she calls the Pendulum of Life, she labels the ball of the pendulum "YOU" and the top as the Unconditioned Consciousness, meaning seeing with the Single Eye of God. She equates the extreme pendulum swings of time that we call positive and negative as the Conditioned Consciousness that limits our judgment of the material to duality. Dr. Gray added that:

> "With our two physical eyes we will always see duality—good and evil—but when we understand that we see this way because of our conditioning, we learn to correct our vision and see with single eye of God—the eye that is too pure to behold evil."

This three-way insight is another means for envisioning the possibilities of tri-tuning with a triality conscience through holitude.

Blame and Shame

> *"Looking down on others is a lazy man's way to self-esteem."*
> Author unknown

"Love your enemies…" (Matt 5:44) is a confusing New Testament precept for Westerners to decipher. It goes against our dualistic pattern of fighting the opposites. We tend to blame and shame our *enemies* as a means of exalting ourselves and hiding our fears.

We want to believe that it is possible to "love your neighbor as yourself" (Matt 22:40). How to accomplish these admonishments in the overcrowded turbulent world that we as humans have created, is a dilemma that needs our full attention.

We tend to label anyone or anything that causes us to be fearful as "our enemy." Instead of focusing on the enemy, real or imagined, we can focus on an appropriate action. That is, how to turn a stressful situation into harmony. There are no enemies unless we bring them into being.

Some of Jesus' New Testament teachings are obscured by interpretations that bolster blame, shame, guilt and punishment. These four judgments spring foremost in our minds when anything is said or done that is considered to be negative. They represent our defenses of protection against those we consider a threat to our particular interpretation of social justice.

This sentiment does not intimate that wrongdoers shouldn't receive lawful punishment. We are responsible for our unlawful actions. Like the Oriental warrior in the story in Chapter Three, under The Mind of a Martial Artist, it is our attitude toward guilt and punishment that is most important.

The universal law of justice can be understood through a quote from Fyodor Doftoevsky's *Crime and Punishment*. "You must accept your punishment or the guilt will kill you." (*See* Part II, GUILT and PUNISHMENT.)

Victims sometimes feel that to forgive their attackers, they must help set the convicted person free with no punitive consequences. Forgiveness has more to do with replacing the vengeance we harbor in our hearts than what kind of sentence the guilty person receives. Our task is to forgive in our hearts, knowing that except by the grace of life's circumstances, the perpetrator could have been us.

It is said that not being able to forgive is like being handcuffed to the unforgiven; only you have the key. The late President Nixon said "Those who hate you don't win, unless you hate them."

How to love our enemies baffles most of us, because humans have a tendency to delight secretly or blatantly in blaming and shaming others; watching them get their comeuppance. Historically, acts of torment and punishment by death have drawn record crowds, most of whom consider it entertainment or vengeful satisfaction.

There is evidence of how much we love to judge the supposed sins of others by the very media coverage that draws our attention. A sex scandal will draw mass attention, while an economic or political matter that affects everyone's tax pocket may go unheeded by the general public. During the hearings for approval of a Supreme Court judge, Americans were transfixed by the TV coverage while a co-worker accused him of having uttered sexually harassing words. If his appointment had depended on public opinion, Clarence Thomas' chances of being approved would have been jeopardized.

A Unity Church minister relates the story about a potential new member. She liked everything about the church except that he as minister didn't preach about guilt and punishment for sinners in this world or the next. She wanted to be assured that those sinners burned in hell.

Dan Frank, Chief Instructor of the Maryland Ki Society, tells the story of a policeman who came to learn the merits of *aikido*. Even though he was a big guy, he was experiencing resistance to his arrests. He learned to focus on the objective—to get compliance through the attitude that, "If I'm not belligerent, they don't have to be." Later, he remarked that the more *aikido* he learned, the less he had to use it.

The reverse of this story calls for the same consideration on the part of those arrested. The accused citizen who is cooperative will have a much better chance of getting extra consideration than the hostile person who views any policeman as an enemy.

Both blame and shame escalate a fighting conscience or cause a slave conscience reaction. A triality conscience helps to release personal trauma. When mind and body are coordinated, we tend to exude compassion. We attune ourselves with our surroundings. Conflict is replaced by harmony when we use our spirergy in a manner that is appropriate to the particular situation.

> Two monks set out on a meditative journey. They saw a woman who was stranded because a recent flood had washed out the bridge. One monk picked up the woman, carried her across the stream and sent her on her way.
>
> The two monks continued in silence until evening when they made camp for the night. At sunset, when they were allowed to break their meditative silence, the other monk spoke in an angry tone.
>
> "Don't you know that we are forbidden to touch a woman, much less pick her up and carry her?"
>
> His companion replied, "I carried a helpless woman across a stream and left her there. You have carried her all day."

The stories of bravery and compassion from Eastern and Western cultures included in this chapter were chosen from the many possible examples showing that while cultures differ, humanity is basically alike. Inspirational writings, customs and experiences from both the East and the West can motivate us to look at all sides of any situation for the best solutions.

We need to evaluate our impressions and actions toward those who live a different lifestyle, subsist on another economic level, practice a fringe religion, belong to an opposite political party, have the features of a different race, were born in another country or speak a different language. Do we judge them through fear or attempt to understand the source of their convictions and the reasons for their actions? The more we develop our triality conscience, the less we will have to contend with the conflicts that those who lived by traditional fighting and slave consciences in the past have handed down to us.

The Epitome of Tri-tuning

> *"We must live together as brothers or perish together as fools."*
> Dr. Martin Luther King, Jr.

Favorite stories that reflect individual deeds of courage and virtue are an inherited part of every culture. They tell of times when everyone could have walked away, leaving someone unaided. Instead these heroes pushed aside the temptation to avoid getting involved in something considered beneath their dignity or beyond their obligation to humanity.

We would not know about one such story if Terry Dobson, an American studying *aikido* in Japan, had not humbled himself to tell about an incident on a train in Tokyo. The following is an account of the chapter entitled "A Kind Word Turneth Away Wrath," from Richard Strozzi Heckler's *Aikido and the New Warrior*.

> When the rickety old train came to a stop, the quiet of a spring afternoon was shattered by a loud-mouthed drunk who stumbled into the comparatively empty car where Terry Dobson was seated. While screaming extreme profanities, the intruder's blow sent a woman holding a baby spinning into the laps of an elderly couple. They scampered to the other end of the car while other passengers froze with fear. When the filthy-clothed Japanese laborer with bloodshot

Gleaning the Best from East and West

eyes and a face that reflected his rage and hatred tried to wrench out the metal center pole, Dobson stood up.

The young six-foot, 225 pound *aikidoist*, who had been training eight hours every day for three years, was itching to try his skill in actual combat. Though students had been warned that they were not to use the martial art techniques in public unless it was absolutely necessary to protect other people, Dobson felt that his opportunity had presented itself. Despite the daily teachings by *Ueshiba Sensei* that *aikido* was a non-violent art of reconciliation, with a mission to resolve conflict rather than generating it, Dobson felt that this scene warranted his contribution.

Seeing him stand up, the drunk roared, "Aha! A hairy foreign twerp needs a lesson in Japanese manners!" Their attempted swings into combat were interrupted by a loud, ear-splitting but strangely joyous "heeeeey!" Both looked down at a tiny Japanese man, well into his seventies, immaculately dressed in a *kimono* and *hakama*.

With no notice of Dobson, he smiled delightedly at the laborer, "C'mere and talk with me." Instead, the confused drunk swore at him and readied his fists. The old gentleman, still beaming and with no trace of fear, asked lightly, "What you been drinkin'?"

Amid profanities the laborer said he was drinking *sake*, and that it was no one's business.

Ignoring the slurs, the old man said, "Oh, that's absolutely wonderful," and proceeded to tell the drunk how he and his 76-year-old wife drank warm sake in their garden every night, sitting on an old bench his grandfather's student made for him, and admiring the persimmon tree his great-grandfather had planted.

His delight in sharing the story affected the drunk, whose face began to soften as his fists slowly unclenched during an agreement that he too loved sake.

The soft-spoken man went on saying he was sure the laborer also had a wonderful wife. This brought a sad and tearful admission by the drunk had he had no home, no clothes, no tools, no money, and ended with, "I'm so ashamed of myself."

The old gentleman sympathized, inviting the drunk to sit down and tell him all about it.

When the train stopped at Terry Dobson's station, he was feeling dirtier and more ashamed "in my clean clothes and my make-this-world-safe-for-democracy righteousness than that laborer would ever be." His last glance took in the scene of a compassionate old man stroking a filthy matted head of the drunk who had tearfully sat down beside him.

Upon leaving the train, Dobson sank onto a bench to sort out the experience. He admitted to himself that, "what I was prepared to accomplish with bone and muscle had been accomplished with a smile and a few kind words. He had just witnessed *aikido* in action and knew it would take a different sense of spirit for him to "speak with knowledge about *aikido* or the resolution of conflict."

In 1978, the now late Terry Dobson, along with Victor Miller, authored *Giving In to Get Your Way—The Attack-tics System for Winning Your Everyday Battles*. They dedicated the book in memory of *Morihei Ueshiba*.

This story is an example of the many virtuous acts by those who have surmounted the usual human fighting and slave conscience around the world. They have ascended to the sense of triality that beckons from deep within all our minds or souls.

Bridging Western Logic and Eastern Feeling Nature

> *"Science as epitome of Western thought and spirituality as the epitome of Eastern thought are not separate disciplines; they are different aspects of the same whole, each dancing around the other, waiting to be merged in human awareness."*
> Norman Friedman
> *Bridging Science and Spirit*

There are advantages and disadvantages to the actions of both the predominantly group-oriented cultures in the East, and the individualism expressed through the collective consciousness of Western cultures. There is an underlying wish for peace of mind among all peoples whether considered Eastern, Western, Northern or Southern. The attainment of "the peace that passes understanding" can serve as a goal when we attempt to glean the best ways to serve humanity. East and West are two sides of the same coin. To gain the essence of both, we need bridges, instead of the walls that have resulted from cunning and deceit.

Despite all the sage advice rendered for millennia, humanity has not come to terms with life enough to successfully bridge the opposites and allow ourselves to live beyond fear. We have yet to succeed in living in a manner that prevents war—between nations or within the hearts of humankind. The treachery that humans commit upon each other is unbelievable. Even some of the customs that are meant as solutions to man's barbaric habits, produce a predominately dark side. (*See* Part II, POWER.)

In the East, the tradition of "save face" is a form of response intended as compassion to prevent embarrassment and the escalation of conflict. However, the unexpressed resentment is often internalized, where it boils to the point of devious explosion.

Hua, a friend from Vietnam, explained the two hemispheric codes of ethics by comparing the Eastern warrior with Western cowhand traditions. In the Old West, it was considered cowardly to shoot a man in the back. An Oriental might bow to the face, but stab in the back. Hua said that many Vietnamese men were knifed in the back by wives who never would have dared to rebuke them face to face.

She added that her own grandmother never once spoke directly to her mother. It was a subtle reminder to Hua's mother that her mother-in-law disapproved of the fact that her son (Hua's Vietnamese father) had married a Chinese woman. Hua said, "Grandmother would tell one of us children what she wanted mother to know and we would relay the messages back and forth."

Similarly, when there is a split among martial art groups in Japan, the custom is that neither the group nor its individual members have any communication with the other group thereafter. Some will go so far as to forbid their students to associate with the other group in any manner.

This trait often spills over among Western *martial arts* groups. Coupled with the Western emphasis on stiff competition, this practice can cause even more animosity. In the West, blame for these resentful habits is passed off as the "politics" of organization. It is easy to make politics the scapegoat for human egotistic selfishness and jealousy when the narrow-mindedness that loves to ally itself with fear is the real culprit.

These short-sighted practices set poor examples for young martial art students who have a natural desire to follow in the footsteps of the adults they admire. The Mahatma Gandhi said, "If we wish to create a lasting peace, we must begin with the children." Just as we do not always set good examples concerning our religious convictions, we sometimes fall short of our goals in fulfilling our moral ethics as well.

Ancient Japanese enhanced the traditional arts they borrowed from China. We can only hope that as those artistic techniques are accepted in the Western world, they will not be corrupted or watered down by Western logic to the point that they lose their Eastern essence.

Many Westerners feel that to choose an Eastern philosophy means abandonment of Western theology, instead of blending the merits of both. Comparatively speaking, Westerners need a dose of calm to balance our hyper-mania, while Easterners could learn to enjoy the enthusiasm of more individualism.

Opposite shortcomings can be noted between the East and West. Easterners are more passive and patient, but tend toward cunning and treachery. Westerners are more aggressive and outspoken, with a tendency toward belligerent mannerisms that cause hyper, stress-related rash decisions. The Japanese are pompously proud of their tradition that the sun rises upon them first. As Americans, we tend to burden ourselves with the egotistic ideal that we must be #1 in every way. Worse yet is our impression that the rest of the world must copy our lead in whatever and however we decide is best for them.

All too often one nation judges another through fear that is caused by misunderstanding. More harmony can be created when each citizen at least attempts to understand the source of the moral convictions of other cultures as well as the reasons behind their shortcomings.

Everyone deserves the liberty to be responsible. By contributing to each other's welfare, globally and locally, we enhance our own freedom. To think globally and act locally is sound advice.

The extent to which the whole world replaces a fighting and slave conscience with a triality conscience, will determine which will prevail. In emerging countries, where the ruling class has historically become rich at the expense of the poor, the down-trodden will need time to learn how to overcome their slave consciences.

Moses kept the Israelites in the wilderness until they learned to rise above the slave conscience they had grown accustomed to in Egypt. Slaves or subjects who suddenly experience a change to the freedom of democracy and socialism, usually have little comprehension of how to handle the newly-found liberties. Either they learn to balance freedom and responsibility, or they breed spoiled unreliable citizens. This is the chief argument by those who believe that democracies will not endure; that the average citizen lacks the intelligent to make responsible decisions.

When what is freely provided gets out of balance with citizen acceptance of responsibility, freedom is short-lived. Much of our globe is experiencing a pendulum swing to democratic government. The test of its endurance will rely as much on citizen reaction as on the governing bodies.

Both the Eastern and Western hemispheres, including the Northern and Southern continents, have great knowledge and material resources that can benefit each other. An understanding and blending of the best from the entire world, in a harmonious way, will escalate humanity in a New Direction. The complementing of opposite mindsets by blending all sources of achievement and contentment, around the globe, can bring good fortune to all.

Review of Tri-tuning skills in Chapter Four:

1. Aikido Tenkan Technique, p. 92
2. Relationships and Family Conflict, p. 95

Tri-Tuning

PART II

PART II

Ways to Tri-tune our Everyday Lives

"The important thing is not to stop questioning."
Albert Einstein

An Alphabetical List of Reasons and Ways to Tri-tune

*"It is right to be content with what we have,
never with what we are."*
Sir James Mackintosh

AN ORIENTAL SWORDSMAN seeking enlightenment, asked his master whether he should put away his sword since he did not want to kill anyone any more. The master's answer; "Wear it until it becomes a burden." When we learn to handle our problems by getting beyond fear, we will no longer need our defensive encumbrances.

Some of the words and topics mentioned in Part I will now be further explained and arranged in alphabetical order for easy cross-referencing. Additional ways to ease the challenges of daily life through tri-tuning will be explored. Volumes of information have already been written on most of these subjects. Part II is an elaboration on the meanings of these words and their connotations relative to the concepts defined through spirergy, tri-tuning, triality and holitude.

Compare the ways you normally relate to each word, with what you experience while tri-tuning. Some of the analogies suggested as solutions may not reflect your values or insights. The examples used to explain the topics are not necessarily the only answers. They are meant to stimulate your quest for solutions concerning these issues as they apply to your life. Follow the advice of Benjamin Franklin and "open your mind, for the doors of wisdom are never shut."

Develop your own holitude and triality manual as a reflection of your own conclusions. Evaluate all viewpoints and choose the best ways to improve *your* daily routine. Change your opinions according to your *gut feelings,* rather than as an obligation to believe something that counters your *wee small voice.* Evaluate each topic from your own perspective. How well do you "know thyself" now and how much better can you come to know yourself?

Review your journal listings of how you already tri-tune and the list of new tri-tuning habits you would like to develop. Occasionally, set a timer. When the bell rings, observe whether you are stressed, collapsed or tri-tuned. If you feel you are not accomplishing enough, recall how you would have reacted before your were aware of tri-tuning. Compare the two. Likely, there has been more improvement than you realized. Be good to yourself, no matter what. Be patient with your progress while developing your potential personal growth. Enjoy the challenges of life's see-sawing ups and downs. Do not wait for ultimate happiness; begin where you are and enjoy the ride!

ANGER, Hate, Vengeance, Resentment

> *"Anger is a wind which blows out the lamp of the mind."*
> Robert Green Ingersoll

Tri-tuning helps us make level-headed decisions; to know when to repress, express or release anger through our *one point*. (*Refer* to the Ki Meditation section in Chapter Two.) At crucial moments we can simply release our anger by replacing it with an appropriate solution. It may take lots of practice to replace a normal tendency to act defensively but it will be worth the effort.

According to Chinese medicine teachings, repressed anger is harbored in the liver; the largest and one of the most important organs in the human body. From a holistic medicine point of view, the liver is the human garbage can for toxic matter and thoughts of anger. New scientific evidence is beginning to influence the Western medical profession to consider these possibilities.

Some medical professionals, including Dr. Dean Ornish, emphasize the fact that anger and hidden mental grudges manifest as physical illness. Practice releasing anger in an appropriate manner, rather than repressing it inwardly. (*Refer* to Chapter Four, Blend and Mend.)

Before the discovery of microbes, illnesses were thought to be caused by spirit demons as punishment for sins. This interpretation is still held by some religious groups. The illnesses caused by microbes also can be seen as Nature's means of expelling toxins to restore balance between the mind and body. St. Francis of Assisi said that "illness of the body benefits the soul." This does not mean that we should desire illness, but that illness sometimes manifests as a cleansing of anger and frustration caused by congestive fears.

Studies done by Norman Cousins, Dr. Bernie Siegel and others, suggest that we bring on illness by our own inner conflicts. This conclusion is sometimes countered by the argument that "self-accusal" creates self-guilt, which in itself can cause physical and mental illness. Living beyond fear brings these two perceptions into balance.

Beyond these conclusions is the belief in reincarnation that illness is not a punishment, but a karmic correction or the re-balancing of our misdeeds in this or a past life. A triality conscience can help prevent some of these problems from arising and can assist in dealing with whatever materializes.

> The story is told about a mother whose only daughter was killed by a rapist. He was convicted and imprisoned for life. This revenge did not extinguish the mother's anger and grief. It extended into years of self-perpetuated misery. One night, as she lay awake suffering from her usual insomnia, her thoughts turned to the young man's parents. She wondered whether they too were suffering.
>
> Upon investigation, she learned that they and their imprisoned son were living with terrible guilt. After visiting and later forgiving him in her heart, they became friends. The deceased daughter then appeared to her mother in a dream. She revealed that her mission on earth had been to teach her mother to overcome the lifetime of bitterness that had kept her chronically and emotionally ill.

The reference to reincarnation in this story may be incompatible with some religious beliefs, but the scenario of harbored hate and unrelenting vengeance is played out in court cases every day. The opposite extreme is witnessed when victims feel that they must forgive to the point of not prosecuting the accused villain. Forgiveness is one issue; correctional measures under the law—for public safety of the innocent—is another matter. Forgiveness is a satisfaction within the heart.

We are responsible to the laws of Nature, as well as civil law, for our misdeeds. Civil laws, though unfair in some cases, are necessary to protect the innocent and to serve as guidelines for permissible behavior. Forgiveness lies in the realm of understanding and the release of personal vengeance. To "love our enemies" is an internal release from personal vengeance. Whether we view the matter as karmic cause and effect, or "as we sow, so shall we reap," resentment gnaws away at our physical and mental well-being. Those on whom we waste our emotional hate may be completely unaware that they caused a problem or may actually be innocent. They might even be glad to see us in turmoil. The need for forgiveness can be seen as being handcuffed to the accused while we hold the key.

If the human liver is a garbage pail for physical and mental toxins, then toxic overload contributes to the explosive eruptions of such responses as violent road rage and physical abuse. Dependence upon synthetic drugs, in many cases, helps suppress the anger and hostility. They can also spawn side effects that magnify the tendency toward vengeance. Learning to live beyond fear is a more stable and permanent cure.

Suggestion: Survey your patterns of anger and practice replacing them, one by one. Learn through tri-tuning to respect the feelings of others and how to release personal emotions appropriately.

BALANCE

> *"Only when we have tuned ourselves and strengthened our ability to maintain balance in motion, can we respond to imbalance brought on by opponents."*
> Ming Shi
> *Mind Over Matter: Higher Martial Arts*

Balance is a correction of extremes. It is Nature's pivotal point which allows for extremes and uses them as pressure valves to be followed by the regaining of cosmic balance. When extreme pendulum swings propel us out of balance, Nature does the necessary re-balancing.

Fears associated with the usual chaos created by change are normally labeled "punishment by God" or looked upon as natural disasters. What we often think of as punishment is simply Nature's means of bringing into balance the extremes that are caused mostly by human negligence or over-indulgence. We live in cultures of extremism. Our actions either accentuate the problem or help Nature perform her cosmic balancing act. Most extreme imbalance is caused, unwittingly or on purpose, by human greed and selfishness. Nature pulls one way and human nature pulls the other.

One of the main objectives throughout this publication is to point out how our obsession with extremes keeps us out of balance within ourselves and with the rest of the world. The particular suggestions that I use to demonstrate a point are merely examples to bring awareness to the reader's mind.

To understand balance, consider how the universe operates. Nature uses balance as a means of adapting life to evolutionary change. The more we respect and harmonize with Nature's laws of balance, the less we will have to fear. When we purposely fight Nature instead of helping, we cause an unnecessary breach of natural extremes to swing wider and wider.

The pendulum of change is not intended to remain stationary in the middle. Nature embraces the ebb and flow to rebalance our actions that either cause or prevent unnecessary chaos.

Paradoxically, this does not mean that we throw out extremes or stay on the fence of indecision and fear. Like negativity, extremes have their place but we need to learn how to deal with them and their opposites. The chaos of extremes can best be avoided by weighing the balance of both sides of a situation. It is a matter of appreciating and complementing the opposites.

Since around the thirteenth century, Oriental art has reflected the perception that "there is balance in imbalance." Decorative objects are not placed in the middle of a table. To center something makes it divisible by half, which severs its oneness into halves. A larger decoration, off centered, with a smaller one near the opposite end, lends balance.

In the East, the even numbers (2, 4, 6, etc.) are considered unlucky, because they are divisible. In the modern West, we accentuate even numbers, but hang on to our ancient guard against the divisible number 2. We dread a $2 bill, and distrust the two-faced person who might double-cross us with double-dealings.

The duality of mind and body in the West is only recently being replaced by a sense of unity. The Western separation from Nature may be a subconscious reflection of the Genesis Biblical Story of separation from God. Traditionally, being driven from the garden of Eden is pictured as humanity being driven into a harsh wasteland that God has little to do with, except as a means to punish humans for their sins.

In his lectures, the late author Paul K. Chivington expressed an opposite interpretation of the Genesis story. He equated humans being driven from the Garden of Eden, to parent birds pushing the young out of the nest so they can gain the courage that is needed to develop wisdom through maturity. It may seem harsh but it is for growth, not punishment.

Balance is also needed between the mind and body, the two sides of the body and including the two hemispheres of the brain. Balance in the human body is largely equalized through the spinal column. Wellness depends upon the restoration of balance. Chinese medicine is based on restoring this healthy balance.

BREATH

"Breathing deeply, fully and completely energizes the body, calms the nerves, fills you with peace and helps keep you youthful."
Paul C. Bragg

One of the most important ways to maintain good health is through proper breathing. Breath is our most precious commodity. Not only do we share the balance of oxygen and carbon dioxide with all life on earth, we are interdependent upon this balance. A reduction of plant life will decrease the supply of oxygen necessary to sustain animal life. Without the exchange of carbon dioxide and oxygen between plants and animals, life on earth—as we know it—will disappear. Water, food and sleep are essential, but human life lasts only a matter of minutes without breath. When we plant trees, we not only provide shade for future generations but their oxygen supply as well.

Do you breathe correctly? This question may sound absurd since all animal and plant life unconsciously breathes continuously from birth to death. That fact does not guarantee that we breathe correctly. Do you sometimes find yourself holding your breath or taking shallow breaths?

We deprive our bodies of a healthy oxygen/carbon dioxide exchange when we are stressed by fear. Fear causes tension and tension causes shallow breathing. This habit deprives the body of the vital energy that is metabolized from each breath we breathe.

The fight/flight syndrome, a decision whether to stay and fight or to flee from danger, signals the body to send more oxygen-filled blood into the muscles. This reflex action transpires when we fear confrontation in any form, whether imagined or real. When we are fearful and tense, the same reaction occurs whether the anticipated attack is physical or mental. It is suspected that diseases of the muscles, nerves and blood circulation, such as arthritis, shingles and high blood pressure may be affected, or even caused, by chronic rigidity resulting from worry and fear.

When stressed or scared we resort to quick, short breaths and extra blood is summoned to the muscles. When relaxed, we breathe smoothly. The over-abundance of blood in the muscles then streams back to resume its usual chores, such as aiding digestion or replacing dying cells. Is it any wonder that we get indigestion when we are upset from stress and our blood supply has been called away to active duty elsewhere?

Oxygen is an essential energy source for the body's numerous functions. The body heals itself, mainly through turning the oxygen we breathe into healing energy. Deep breathing is useful for everything from relaxation to body-cell replacement.

Tohei Sensei developed *ki* breathing, which he calls *whole-body breathing*. We breathe through our lungs and skin as well as through the bloodstream at a cellular level. It takes less than 30 seconds for our blood supply to circulate the entire body. Whole-body breathing is not so far-fetched as it may sound.

Comparing Ordinary Deep Breathing

Usually, deep breathing instructors begin by saying, "Take a deep breath."

1. **Breathe in as long as you can, and follow it by an out breath.** Think about how that deep breath felt.
2. **Now begin by exhaling for as long as comfortable.** Then allow your body to breathe in as long as comfortable.

Which way took the most exertion and caused the most stress. Likely, you chose #1.

You probably lifted your shoulders with that first in-breath, which automatically caused stress. During the second breath (#2), your body welcomed the in-breath that filled the vacuum that had been created by the out-breath. You breathed without exertion.

The next time you are instructed to take a deep breath, breathe out quickly before taking the deep breath. Accent each out-breath and allow an *equally long* in-breath. If you breath out longer than in, you hyperventilate. This imbalance can cause dizziness.

Whole-Body Breathing Exercises

To practice whole-body breathing:

1. **Tri-tune while standing, sitting or lying comfortably.**
2. **Breathe *out* through your open mouth, with the jaw relaxed.**
3. **Breathe in through the nose.**
4. **As you breathe out again through the open mouth, visualize your body as a vessel that you empty slowly from head to foot.**
5. **As you breathe in, visualize slowly refilling the vessel from toes to head.**
6. **Repeat the out-breath, counting the seconds as you exhale, and inhale an equal number of seconds.**

Use silent counting to measure the increase in seconds that will become comfortable as your lungs expand with practice. When you are ill, be sure to *whole-body breathe* for at least 20 minutes, as many times each day as possible, to aid healing.

Correct breathing is beneficial during any activity. Breathe *out* during exertion and *in* upon recovery. While playing golf, tennis or any sport, release the breath rapidly, but smoothly, as you exert energy during contact. Any activity is less strenuous if performed on the out-breath.

This does not mean using the vocal cords. Just use an accentuated (not gushed) out-breath. Vocalizing the release of breath is a waste of energy and an irritation to the throat, unless intended as a scare tactic.

The "rebel yell," used by Confederate soldiers during the American Civil War, served as a tension release for those yelling—while striking fear into the enemy. A scream or cry for help is also an emotional out-breath of fear release.

The Japanese warrior **kaia** is a projection of focused *ki* through the voice. It resonates as ee-yee-e-e-e, with a staccato ending that can stop someone in their tracks. It is also effective as a silent or compassionate soft sound.

In *Illuminated Spirit,* Dan DeProspero tells how he voiced a soft *kiai* into the ear of his *Kyudo* (Japanese archery) *sensei* on his death bed. It was a respectful acknowledgment of the bond between them. The pace of Onuma Sensei's heart monitor quickened for a few moments before gradually fading away, indicating death.

A healthy expending of the out-breath is experienced through singing, laughing and talking but a balance of in-breath is required. When singing correctly, the sound is correlated with the breath and correctly spaced in-breaths are important. Shirley MacLaine commented about the importance of getting the breath out while dancing. A dancer must learn to equalize the out and in-breath to prevent stress build-up and exhaustion.

"Breathe before you speak," is one of Richard Carlson's suggestions in *Don't Sweat the Small Stuff...and it's All Small Stuff.* He advises that taking a second, (that at first seems like an eternity) to breathe instead of anxiously answering, will release stress for both the stressed speaker and the up-tight listener. Taking a breathe, in this situation, will assure enough out-breathe to complete your answer.

Remember to emphasize the out-breath during fearful times of danger, stress, anxiety and injury. When short of breath, instead of submitting to the inclination to breathe in, breathe *out* to empty stagnate air from the lungs. Then the body will automatically invite an extra health-support of in-breath.

We refer to the out-breath as *a sigh of relief*. It is just that. An awareness of the out-breath can be used for calming after any sudden reaction. Breathe out after you have quickly prevented something from falling or during a precarious situation that leaves your heart pumping. At the scene of an accident, encourage those in shock to breathe out for relaxation and to continue a rhythmic deep breathing.

Remember to deep breathe when you are injured or ill. This will ease the state of shock by relaxing the body. In case of a heart emergency, correct breathing can be your "first" aid—before and after 911 help arrives.

According to Ed McCabe, an investigative journalist on oxygen therapy:

> "Viruses and microbes (such as flu, AIDS, arterial plaque, and cancer cells), live best in low oxygen environments. They are anaerobic. That means 'increase the oxygen level around them and they die.' Deep breathing can restore and maintain health."

Paul Bragg, the originator of Health Food Stores in America, used this quote in his book to point out that shallow breathers do not adequately expel body toxins. When impure blood is re-circulated through the body, it cannot replenish the body properly.

We live in a sea of air in which oxygen decreases as pollution increases. Attaining extra oxygen by increased breathing will become more essential, according to amount of toxicity in the air.

Other than highly-polluted places, deep breathing can be practiced anywhere. Extra breathing will increase energy and relieve tension. Utilize anxious times; waiting impatiently in a checkout line or at a traffic light. In conspicuous places, breathe out *and* in through the nose.

We need never be bored after learning to deep breathe. Practice deep breathing during a lecture, while waiting anxiously or before any performance. Time is never wasted while deep breathing. Take advantage of those uptight times: waiting for the computer to boot up, anticipating an important phone call or during the lulls between thoughts while composing any form of writing or artistic creation.

Athlete Ian Jackson, and author of *The BreathPlay Approach to WholeLife Fitness,* accidentally discovered that when he "pushed the breath out, and *let* it in," breathing brought extra enjoyment to his running and to his life. He called it *upsidedown* breathing, a technique he teaches as a means of handling stress.

Our bodies benefit from proper deep breathing at any time. Deep breathing practice is best done alone. Each of us has a different breathing capacity. Among its many benefits: breathing massages internal body organs, releases stress and calms the mind. Deep breathing and correct posture go together as two of the most complementary means of restoring and maintaining good health.

Suggestion: Give some attention to your posture and breathing habits. You may be surprised at what you discover about yourself and how deep breathing can improve your health.

CHANGE

> *"Change is often desirable, frequently necessary, and always inevitable."*
> Author unknown

"Energy itself is change and change is motion." To these words Professor Gerard Lamothe added:

> "Whatever *is*—is motion. When I accept this notion, I have adopted my role of being changed by my environment as well as my role in parenting my environment. Through this notion of motion, I am at once a child of the universe and parent to the universe. We are not just products of change, we are directors of change."

Much of our personal energy is wasted, either through fighting change or becoming slaves to misdirected change. When we accept the challenges created by change, we can flow and grow beyond the pain of dueling the opposites. By the complementary use of positives and negatives, we can fulfill our need for complacency in one set of circumstances and our curiosity in another situation.

Any change creates its own opposite. There are advantages and disadvantages in every situation. Cultural norms change over time in every society. Fads come and go quickly, while long-standing mores usually die a lingering death. However, cultural norms that have withstood the flux of change for extended periods can reverse themselves unexpectedly. Examples include the fall of Communism in Russia and our national attitude toward smoking.

These changes parallel *The Hundredth Monkey* by Ken Keyes, Jr. He equated the results of Lyall Watson's report on the unusual actions of wild troops of macaca fuscata monkeys living on an island in Japan, with simultaneous similarities of change, discoveries and inventions the world over.

> In 1952, primatologists provided the monkeys with food, including sweet potatoes, to discourage them from raiding the farmers' produce. Several innovative changes on Kishima Island in 1953, concerned an 18-month old female named Imo. She somehow discovered that sand and grit could be removed from the sweet potatoes by taking them into the water and washing them. This was soon imitated by Imo's playmates and her mother. By 1958, the juveniles and some adults, who had learned from the children, were washing their sweet potatoes.
>
> Then something unusual occurred. One day it was discovered that all the monkeys, including those on islands too distant for audible communication, had developed the habit of washing their sweet potatoes.

Ken Keyes concluded that "there is a point at which if only one more person tunes-in to a new awareness, a field is strengthened so that this awareness is picked up by almost everyone!" This concept confirmed his basic intuitive tenet "that the appreciation and love we have for ourselves and others creates an expanding energy field that becomes a growing power in the world." He used the hundredth monkey phenomenon as a "counterbalance of hope to off-set the doomsday story of nuclear destruction."

Watson's paranormal conclusion has been challenged because of its supposed lack of proper scientific data. Soundly based or not, the premise of the "hundredth monkey" pendulum swing reflects the simultaneous inventions by two or more individuals and the identical developments in cultures living at great distances from each other. Perhaps not in one day or year, but when enough like-minded people jump on one end of the see/saw of a social trend, that momentum leads to quick replacement of outmoded norms.

One day in the 1957, only a few children had Hula-Hoops. Almost overnight the craze was on. The energy of change causes this and other phenomenal changes to happen. Many inventions, such as the telephone, that have been simultaneously created by persons unknown to each other, is—so far—unexplained by the scientific world.

We need to understand that every fad creates its opposite. When we were warned that butter was harmful to our health, we switched to margarine. The body's incompatibility with the toxins caused by artificial chemicals in oleo, has not been equally disclosed.

Apparently it is a normal human reaction to look upon present norms or beliefs as the ultimate and only absolute truth. Change is looked upon as either unwarranted or forced, without consideration of its positive and negative consequences. Fundamental beliefs become dogmas when believers doggedly reject the inevitable changes that result from outmoded so-called *truths*. The opposite—change just for the sake of change—causes just as much unnecessary conflict and trauma. It must be remembered that "hundredth monkey" trends can sway the populous toward ideas and deeds of destruction as easily as those of construction.

When the earth was thought to be flat, it was laughable and sacrilegious to claim it was round. In the early days of aviation, comments such as, "If God had meant man to fly, he would have given him wings," were commonplace. Presently, a similar comment is, "If that were true, scientists [all professionals] would accept it." More radical still, we sometimes hear, "I wouldn't believe that, even if it were true."

Dr. Ignaz Semmelweiss, a Hungarian obstetric physician, died in 1865—a broken man. In fifteen years, he could not persuade the medical profession to change it's practice concerning hand washing between patients. His practice of requiring medical students in his hospital to wash with chlorinated lime when going from the morgue to the delivery room, sharply reduced the mortality rate for mothers and babies.

What he had practiced from 1850 on, combined with results from the works of Louis Pasteur, led English surgeon Dr. Joseph Lister to introduce the principle of antisepsis. By the time of Lister's death in 1912, hand washing and antiseptic surgeries were common practices—over 50 years after Dr. Semmelweiss's desperate plea had been ridiculed. Dr. Elmer M. Cranton used this account in *Bypassing Bypass, the New Technique of Chelation Therapy,* as an example of how long it sometimes takes for the values of new or unorthodox medical practices to be recognized as having value.

Ironically, the discovery of bacterium through the simply constructed microscope of Dutch naturalist Anton van Leeuwenhoek had been reported to the Royal Society of London in 1683. Before Pasteur's discoveries in 1860, it was generally believed that bacteria were produced by spontaneous generation. Consider how many lives were lost in 200 years because of stubborn resistance to change by the most educated of professionals.

In the latter half of the twentieth century, we have experienced the same reluctance to change because of an inability for Westerns to grasp the mind-set required to understand the basis of Eastern medicine. Neither system is flawless but each can learn from the other. In *Mind Over Matter: Higher Martial Arts,* Ming Shi explains how diseases are produced by the seriously ever-growing imbalance between the various levels of body and mind. "When environmental conditions are beyond human control, the only practical thing to do is to change the ability of humanity to adapt to the environment."

Open-minded scientists refer to change as the only constant. *Tohei Sensei* feels that it is most important to prepare children to adapt to appropriate and necessary changes. One of his favorite sayings was, "be content but never satisfied."

Problems are caused by those who are extremely fearful of change and by those who force change merely for the sake of change. Rev. Myles Monroe told his congregation, "Not all change is improvement, but there can be no improvement without change."

Ways to Tri-tune our Everyday Lives ▲ 131

When tri-tuned, we can face appropriate change with calm introspection. The young are innately curious—which naturally leads to change. Adults are more prone to be complacent and satisfied with the status quo. To an extent, youth desires change just for the sake of change. The opposite—those who are more experienced and mature, don't want to rock the boat. Broadmindedness and a balance between these extremes can create contentment through serene enthusiasm. Visualize a tri-tuning triangle with curiosity on the right, complacency on the left and contentment at the top.

When a decision whether to accept or reject a particular change becomes necessary, it is essential to look at both sides with an open mind. Those who are close-minded, do not want to hear the other side of an issue. They will avoid becoming involved and usually will refuse to face the controversy. They typify an extreme mental rigidity, "I wouldn't agree to it, no matter what."

This close-minded attitude is displayed by those who see a situation from their point of view only. They will lie and manipulate to get their way. They are reacting through a fighting conscience. Those who act through a triality conscience are willing to study the situation and listen to the other side. They will state both their concerns and their fair-minded convictions.

Suggestion: Do you fear change or do you view it as a challenge, for better or for worse? Some changes leave us refreshed while others are devastating. Take inventory of your procrastination toward change and list new habits that will ease your life, either presently or in the future. Rather than expecting instant change, be thankful for any improvement. Continue to do your best a little better and enjoy the results.

CONSCIOUSNESS, Subconscious

"In the long run…
no conscious will ever replace the life instinct."
Carl Jung

Consciousness is the awareness of what we think, feel and do; our relationship with, and our reactions to, the external world. The subconscious, or unconscious mind, was seen by Sigmund Freud as inherently evil, while some scientists saw it as the source of creative genius. Carl Jung mediated between these extremes. He concluded that the unconscious is "perfectly neutral as far as moral sense, aesthetic taste and intellectual judgment goes." (*See* Part II, SPIRIT.)

According to most psychologists today, the subconscious mind stores all awareness, real or imagined, without judgment. The conscious mind perceives right and wrong according to each of our *perceptions* of what happens and what should or should not have happened.

A bold and enlightening statement in *The Holotropic Mind* by Stanislav Grof and Hal Zina Bennett reveals that—

> "We are not just highly evolved animals with biological computers embedded inside our skulls; we are also fields of consciousness without limits, transcending time, space, matter, and linear causality. As a result of observing literally thousands of people experiencing non-ordinary states of consciousness, I am now convinced that our individual consciousnesses connect us directly not only with our immediate environment and with various periods out of our own past, but also with events that are far beyond the reach of our physical senses, extending into other historical times, into nature, and into the cosmos."

From his search for the source of the human life-force, the late Dr. Marcus Bach concluded in his publication, *The Chiropractic Story:*

> "The coil of life is in the spine. I am speaking for myself as a researcher in the field of man's total quest for meaning when I say that every religion no less than every spiritually-oriented approach to health and healing believes in the existence of this life force. Call it Consciousness. Call it Innate. Call it God."

It is in this same vein that Tohei Sensei equates ki with God. Neither he nor Dr. Bach are referring to God simply as a superhuman. They are speaking of the visible and the invisible consciousness that is formed and unformed—all that exists. (*See Ki* in Glossary.)

DEATH

> *"The fear of death is like a worm dreading to spin its cocoon, not realizing it will emerge as a butterfly."*
> Author unknown

Every bit of matter or material thing has a birth, life and death. Our sun is a middle-aged star. Imagine what life on earth would be like if there were no life and death cycles; no recycling between motion and matter. That stale, stagnant existence would lack all the dynamic vibrancy we now enjoy. With no death there would be a staggering overgrowth of original life on planet earth, with no room or reason for evolution beyond the first single-celled existence.

Death assures the renewal of life. Imagine the results if human beings, animals and plants did not die. Over-population, along with the human tendency toward the greed that many of our present habits breeds, would lead to uncontrollable violence.

Our normal attitude toward death is fear and grief. Even those who are steeped in promises of a heavenly hereafter, look upon life as being so precious that it must be maintained at all cost. At the time of death, our traditional care and preservation of these earthly space-suits that we call bodies becomes so paramount that it tends to take precedence over concerns about the mind and soul.

Those who do not understand Nature's balance of life and death sometimes become overzealous about preserving the environment just as it exists at present. They forget that changes during the past have led to present and future change. The mental stagnation caused by honing in on the status quo, without consideration of Nature's laws of change, is another form of separation from the oneness of the cosmos. Birth, life and death are evident, even among the stars. The death of one life or species opens the way for a new life or new forms of life. If we continue to fight Nature's recycling, this extinction will be more likely to include humankind.

This natural balance of chaos and order does not excuse the malicious and careless acts of destruction that humans cause through greed and lack of concern for the future of our eco-system. When too many species die off too quickly, another imbalance is created. The rape of

Nature by humanity has caused a domino effect of destruction throughout our planet.

Considering both extremes, environmentalists can do more for the future of the earth by recognizing the necessity for balance than short-sighted visions of preserving life at all cost. In their zeal, modern "do-gooders" often lack a sufficient *ball of knowledge:* the understanding necessary to recognize Nature's methods for balancing life and death. Death plays a role that is just as important to the cycle of continuum—as life itself.

Forest rangers at Sequoia National Forest tell how in years past the sequoia trees were overly-protected. Every fire that crept near these cherished trees was extinguished. The sequoias began to show signs of stunted growth and disease. Only after the examination of a fallen tree, did the age rings detect evidence of fire about every seven years—until they had been overly protected by humans. On further investigation it was learned that the bark of the sequoia contains a natural asbestos against devastation by fire. The natural periodic fires had destroyed the smaller trees and underbrush, leaving sufficient nourishment for normal growth of the massive sequoias.

New environmental policies have been put into practice at Yellowstone National Park. Hopefully they will replace the former errors of over-protection that set in motion the conditions that caused the park's latest devastating fire.

We, as mere mortals, must learn Nature's ways by trial and error. We can learn more accurately through a better understanding of the *oneness* of Nature. We can also learn from those who live close to and understand Nature. We will learn little by fighting each other or blaming the natural extreme changes that we do not understand. We can learn Nature's secrets of balance more easily by complementary understanding, than by the shortsightedness of dogmatically insisting on preserving all life at any cost.

The opposite of an extreme concern about death in Nature is seen in the careless, vicious slaughter and irresponsible lack of concern about preserving our natural world. We tend to forget that *we* are included among Nature's vulnerable creature's who depend on earth's oxygen-generating plant life. There are those who kill and maim with no consideration for the balance of Nature or extinction of a species. Most sportsmen abide by the laws that are based on animal population balance.

Many animals, such as bats and whales, have been killed as a result of story-book tales that induce fear. The bat's diet provides a natural way to reduce the mosquito population. They could serve as an alternative means to decrease the use of harmful toxic sprays that also kill beneficial insects and threaten human health as well. We should be more concerned about the over-use of herbicides and insecticides that upset the entire eco-system.

To the opposite extreme, if Nature imitated our present social attitudes toward preserving life at all cost, human life would be unlimited and death would cease to be. We have lost the sense-of-oneness that regulates the cycles of life and death. This sacred continuum is meant to benefit *all*—the past, present and future of living existence.

"We are mortal beings and will all eventually die," writes Tom Harpur in *The Uncommon Touch*:

> "Indeed, properly understood and prepared for, death can be understood as a form of healing. God, whose nature is love no matter how much this love may seem to be obscured at times of crisis, does not send illness. Sickness is not a divine punishment nor is it sent as a lesson or as a means of purifying character. Such a view would make a sadist monster out of God instead of a loving source of light and energy revealed by Christ."

Whether we believe in a form of reincarnation, heaven or a hell of damnation, we know that death will someday be our inevitable demise. If we spend our lives fearing death, we have little time for the joys of living. The early Greeks, who had no belief in the hereafter, found *honor* in fighting to their death in the Olympic games, over and above the dishonor of losing the fight. Neither the extreme of death as honor and sacrifice, nor an unnatural fear of death, measures up to a preparation for death through spiritual healing.

One part of Bill Moyers' TV series, *Healing and The Mind*, dwells on the value of a personal contentment within the patients themselves, whether or not their illness ends in death. The popularity of Hospice care, faith healing and assisted dying, induces new controversies concerning death. Whether the illness is reversed, or if it ends in death rather than cure, a healing of the spirit appears to be the ultimate satisfaction. Attaining peace of mind is sometimes a greater miracle than restoring health.

DEFENSE, Defensiveness

> *Nothing is as strong as gentleness,*
> *Nothing is so gentle as real strength."*
> St. Francis de Sales

We look upon defense as a necessary means of staying alive and well. When we speak of someone being *defensive*, the word takes on a different connotation. When we act defensively, we tend to lash back quickly. If taken to extreme, we have little regard concerning the feelings of others or the results of our actions. When this attitude toward defense is used by an attacker or a defender, neither is calm nor alert. Concerning a defensive attitude, Dr. Deepak Chopra has said that we spend 99.9% of our time defending our point of view.

When the martial arts are referred to as self-defense, defense is a misnomer in the deepest sense of Oriental meaning. The real overcoming takes place within ourselves. A warrior is one who is willing to overcome his or her own fears. The real aim is to be compassionately decisive, not defensive. The ideal goal of warriorhood is resilience, not resistance.

When interviewed for *Aikido in America, Sensei* Simcox summed it up, "We teach attitudes leading to actions. This is different from an attitude of defense."

DUALISM, Dueling, Separation

> *"Duality is the source of fear."*
> Deepak Chopra
> *The Way of the Wizard*

A fighting or slave conscience leaves us feeling separated and alienated from the togetherness that we so innately desire. Dualism is used as a competitive duel of wits and physical combat. The *two,* that is sometimes seen as duality, can be viewed more appropriately as coupled, joined and complemented—for the benefit of both.

The usual fighting or slave responses through a duality mind-set is so much a part of the human psyche that we think of them as normal. Of course we don't expect to go through life in perpetual harmony but to exist in constant conflict is a sign of further separation of mind, body and spirit. The extent of disharmony in each person's life depends upon how we treat each other—beginning with the relationship between child and family. It extends to the playground, school, community, career, family and relationships. As adults, we face the challenge of dealing with our conflict versus harmony problems.

Many marriages are lived out in a state of separation. Not separate as a matter of not living together, but a lack of team spirit. The typical scenario of love and marriage begins with a scientifically unexplained chemical attraction that overshadows our rational thinking. If the emotional desires to please during courtship are not gradually replaced by a compromising of give and take—trust and understanding—the magical attraction is replaced by discontent. The sense of togetherness dwindles and a sense of separateness mounts. The intensity of romance is replaced by defensiveness.

The rivalry begins mentally, "If he [or she] is going to do that, I will defend myself by doing this." Or "If I don't do as he [or she] wishes, I will lose him [or her]." When partners react with either of these fighting or slave conscious reactions, the situation escalates into intolerable endurance by the increase of ever-deepening conflicting incidences.

If one partner attempts to tri-tune the situation, again it is a matter of whether the other partner responds through a triality conscience or continues with a fighting or slave conscience response. When a mutual team spirit is established, the situation is reconcilable.

By replacing duality with triality, couples and cultures can base their ethics on unity amid diversity, instead of dueling duality. Although H. G. Wells is better known for his science fiction thrillers, his chief concern was that humankind would annihilate itself before learning how to preserve itself.

EGO, Id, Super-ego

> *"Why show off?*
> *Heart say you brave, display says you lucky."*
> -from the movie, *Karate Kid II*

From a body, mind and spirit standpoint, the psychoanalysis terms—id, ego and super-ego can be related to: body as id, mind as ego and spirit as super-ego. Rather than striving to get rid of the ego and id, they can be balanced through the support of the super-ego. Without ego drive we would not have enough ambition to face the normal chores that confront us each day. Without id, human instincts would be repressed.

The ego protects us from becoming overly aware of too many of our shortcomings too quickly. Complementary support between the id and ego, invites the super-ego to join in to help replace our shortcomings without blame, shame, guilt or punishment.

A triality conscience does not concentrate on getting rid of something. It coordinates the fighting conscience of ego with the slave conscience of id, through the intuition and integrity of the super-ego. (*See* Part II, INTUITION.)

EXERCISE (physical)

> *"He who cannot find time to exercise*
> *will have to find time for illness."*
> Lord Derby

The importance of physical exercise is being emphasized more and more. Tests concerning the bone marrow loss in the early astronauts' bodies revealed the results of a lack of both isometric and aerobic exercise. Because of anti-gravitation in space, bodily movement is experienced differently. Here on earth, the opposing gravitational tension created by the movement of muscles, most of which are attached to bones, somehow stimulates the formation of bone marrow. Many of the essential components that sustain life, such as red blood corpuscles, are produced through the creative interaction of bone marrow.

The age of button-pushing technology is rendering us flabby and sick. We work hard at earning money to buy timesaving and laborsaving devices. Then we spend even more to get the exercise that our energy-saving technology denies us. The recent rush to fitness gyms would amuse our hard-working ancestors. They were obligated to walk and exert themselves physically—just to accomplish their everyday activities.

In a letter to Dear Abby, a reader wrote that her mother would have advised getting exercise by taking a gift to a friend or doing something for someone in need. Jumping around to loud music did not impress her as an ideal way of exercise.

Putting the humor aside, routine exercise in some form is advisable for everyone. We especially need techniques that move muscles in the opposite direction than normally used. If most of our exercise comes from one source, such as a sport or particular type of manual labor, that movement should be balanced with an opposite type of exercise. It is important that exercise—whether patterned, free-style or through helping someone—should be done with a calm/alert frame of mind. Begin with a smile and turn exercise from boredom into fun by a state of tri-tuning.

Anything worth doing is worth enjoying. "Exercise with a receptive body, not a striving mind," is Paul Bragg's advice in *Bragg Super Power Breathing for Health & High Energy*.

An ideal time to exercise is before getting out of bed in the morning, when muscles are warm. Mimic the stretching exercises performed by a cat or dog when they awake. Experience how good it feels! P.S. Be careful that it doesn't relax you back to sleep.

It is possible to find time to exercise, even amid a busy schedule. Exercise head and neck muscles while waiting for computer information to appear. Stretch the arms high in the kitchen while waiting for a pot to slowly come to a boil. Exercise legs and feet during TV advertisements. Utilize boring minutes and waiting periods by exercising or deep breathing.

Stretching the arms high or wiggling the feet and toes can stimulate both the lymph and circulatory systems. When the arms haven't been stretched high for a length of time, sudden reaching for an item can tear weak muscles that may take weeks to heal. Our bodies are slower to react to anything that hasn't been practiced over a period of time.

Hawaiian *Ki-Aikido sensei* Harry Eto, now in his nineties, credits *Tohei Sensei's Ki Development* exercises for his longevity. After an operation in his seventies, he began practicing the exercises regularly.

FAIR-MINDEDNESS, Honesty, Negotiation, Arbitration

> *"Fairness is what justice really is."*
> Potter Stewart

Fairness is simultaneous cooperation and competition amongst ourselves and others. When those whose chief goal in life is to be #1, in control, top dog or glorified, they are tempted to minimize the importance of fair play. Fear that their competitiveness will boomerang, alienates them from the fair-minded interactions they expect and sometimes demand from others.

A sense of fairness can radiate from one person to another without a conscious awareness, even during a phone conversation of great distance. By tri-tuning, we emit vibrations that invite harmonious transactions before problems have a chance to interfer and/or take over.

FEAR

> *"Don't get scared, get skilled."*
> Oprah Winfrey Show

Fear is the lowest common denominator for all the causes of separation between mind, body and spirit. Fear is said to be the seed of every worry. Worry is stagnated fear. It is the result of being out of sync with the opposites.

On the lighter side, someone said, "Why worry? Half the things we worry about never happen and the other half will happen anyway."

Normally life is a game of attack and defend. The universal law is, "What we give, is what we receive."

Living beyond fear does not exclude a sense of danger, which is our ultimate life preserver. The English definition of fear, as "being frightened," surfaced around the thirteenth century CE. According to the *Arcade Dictionary of Word Origins,* by John Ayto, the ancient meaning of fear was related to danger, what one undergoes and experiences, rather than being frightened.

From this perspective, fear can be seen as a challenge that elicits courage and accomplishment. We can sense a real danger intuitively when we are not in a frozen state of fear. When we are chronically fearful, everything is interpreted as frightening. When we remain in a state of fright, fear becomes our enemy. Shakespeare said, "Extreme fear can neither fight nor fly." The alternative is an immobile state of freezing.

Scientific theories concerning the role of the nervous system and its relationship to fear range from a belief that fear energizes the individual for fight or flight, to the conception that fear causes the person to freeze and become weak. The main conclusion is that a fearful person becomes helpless when there is a lack of balance between the sympathetic nervous system's guarding of muscles and glands—and the parasympathetic system that governs functions of the eyes, heart and digestive system. Repetition of this imbalance becomes habitual.

Many have found solace concerning fear-filled habits in group or individual counseling, self-help recommendations and through religious faith. Religions that are *based* on fear interpret the fear messages in the Bible on the modern definition of fear—being frightened. More theologians are interpreting Old Testament references to fear of God as *awe*, which places it in the category of reverence and respect. Except for those preachers who use fear as a weapon to control their followers, references to fear in the New Testament are usually interpreted as love.

Tri-tune Your State-of-Being

To understand Amy's tri-tuning test experience (*Refer* to page 1.) about thinking beyond fear, practice the following:

1. **Think of something frightening.** Have someone test whether you are stable or unbalanced. Most likely you failed the test because you felt a lack of security and confidence.
2. **Now think of something pleasant.** Ask your partner to test again. In all likelihood you passed the test and recognized a sense of well-being and stability.

3. **Exchange places with your partner.** While testing, observe that each of you can detect the extent that the one being tested is tri-tuned.

Fear can be replaced naturally by the way we think and our state of tri-tuning. Whether real or imagined, fear is an emotional reaction. Fear is contagious!

The actions of one fear-filled person can create mass hysteria. Fear radiates vibrations that subconsciously affect everyone. We can walk into a room where an argument or violence has ceased and still recognize that something is amiss. The energy vibes remain and can expand like ripples from stones thrown into still water, even after they are replaced by appropriate thoughts and actions.

Retrieve the Sense of Tri-tuning

1. **Close your eyes and tri-tune.** That is, focus at the center of your body (in the lower abdomen) and release your body weight to gravity, just as you did in previous tests.
2. **Experience pleasant thoughts for at least 15 seconds.** *Feel* the pleasure as well as thinking about it.
3. **Continue in that state.** Retrieve the tri-tuning if you have lost it.
4. **Now think of something troublesome for an additional 15 seconds.** Were you able to maintain the tri-tuning? It is doubtful. We tend to lose mind/body coordination when fear-related problems come to mind.
5. **Now, in that uncoordinated state, tense your body with eyes closed.** For another 15 seconds or so, think of something that has been troubling you. Easy, wasn't it? But it didn't feel so good and it probably didn't promote appropriate thoughts.
6. **Tense your body again and try to think of a possible solution to your problem.** Likely you found it difficult to concentrate.

7. **Retrieve the tri-tuned state and think of a solution.**
    Easier, wasn't it? Practice regaining and maintaining the state of tri-tuning until you can attain or retrieve that sense-of-being at will.

Prepare for dangerous situations by looking for solutions through the awareness of possible danger. When you are in an unfamiliar situation, inquire about the precautions you should take. Be aware of danger, but not consumed by fear.

Campers have died who unwittingly used the poisonous branches from oleander bushes to roast their hot dogs. In strange places or when learning any new skill, ask about the possible dangers and practice the actions necessary to surpass them. When learning to snow ski, it is as important to learn how to fall safely as it is to know how to maintain balance. Look at the dangers as precautions—not through fear—but as a reason to seek better solutions.

Adult fears are mimicked by children. Baby monkeys whose mothers are abnormally fearful, will tend to mimic their mother's fears. In experiments where the baby monkey is put in the care of a normal mother, usually the baby will gain confidence.

Fear attracts enemies. Animals, particularly, can detect fear in humans. Any attacker, whether verbally or physically, either consciously or subconsciously senses the fears of the opponent.

In *Ki in Aikido,* C.S. Shifflett related an incident she had witnessed:

> "I once saw a man wandering through the street drunk or on drugs. Passersby observed him with a watchful calm that offered him no point of focus until one young woman panicked. She shrieked, 'Get away from me!' and darted wildly about in confusion. Her noise, random motion, and terror made her everyone's focal point—and his. He set off in hot pursuit. She was grateful to be rescued but others did not need rescuing, due not to size, martial arts training, or weapons—but attitude.
> The attacker is amazingly dependent on the 'victim.' "

The subconscious mind of any habitual worrier will conjure up a new reason to worry when an old worry subsides. Fearful worry is a waste of energy. Concern over circumstances while seeking solutions is a productive use of energy.

An unknown author said, "Fear is false evidence appearing real." Dr. Karl Menninger assured that "Fears are educated into us, and can, if we wish, be educated out."

Suggestion: Think of the chronic responses of someone who is constantly worried about one thing or another. Be patient with yourself if you detect this as one of your own habits. Replace the worry habit by retrieving your tri-tuning.

FIGHTING and SLAVE CONSCIENCE

> *Don't fight forces; use them."*
> Richard Buckminster Fuller
> *Shelter,* 1932

If less time were spent in a fighting conscience mode, we would have more time to solve local and global problems. The unfairness of humans toward one another can be rectified. There has never been a better opportunity to make a quantum leap into unprecedented humane-ness by the development of a triality conscience.

Contrary to common belief, throughout most of history, humanity has been plagued by far more world-wide violence than we endure at present. Travel throughout the world is comparatively safer than during most past historical times. We are now very aware of violence closer to home because in the United States we have experienced an unprecedented increase in turmoil that has slowly developed during the past 50 years.

We use our fighting conscience as a defense against what we perceive as wrong or evil. We resort to our slave conscience when we feel powerless or over-powered. The victim and the victimizer create a vicious cycle of aggression and vengeance.

We are constantly caught in the cross-fire of change. Too many changes too quickly can cause mental phobias and depression. When the manic stage strikes, the manic-depressive person responds by lunging head-long into the unknown without caution. A pendulum swing to the depression stage causes the same person to slink away in a state of uncontrollable fear. These extremes portray an extreme fighting conscience, followed by the opposite—a slave conscience. The normal fighting or slave conscience indicates various forms of neuroses. A triality conscience is a healthy sense-of-being.

If a reader feels that he or she must agree with everything written in this book in order to benefit from tri-tuning, this submission reflects a slave conscience. Anyone who thinks that if he or she disagrees with anything herein and that fact proves that the entire book should be considered rubbish, is displaying a fighting conscience. Anyone who chooses to practice whatever is comfortable to him or her at this time, is acting with a triality conscience. In the future, some suggestions that seem foreign now, may become better understood and more respected. Likewise, foods that are repulsive at first taste, may sooner or later become our favorites. Strange ideas can develop into normal attitudes.

The examples of tri-tuning and the suggestions for developing a triality conscience represent my own outlook at this particular period in my life. Each reader's experiences and conclusions will naturally be somewhat different, just as the outlook by members of a particular religion or culture will differ and may change over time.

Replacing a fighting/slave conscience with a triality conscience does not restrict us to a particular set of ideals. It is reminiscent of the cliché, "I don't agree with what you say, but I will defend with my life your right to say it." A triality conscience elevates us above our fighting/slave fears. In turn, our attitude of holitude will help others through their fears as well.

Adlai E. Stevenson said, "It is often easier to fight for principles than to live up to them."

FLOW

"This is but a moment in the flow of Eternity,"
Author unknown

Flow is a matter of being in sync with the state-of-being that some authors, including Joseph Campbell in *The Power of Myth*, call bliss. It is the epitome of a synchronization of mind, body and spirit. When we flow, we glow!

Flow, according to author Mihaly Csikszentmihalyi, is the merging of action and awareness. In *Flow, The Psychology of Optimal Experience,* he describes it as a state of concentration so focused that it amounts to absolute absorption in an activity.

> "Flow is the key element of an optimal experience…. The task is to learn how to enjoy everyday life without diminishing other people's chances to enjoy theirs…. The 'autotelic [self goal] self easily translates potential threats into enjoyable challenges, and therefore maintains its inner harmony."

Our solar system has its own rhythmic flow. Each organ in our bodies operates to a slightly different rhythm. When our body rhythms are in sync with the cosmic vibrations, we are healthy.

The term "just be" describes the sensation of flow. When we learn to know ourselves, that sense of *knowing* will allow us to *just be.*

FREEDOM, Responsibility

> *"We hear them cry 'Freedom, freedom,'*
> *yet they demonstrate little awareness*
> *that with freedom goes responsibility."*
> Edvard Kuhn

Responsibility is the balancing act of freedom. We are responsible for anything we possess. Anything worth having is worth our care. When each citizen within a political system acts responsibly, fewer laws are needed. If rights are balanced by responsibility, many strict laws can be reduced to rules and guidelines.

There are always exceptions to the fairness of any law. Every law is both protective and restrictive to law abiding citizens. The flexibility of law within a democratic system is an advantage over and above any other type of government achieved so far, but a balance of responsibility is required.

The phoenix we call freedom, that found its embodiment in the Constitution of the fledgling United States, was conceived and born from the ashes of religious strife in Europe. It was seeded by the desire for freedom from the religious and political tyranny the New World immigrants had endured during and after the Protestant Reformation that began in the1500s.

Ways to Tri-tune our Everyday Lives ▲ 147

The pioneers who settled the New World would not have been so tolerant of different religious beliefs had it not been for their own torturous religious experiences in Europe. They had been driven from province to province in Europe because of the continuous changing of rulers, whose chosen religious dictates they were compelled to follow.

Recent laws against prayer in schools, classes on religion or the display of religious symbols in public and state domain, are a far-cry from the original reasons for establishing freedom of religion. It concerned the domination of governments over all religious practices, not as an exclusion of religious practices in public places.

The upheaval in Europe, caused by the schism of Christianity from the dominance of Rome, to Reformed beliefs, left the populace in a sense of religious slavery to whomever ruled the area where they were living. Either they followed the religion chosen by the ruler or they were forced to move to another jurisdiction.

Despite their awareness of the hardships and dangers they would have to face, many chose to move to the New World. They brought with them a determination that no ruling Monarch would control their religious beliefs. It took the Revolutionary War and the Constitution to completely achieve their goal. Now, petty misunderstandings about these original motives place new threats to the security of religious freedom.

Our founding fathers looked upon the Constitution as giving individual's the freedom to be responsible. Our present form of democracy is expressed through majority rule. If we ever advance to complementary rule, we will be living in a stage of pure democracy. By an appreciation of what has been accomplished so far, we are more likely to achieve complete democracy. We have the responsibility to maintain the freedom of government, community and for ourselves.

When parents fulfill their obligations to guide and teach children responsibility as well as rights, the whole world benefits. When children are taught gradually about responsibility and the ability to make sound choices, fewer laws and social control will be needed for everyone's protection. Either too much permissiveness or unreasonable responsibilities too soon creates fearful confusion for the child and repercussions to the parents.

Citizen irresponsibility creates a demand for more laws and additional punishment. This, in turn, promotes both fighting and slave mentalities. The time and money spent arguing over government or group control of such controversies as smoking tobacco, drinking alcohol, abortion, use of guns, expression of religion and a whole host of other disputes, could be better used for education, inspiration and guidelines for civic understanding and expectation. Ultimately, civil behavior becomes an individual responsibility. Irresponsibility causes social collapse.

More and more laws cannot take the place of respect and responsibility. When children are taught more about sex, for example, and less about moral and health values, additional laws become necessary. Both too many prohibitive laws and too much freedom apparently make human indulgence more inviting. Full knowledge of both sides of an issue invites common sense decisions.

To be forbidden without reasonable explanation somehow tempts disobedience, especially among the young. Either too much discipline or uncontrolled permissiveness creates underlying childhood fear. What is strictly denied children, without example and training to understand the situation, is exactly what they will try to do. Fortunately, in many cases, experience proves to be an ultimate teacher that kindles the responsibility necessary for the young to learn how to override temptation. More personal responsibility equals less restriction by laws. Every law protects some, while hindering others.

The tug-of-war between rights and responsibility has swung the extremes of discipline from harsh corporal punishment to a "touch-me-not" generation. Permissiveness has swung the double-edged sword of extremes from strict discipline to "don't tell me what to do" and "I can do as I please."

The healing benefits of compassionate physical touch that was limited by Puritan and Victorian rules, is being reexamined and beginning to be recognized scientifically. Conversely, illicit and irresponsible touch is creating fears that cause new laws to be enacted.

We tend to put the blame on such problems as overpopulation, natural disasters or a lack of religious faith. All have a bearing on our future but, ultimately, *it is human behavior that will determine our personal and global destinies.*

We cannot blame others for the temptations we do not resist or the responsibilities we do not handle. A quotation credited to both Pythagoras and first century Roman philosopher, Epictetus, reads: "No man is free who is not master of himself."

GUILT and PUNISHMENT

> *"May the words I speak today be soft and tender for tomorrow I may have to eat them."*
> Author unknown

When something happens, we look for the fault. Our egos try to prevent the blame from falling on us. To determine the cause and find a solution, knowing the facts about what happened is important. This necessary investigation sometimes fosters delight in blaming and great satisfaction in shaming those who are blamed. Innocent victims have suffered because of rash remarks that resulted in baseless blame and pronouncement of guilt and punishment.

As a society, we tend to blame *things* for our problems. Violence is blamed on TV, shootings are blamed on guns, smoking is blamed on tobacco and alcoholism is blamed on alcoholic beverages. A TV set cannot turn itself on or pick an appropriate channel. A gun cannot pick itself up and shoot someone. There is no law forcing anyone to buy cigarettes and alcohol. Cigarettes cannot light themselves and alcohol can't pour itself into a glass.

Only we humans, who possess marvelous brain structures and minds, are capable of making the choices that enhance or destroy ourselves as well as other species. Laws concerning the production and use of anything, take away advantages that responsible citizens have a right to enjoy. Excessive laws allow irresponsible persons to rely upon someone else to make the decisions they should learn to make for themselves.

When children are raised with no sense of restraint, their adulthood will reflect this parental irresponsibility. Children whose families live near water must be protected until they learn to cope with the dangers of water. Especially in rural America until the middle of the twentieth century, available guns in homes were quite normal. Yet, the usual harsh discipline in one-room school houses and equally strict parents, did not elicit the increasing violence that is suffered today. The lack of home and community responsibility for child guidance must be examined as the basic underlying cause. The advantages of Victorian proper actions by discipline that was forced by fear through strict religious home and community rules can be accomplished through a collective triality conscience with a sense of holitude.

The sources of potentially harmful drugs existed long before humans evolved from instinct to reasoning. What modern man has extracted and produced as potent and potentially killing drugs were used in their milder natural forms. Usually they were allowed under the strict guidance of the shaman medicine men and women or by some sort of cultural rules. While overindulging did occur, it did not result in the epidemic proportions that modern blends of natural and synthetic drugs have produced.

Children need to be taught to make beneficial choices and to form the habits that help them make responsible and reliable decisions as adults. Too much reliance on someone else's authority or succumbing to our own irresponsibility, creates a slave conscience. Injuring our bodies by the misuse of what animals would instinctively know to avoid, is an insult to the limitless potential of our natural human mental ability to choose.

Our overly-protective egos can cause us to put guilt trips on ourselves when tri-tuning awareness exposes our shortcomings. We turn to blame, shame, self-guilt and punishment to *reason out* these fears. They are the so-called "sins" that our egos have masked and hidden from the conscious mind.

The word sin originally was associated with "missing the mark." When we fail to hit the center of our targeted ideals, tri-tuning can be used as a way to improve. Aiming to do better next time is better than wasting energy on self-blame and shame. When we try to correct our habits or the habits of others through guilt and unjust punishment toward ourselves and others—we are not tri-tuned.

Through a triality conscience, we can experience the *awe* of awesomeness rather than resorting to awfulizing. Dr. Joan Borysenko, author of *Minding the Body, Mending the Mind*, aptly uses the term *awfulize* as a means to describe our usual tendency to ridicule with vengeance rather than seeking solutions.

Blame and shame were dominating factors for most of us, from both our heritage and upbringing. First we need to accept ourselves as we are and to begin where we are. Acceptance and patience with ourselves are prerequisites and necessary companions in our self-remodeling. Be kind to yourself! Reverse the Golden Rule and *"Do unto yourself as you wish that others would do unto you."*

HABITS

> *"Habitual defensiveness and worry can fall away.*
> *It can all be otherwise."*
> Marilyn Ferguson
> *The Aquarian Conspiracy*

Until each of us establishes more desirable habit patterns, our undesirable traits will control us. Sometimes we react to conflict by lashing out at one another, or against ourselves, through a fighting conscience. Otherwise, some of us submit to these shortcomings with frail excuses and succumb to demands through a slave conscience.

Each of us has thousands of habit patterns. Every conscious or unconscious move we make, or thought we think, is linked to automatic memory patterns. Many are beyond our conscious awareness. We are creatures of habit and we react according to past experience.

Subconscious Reaction Ki Test

A Ki Wellness student asked how our muscles can work if we don't purposely tighten them. I held her wrists and told her to get lose from my grip. She pulled and twisted but couldn't free either arm. I told her to scratch her head. She automatically broke from my grip and scratched her head.

We reversed roles so she would know that I hadn't faked the *ki* test. **Experience this for yourself with a partner.**

Whatever we know instinctively or what we have learned to do unconsciously, our bodies can do—without our conscious detailed instructions for every movement. We marvel at the incredible skills of ski jumpers or experts in any field. Their bodies and minds have been trained to do their conscious and subconscious bidding by persistent practice of mind/body coordination with accurate intent.

Our marvelous bodies know how to perform anything we have learned so well that it comes as second nature. What would our day be like if we had to consciously instruct each muscle how to move and synchronize with every other muscle, simply to scratch our head? When we become fearful, we deny the body its natural flow and balance with the cosmos. When we consciously tighten our muscles, the body goes into a stress mode.

Each habit forms its own memory pattern. When the student in the example scratched her head, it was an unconscious move. She had tri-tuned naturally, combining natural tension and relaxation. When she struggled to free her arm, she was *trying to tell* her muscles what they must do. The fearful awareness of her captured arms caused the usual stress reaction.

When we tri-tune, we replace *try* and *make* with *let* and *allow*. We react naturally. By the same token, our innate ability to latch onto first impressions and form habits quickly can also spawn potential phobias when linked to unnecessary fears. Our minds remember our every reaction and will repeat it again and again, unless we rationally discourage it. A repeat action can provoke more fear and each repetition can magnify the fear.

At this point the advantage of human reasoning comes into play. We have the mentality to determine whether or not our fears are legitimate. We can decide when something is too dangerous to attempt, or if it is a challenge to be surmounted. When attempting to get rid of an unwanted habit, don't focus on never repeating that habit again. Instead, decide on a desired replacement and develop that new habit. The old habit will simply fade away.

After burning its hand on the stove burner, a child might be afraid to touch any part of the stove thereafter. As adults, we can experience an insignificant or severe incident and tend to become more fearful each time we encounter that or a similar circumstance. The habit can quickly escalate into a full-blown phobia if we don't analyze and re-program our reaction. We, as humans, have the unique ability to rationalize our fears, determine our habits and correct unnecessary fears. We proudly rank ourselves above other animals that, supposedly, are limited to instinctive reaction. At least they *use* their instinctive abilities. We tend to let fear dominate our rationality.

Suggestion: Pick a habit you want to erase. Think of a desirable replacement. Practice the replacement each time you are tempted to repeat the old habit.

HAPPINESS, Joy, Humor, Laughter, Contentment, Smile

"Happiness is an inside job".
Wally Amos

Happiness is a habit. It depends more on attitude than circumstances. Anything worth doing is worth enjoying. When we do something that we loathe, more energy is wasted than would be used if we enjoyed the experience. Think of some way to turn an undesirable job into a satisfaction. Singing, whistling or even humming might do the trick. If you detest your employment, be thankful for whatever advantages do exist while preparing for something better. Purposely list the present benefits and be open to the new opportunities that might spring seemingly out of nowhere.

Sometimes, it's only when we look back on certain circumstances in our lives that we can begin to realize the opportunities that our resentments hid from us at the time. We miss out on the joys of life because of fears associated in so many forms: worry, resentment, jealousy, hate, control and ridicule—all based on our fears.

Cliché's like "Don't be a Pollyanna," reflect the usual response to the story *Pollyanna* that Eleanor Porter penned to show us how to extract joy and happiness from the strife and boredom of everyday relationships. Her theme was misunderstood and Pollyanna is seen as a "cockeyed optimist" with little awareness of the "real world." Our fighting and slave consciences blind us from recognizing Pollyanna's triality conscience.

Unlike the judgmental and gossipy townspeople, Pollyanna could see beyond the old man's eccentric and reclusive unhappiness. She overlooked a bed-ridden woman's self-pity. She didn't look down on her orphaned friend's station in life. Instead, through the innocent "glad game" her deceased father had taught her, she helped them as well as her Aunt Polly to lift themselves above their habitual resentments.

Hidden fears clouded their recognition of the value of finding some gladness in every situation. In the latest movie version, when asked how she could be glad about Aunt Polly's rigid Sunday routine, Pollyanna rebuffed, "We can be glad it isn't Monday, when next week's work begins."

After a tragic accident, Pollyanna's own fear of never walking again became overwhelming. The townspeople finally adopted her "glad game" approach to life to help her recover. The universal law that giving is receiving, was proven. Our actions boomerang and, sooner or later, whatever we give comes back to us.

Eleanor Porter wrote *Pollyanna* in 1913. She would be appalled at the down-playing of the story's moral objectives in the most recent movie version. In a black-casted TV version, among other discrepancies, children talked-back sarcastically and belittled their elders, reflecting the opposite of the original story version.

Pollyanna's "glad game" gained her a triality conscience. It helped her overcome life's disappointments and to glean strength from her stressful circumstances in life as the orphan of poor missionary parents.

Sad Face and Happy Face Ki Testing

Experience happiness with a **ki** test concerning the value of a smile. Place photos or drawings of a happy face and sad face on a wall a few feet apart or have a third partner make a sad and then a happy face.

1. **Concentrate on the sad face while your partner ki tests.** Did you test weak?
2. **Now concentrate on the happy face and repeat the testing.** Likely, you tested stable.

3. **While tri-tuned, look at the sad face again and see beyond your fear.** When tested this time, you probably projected beyond your fear and tested stable. You *lived beyond fear.* In a tri-tuned state-of-being, we can help others get beyond their fears by our pleasant faces and words.

In his *Book of Ki*, *Tohei Sensei* relates an incident that happened when he began teaching *aikido* in Hawaii. During a demonstration, he threw five men who had been instructed to attack him simultaneously. Afterward, someone in the audience remarked that when one of the men was holding him as hard as he could, *Tohei Sensei* was smiling. He wondered how it was possible to smile in that situation. *Tohei Sensei* answered, "I have a habit of smiling when I am in trouble."

We can measure our normal happiness by evaluating our own "joy triangle." Are we over-confident, afraid or glad? When we face the realities of life we can go with the flow of the ever-changing challenges in our lives with gratitude.

Visualize over-confident, afraid and glad as a tri-tuning triad illustration. When we habitually fall into the left (afraid) category we remain fearful. It takes a lot of outside stimulus to make us even momentarily happy. Chronic unhappiness can be caused by seemingly insurmountable circumstances of sadness at present or from left-over habits from previous troubled times.

If our normal personality falls into the right side (over-confident) of the triangle, we're probably wearing a happy mask to conceal our insecurity. Extreme cases can cause the victim to be completely out of touch with reality. By recognizing the reasons why we fall into one extreme or another, we can rise above the fears we associate with either no confidence or over-confidence. We can be *grateful* and *glad* with holitude. This is the happiness that is defined as "bliss."

No one should expect to be in a state-of-bliss all the time. The world doesn't owe us instant solutions to our every whim. Helen Keller said, "We would never learn to be brave and patient if there were only joy in the world."

There are too many cases of children and adults who have been unduly spoiled. They suffer, and everyone around them suffers from the effects of the superficial happiness that masks their fears.

Our happiness does not necessarily reflect the material circumstances of our lives. All of us know people who live in a frame of mind that boosts them above their economic station or the traumatic events in their lives. We wonder how they can reflect such a sense of contentment.

Conversely, we know too many who have all the comforts of life, yet become disgruntled the minute they are not provided with the continuous external pleasures sometimes referred to as "jollies." "Don't worry, be happy" can mean either the irresponsibility of living in the fast lane or overcoming life's obstacles with a wholesome sense of humor.

Anthropologists have observed that primitive people, and in many cases the economically poor, display more good humor than well-to-dos. Eskimos are known to laugh much of the time. Modern societies tend to display sarcastic, satirized and sometimes sadistic humor with cutting intentions. The so-called humor that is intended to be shocking, can be insulting and degrading. It is a matter of whether we are laughing *at*, or *with* the object of the humor. Laughing *with* someone is humor; laughing *at* someone is reticule and satire. Our attitude, our conception and our intention determine the difference.

Humor, like anything else, depends upon compassion; the triality conscience of the humorist. It is the ideal catalyst for turning conflict into harmony. Those with a natural talent for genuine humor are most fortunate. The King of Blarney, Al Roach, said, "Nobody needs a smile more than those who have none left to give."

Great world decisions, during stressful moments, have been aided by suggestions made with a sense of humor. Fiction writer Donald Westlake says, "There is nothing like absurdity to put things back in proportion."

We can balance our "joy triangle" by taking inventory of our "blame and shame" habits. Sometimes we mask our insecurity by blaming others: parents, government, employers or religions—for our inability to be happy. From the other end of the spectrum, we can get so caught up in the task of self-improvement that we forget to enjoy the process. Work is drudgery only when we forget to do it with joy.

A smile is a natural face lift. Only seventeen muscles are needed to smile. Forty-three muscles are needed to frown. A Chinese Zen monk advised that one minute of laughter is worth an hour of meditation. Research has revealed that laughter is a total-body and whole-brain exercise that releases pent-up stress. Also, happiness equalizes the hemispheres of the brain which helps balance the entire body.

Candace Pert Ph.D., a consultant in Peptide Research in Rockville, Maryland, who was interviewed in Bill Moyers' *Healing and the Mind*, began her career as a basic molecular biologist with a secret interest in studying consciousness. As a student concentrating on subjects from the neck up, she developed ways to measure the "opiate receptor" which led to the discovery that our brains make morphine created by the release of endorphins. The astounding revelation was that these molecules form a psychosomatic communication network not only in the brain, but throughout the body including the immune and endocrine systems. She noted that "One way to think of neuropeptides is that they direct energy."

From a similar perspective, both ancient Eastern and Western knowledge hold that health and happiness go hand in hand. We can begin each day with a smile. Even the muscle formation of a smile stimulates endorphins throughout the body. If we can't muster up a good belly laugh, at least we can start the day with a healthy grin.

Henry Miller wrote in *The Colossus of Maoussi*, "…[to] be happy in the being and the knowing…that is beyond happiness; that is bliss."

HARMONY

> *"Untwisting all the chains*
> *that tie the hidden soul of harmony."*
> John Milton

One of the advantages of a triality conscience is the turning of conflict into harmony. This is not done by eradicating conflict from our lives. Tri-tuning is a skill to produce harmony by blending the extremes of life into harmony. In the orchestra of life, the blending of opposite sounds can be harmonized into stirring, but also soothing, synchronism.

Our relationships in life don't always run as smoothly as we would like but we have more influence on them than we suspect. We may be causing conflict by exerting unconscious or conscious control over others. Whether we realize it or not, our excessive or undue control habits display some form of our own fears. This does not mean that we should ignore the advantages and the necessity of organization, schedules and planning. It does have to do with whether these controls are performed through compassion, teamwork and cooperation instead of domination, conniving or force. The latter reflects a fighting conscience.

Much havoc can result from allowing ourselves to be unduly controlled or depending upon control by others. This reveals a slave conscience. We can do more to heed the conflicts in our lives than we suspect, without fighting, fleeing or freezing. Tri-tuning is the art of flowing with harmonious intent.

Harmony and contentment are to be realized as birthrights. We can get in touch with the universal music of the spheres by tuning into the harmonic flow. Otherwise, we can go kicking and screaming through the black holes of our lives. We will *not* experience harmony by blaming the world for our dilemmas or expecting life to cater to our every whim.

HEALING and HEALTH, Allopathic Medicine, Holistic Medicine, Self-healing, *Kiatsu*

> *"A good doctor,*
> *simply awakens the physician within.*
> *...All healing is self healing."*
> Albert Schweitzer

Hippocrates, the father of medicine, was not referring to medical doctors exclusively when he uttered the words, "Physician, heal thyself." When our fears do not overwhelm the body's natural regenerative processes, everyone has the healing power of body, mind and spirit that can help us restore our health.

Quoting Hans Holzer's words in *Beyond Medicine:* "Disease is not local; it affects the entire organism, body, mind and spirit, and must therefore be attacked on that basis.... In practical terms, all self-healing involves thought processes."

Dr. Holzer, first to document the stress syndrome, is rebuking the limited orthodox medical view that illness is caused either by foreign bacteria or viruses, injury through accidents or the degenerative process of aging and action that weaken the system. The opposite of this view holds that disease is caused by imbalance and vanishes when this imbalance is corrected. He believes it is likely that the foreign invaders can link up with bacteria and viruses already existing, only in an unbalanced system. He adds:

> "It appears that balance between positive and negatively charged electrical particles within a cell and thus within the entire system is at the very heart of the well-being of man."

He suggests that this polarity is the life force for all functions of the system, whether physical, mental or spiritual.

Illness develops at the body's weakest points. The body's resistance can be weakened further by the fears we create in our minds about illness. We can also undo these imagined or real fears with our own minds.

It is startling to realize that our bodies, in their natural state, are healthy. We experience enough aches, pains and sickness that we think of illness as normal. Even our momentary thoughts are a part of the bodily process of self-healing, in a manner that is magnificent beyond explanation. To compare the functions of a human body to a machine or factory and the brain to a computer, is an under estimation of its uniqueness.

Our bodies metabolize the air we breathe, food, water, medicines, sleep and the TLC (tender loving care) that we and others provide. The energy that this process creates, serves to maintain our health. In this sense, all healing is self-healing because the body constantly processes and uses every compatible means to restore our health.

Recently, more recognition has been given to psychosomatic causes of illness. Influenced by those who are convinced of a mind/body/spirit connection (transpersonalization), more scientists are delving deeper into the "know thyself" probabilities of self-healing.

Psychosomatic illness should not be confused with hypochondria; a false personal neurotic view of one's supposed illnesses. Some scientists believe that all illness is psychosomatic, either directly or indirectly. Many patients are falsely accused of hypochondria by doctors who diagnose illness from a purely physical standpoint.

There are three major ways to promote healing: allopathic (modern medical cures); holistic healing (whole-body approaches, including homeopathy and Eastern medicine) and self-healing (taking personal responsibility to listen, learn and care for our bodies). With the great strides in medical cures during the past one hundred years, many people have come to depend completely on the medical profession and to worship doctors as infallible gods. Our health problems are doubled by our slave conscience attitude toward the fighting conscience of the medical profession's emphasis on cures. We have come to the belief that professionals should find cures for all illness, much of which is caused by our personal ignorance and bodily neglect.

We can be grateful for the advancements of modern medicine. However, we will compound ill-health if the curative miracle-drug perspective toward health is not balanced with nature's holistic prevention and our own insightful respect for our bodies. We have forgotten how to listen to our bodies' communication systems and to respect their constant mission to keep us healthy.

Pain is the body's warning signal, telling us that it needs our assistance. All too often we answer with a pain suppresser, which is equal to feeding a crying baby when all it needs is a good burp.

Pain or lethargy may indicate a need for more sleep, exercise or nourishing food to help eliminate the problem. When we learn to interpret our body's language, we can answer our "gut feelings" in accordance with what the body tells us.

Dr. Deepak Chopra, author of many books on mind/body medicine, says that "if we thank our healthy body cells, they will go to the aid of our unhealthy cells." He explains that scientists are now realizing that each cell has its own intelligence. For instance, heart cells know what is happening in the liver. We have more influence on our own health than we ordinarily realize.

As individuals, we hold the key to our health. The medical profession and the alternative practitioners usually stand at odds with each other when they could join and be complementary and integrative healers. As patients, we will continue to be caught in the middle so long as we retain our slave consciences of depending entirely on any type of healer or physician. The information age provides us with knowledge about ourselves that was not available when we began to revere doctors as gods. Our self-understanding and care, coupled with the complementary care by holistic and allopathic physicians, will create a three-dimensional balance of health care. The fears now associated with the dominating fighting conscience side of this equation through insurance fraud and the disadvantages of government control, are costing us money, time and lives.

Illnesses with the latest labels such as: Chronic fatigue syndrome (CFS), phobias and post-traumatic stress disorder, are born out of fear and personal neglect. We may have inherited or we may be habitually predisposed to these illnesses, but their ultimate source is fear. Underlying fears sap the life energy that is so vital to our good health. CFS is now thought to be caused by a virus, but viruses attack parts of the body already in a weakened state. Something caused the weakness and that basic cause is related to conscious or subconscious fear. A viral or bacterial illness is the effect of the cause.

Tohei Sensei claims that CFS is caused by insufficient *ki*. The lack of essential *ki* energy, which can be restored by good physical and mental health habits, leaves our bodies exhausted and subject to invasion by all kinds of Nature's recyclers. The lack of *ki* creates fear, which manifests itself in a guise of imbalance that results in ill-health.

A healthy body/mind/spirit combination can ward off illness. Germs are constantly present in our bodies as part of Nature's recycling program to rid the body of toxins. Illness is a sign that our minds have not treated our bodies properly. An illness eliminates toxins in order to rebalance the body. Death results from an extreme imbalance between vital life energy and Nature's recycling of our improperly nourished bodies. (*See* Part II, NATURE.)

Our modern technology has tempted us to drastically change our sleep, eating and regular habit patterns to the point that we neglect the necessity to replenish our *ki* (life energy). Once upon a time humans slept according to light and darkness, ate food in its natural state and socialized together. The young continually learned from their elders.

In all likelihood materialism is here to stay and technology is a way of life. The human brain has more than enough potential to merge healthy living with modern material changes. Through a triality conscience each of us can choose appropriate ways to adapt or change any situation. Simple tri-tuning can decrease both anxiety and pain in such situations as medical treatments, minor to major injuries and the anticipation of possible physical harm. Tri-tuning is useful in any threatening or emergency situation.

Suspicion about hands-on healing and energy healing arts is a leftover from our traditional puritan sexually-based attitude against touching. Religious and scientific skepticism is another deterrent to the acceptance of unfamiliar and unorthodox healing practices.

When the extreme of too many sexual taboos swung to an overindulgence in sexual promiscuity during the second half of the twentieth century, a new set of problems were born. We are in need of a better understanding of the human body, mind and spirit that is compatible with human sexual needs *and* sexual responsibilities.

Through observance and clinical testing, it has been recognized that without infant touching, caring and bonding, babies are not likely to grow into normal responsible adults. Appropriate touching, like anything else, depends upon a proper perspective in relationship to a particular situation.

Physically abusive adults, however, set patterns of repeated abuse that sometimes continue for generations. The thin line of distinction between natural affection and lurid desires, leaves children and adults with uncertainty whether to "fear" or "revere" the touches they receive.

One grandfather, while rough-housing with his kindergarten-aged granddaughter, was appalled when she remarked that she had learned in school that he wasn't supposed to touch her. This confusion between the detection of selfish deviant intentions and genuine love can be baffling to children, family members and society as a whole. (*See* Part II, LOVE.)

Sometimes the clients of hands-on energy healers are apprehensive about what is actually happening. Those who are not aware of the personal energy (*ki*) that flows from the universe, within and around each body, are even more skeptical.

Since the administering of *Kiatsu* healing touch does not include the circular and other manipulative actions used in massage, clients sometimes wonder why they aren't feeling more action. Those who are not aware of these subtle energies may not detect the healing energy.

Actually, it is not necessary that the client is aware of this energy for healing to take place. This compassionate energy that we are calling spirergy is both motion and matter. Once recognized, it can be appreciated as the visible and invisible world of energy that affects and changes the material world.

Bioenergy healer, Mietek Wirkus says, "Bioenergy medicine is the transmission of human energy from one person to another to improve his or her health. It is like giving a weak car battery a boost." This analogy is also used by *Tohei Sensei* to describe *kiatsu* healing treatments.

HOLITUDE, Attitude

"...moods and attitudes that come from the realm of the mind transform themselves into the physical realms through the emotions."
Candace Pert, interviewed in *Healing and the Mind*

Holitude, a newly-coined word, describes an attitude of oneness or wholeness; a recognition of our interconnectedness to all existence. An attitude of holitude helps dispel the fears of loneliness. When we divide the word alone, it becomes *all one*. We can be alone and whole within ourselves, without becoming a resentful recluse, when we develop a sense-of-oneness. Holitude is a natural result of tri-tuning.

Tri-tuning is an attitude of holitude. Ideally, attitude has been associated with such phrases as an attitude of gratitude. More recently, attitude is being expressed from a negative perspective. The statement "he [or she] really has an attitude," conveys an unacceptable or resentful perspective.

Attitude governs our conscious and subconscious reactions. Sometimes we have to guard our subconscious reactions by checking ourselves before we speak or act. "Think before you speak," we remind ourselves. When our conscious minds have to correct a subconscious inclination, it is proof that our basic attitude needs improvement. As we grow into adulthood, we are increasingly responsible for our attitudes.

A quote by The Rev. Charles Swindoll sums it up.

> "The longer I live, the more I realize the impact of attitude on life....
> I am convinced that life is 10% what happens to me and 90% how I react to it....we are all in charge of our attitudes."

At our deepest mental levels, each of us wishes to improve our attitude. So, if we really want to change, why can't we simply do it? Replacing an ingrained habit requires patience and self-understanding. The source of our attitudes, some buried deep in our subconscious, can be replaced by conscious perseverance to tri-tune ourselves and act through holitude.

Tone of voice is the tell-tale tongue that reveals our attitude. Psychologists say that the tone of our words impresses people more than words themselves. Tone of voice reflects our subconscious thoughts, some of which we are not even aware.

The opposite can also be a factor in our reactions. A subtle fear of exposing our real feelings can provoke masks of protection. The comment, "His bark is worse than his bite," bears this out. Men tend to hide their soft side with a protective macho crust. Women sometimes sugar-coat viciousness with sweet talk. Since the women's liberation movement, these extremes are becoming mixed and sometimes reversed among the sexes. Artificial tones and the masks of pretense that we wear are more easily detected by listeners than we realize.

Our attitude, whether superficial or deeply guarded, can work for or against us. Tri-tuning makes it easier to improve our attitudes. An appropriate attitude can help us maintain a tri-tuned sense-of-being.

Lectures by Professor Halbert L. Dunn, collected in *High Level Wellness,* include his theory that closely parallels holitude and a triality conscience.

"It is only by solving our problems in a *total* way that we can come to solutions for many of the complexities of living. Maturity in wholeness, then, involves a knowledge of one's self, understanding of others, and a harmony resulting from these two realities."

Dr. Dunn's High-Level Wellness Symbol consists of three interlocking orbits representing "the human body as a manifestation of organized energy. They symbolize the body, mind and spirit of man as an interrelated and interdependent whole. A dart through the middle and pointing upward symbolizes the life cycle of the individual's striving to achieve his or her purpose in living and growing in wholeness toward the maturity of self-fulfillment." (*See* Illus. #16.)

High-Level Wellness Symbol

Illus. #16

INTUITION, Instinct, Reasoning (logic)

"We must cultivate the 'halo of intuition' if we are to find a larger wholeness than is possible by mere rationalism."
Georg Feuerstein

Another tri-tuning equation is: instinct plus logic (reasoning) equals intuition. This 3-way elevation of consciousness can also be equated to the *id* (instinctive mind), *ego* (conscious mind) and super-ego (subconscious mind). These three terms explain the holistic workings of the human mind.

Usually scientists and theologians credit only the super-animal, called human, with the ability to reason. Plants and animals live and reproduce according to Nature's laws. As humans, we have unmercifully subjugated plants and animals to our will. Thankfully, many humans show consideration and understanding toward the animals and plants under their care.

In all of Nature there is an instinctive give and take, sacrifice and utilize, contrast that sustains the oneness of all existence. Our misgivings and extreme interpretations concerning the duality of good and bad create confusion. A domesticated animal can live a life of protection and harmony with those who own, care for and enjoy its companionship. The opposite is seen when animals are mistreated and neglected. Enslaved treatment leads to subtle and visible fear between master and animal.

The intention, whether enacted through compassion or selfishness, determines the extent of human care and concern. When humans, animals, and even plants communicate on par with each other, there is a sense of understanding that extends beyond instinct and reasoning.

As witnessed by the devastating destruction of rain forests, the earth itself is being raped of its cycle of interacting nourishment. The animal kingdom, supposedly restricted to instinct, lives by territorial and hierarchical dominance. Animals seem to fare and maintain a more natural population balance that humanity with all its logic does not sense.

Humans are so top-heavy with logic and domination that we tend to ignore, downgrade and mistrust our momentary mental quantum leaps of intuitive warnings about the possibility of our self-annihilation. Ironically, over-population and other irresponsible measures are part of the cause. We stick to the gradual method of acquiring knowledge through the senses, rather than trusting our instantaneous nudges of intuition; our gut feelings or sixth sense. The theory that rational thinking is a left-brained activity and that creative ability is credited to the right brain, is giving way to the holographic theory that all three are present in the brain as a whole.

In his article, *Everyone Does It, Not Everyone Knows It,* Dr. Georg Feuerstein credits Karl Pribram, David Bohm and Henri Bergson, among others, for answers as to how intuition works. "Intuition, for Bergson, is instinct that has climbed to the level of self-awareness and that is capable of genuine detachment from the world of objects and their demands....Intuition transcends intellect, as it transcends instinct."

Comparing the holographic brain theories, Dr. Feuerstein agrees with the Eastern spiritual enlightenment traditional claims "that the genuinely enlightened person is present in the world but not of it; that he or she walks lightly on this planet, having the welfare of all beings at heart." He concludes that we are not merely subject to, but co-creative participants in the evolutionary process, which we can do—

> "only when we call upon our inner knowing, our intuitive function, that will furnish us with the deeper and broader understanding necessary

to act wisely in the World. Intuition and creativity both seem to bubble up from the same living spring within us."

These inspirational probabilities are the crux of what tri-tuning signifies. A holographic state of mind, body and spirit sets the stage for intuitive attunement. Learning to live by a sense of triality and holitude is a university from which we never graduate. It is a perpetual challenge and life's experiences are to be enjoyed by each of us.

KIATSU *(See HEALING and Glossary of Foreign Terms)*

KINESIOLOGY, Muscle Testing

> *"Health is composed of structural, chemical, and mental factors that should be balanced, forming an equalateral triangle."*
> D. D. Palmer

Kinesiology, the science of human muscular movement, is basic in many healing techniques. It is extensively used in the Applied Kinesiology practiced by some chiropractors as a tool for both a diagnosis and treatment. Allergy detection and the toxic threat from food and chemical consumption can be evaluated by the same type of kinetic muscle testing used in *ki* testing. This muscle testing can be used in any modality to indicate whether the mind and body are coordinated, or out of sync.

David Walther, in *Applied Kinesiology Synopsis,* relates how George Goodheart, a Doctor of Chiropractic, brought Applied Kinesiology into being in 1964. By using the Kendall and Kendall technique of muscle testing, he found that the cause of weak muscles that showed no apparent reason, had more to do with the control of the nervous system over the muscle than the power that a muscle can produce. Applied Kinesiology is based on the fact that the human body is a self-correcting and self-maintaining mechanism that many times can be aided without surgical mutilation of the body.

D.D. Palmer, in *The Science, Art and Philosophy of Chiropractry,* points out that the basic principle of chiropractic treatment is that "too much or not enough energy is disease." There is a need for better understanding of the elusive, unseen and underestimated energy that constitutes and sustains life.

LOVE, Kinship

> *"Throughout the universe there can be found a Natural Order which is forever unfolding. It unfolds to its perfection through the expression of love."*
> Count Nils Chrisander

Love is one of the most essential influences in our lives. It is also one of the most complex concepts to define. I have purposely down-played the word love because of its multitude of connotations and expressions. Words like compassion, understanding and complementing have been substituted for the word love throughout this book.

Love can be a many-splendored thing! It is also a multifaceted word, which complicates its definitions and the intentions of its use. Love can be possessive, sacrificial or genuine.

Possessive love reflects a fighting conscience. Sacrificial love shows a slave conscience. Genuine love reveals a triality conscience. Ideal love is not selfish or self-intimidating. Unconditional love is virtuous integrity. Much of what is considered to be love, is conditional: "I will love you if…" or "you can earn my love by…." It is debatable whether these are actually forms of love. They reflect selfish love which is a form of fear. We choose between love and fear every moment, but our understanding of love becomes shallow when we fall short of living beyond fear.

Walter Russell speaks of the relationship between fear and love in *The Message of the Divine Iliad*.

> " The dread serpent of fear of our neighbors which forces us to lock doors, police streets and arm nation against nation, will disappear only through the complete reversal of human relationship practices to conform to Nature's law of love."

The admonishment by Jesus to "love your enemies" parallels the ideal of "blending and mending" instead of "blaming and shaming." His reasoning can be realized more clearly by examining the complete Biblical passage, in Matt 5: 43-48, of the Lamsa version:

43 You have heard that it is said, Be kind to your friend, and hate your enemy.
44 But I say to you, Love your enemies, bless anyone who curses you, do good to anyone who hates you, and pray for those who carry you away by force and persecute you.
45 So that you may become sons of your Father who is in heaven, who causes his sun to shine upon the good and the bad, and who pours down his rain upon the just and the unjust.
46 For if you love only those who love you, what reward will you have? Do not even the tax collectors do the same thing?
47 And if you salute only your brothers, what is it more that you do? Do not even the tax collectors do the same thing?
48 Therefore become perfect, just as your Father in heaven is perfect.

From a tri-tuning standpoint, love can be equated with an emphasis on the *laws* (responsibility) of the Old Testament, an accent on *love* (charity and compassion) in the New Testament, and the evolution of national and personal *liberty* (individual freedom and opportunity) that results when law and love are complemented through liberty. (*See* Part II, FREEDOM.)

The habit of hate and the rewards for love are simplified by Dr. Bernie Siegel, in *Love, Medicine and Miracles;* "To hate is easy, but it is healthier to love."

MAGNETISM, Mysticism, Magi, Hypnosis, Occult, Myth

> *"In each of our lives,*
> *there are moments when we rise to a privileged place,*
> *where everyday acts take on mystical meaning."*
> Dr. Deepak Chopra
> *The Return of Merlin*

Some may dispute the similarity between words associated with magnetism and their relationship to each other. Mysticism, Magi, Hypnosis, Occult and Myth, are classified by various groups through diverse interpretations. Each is cherished by some but feared by others. This leads to alienation and misunderstanding. When we probe into life's mysteries with a *curiosity* toward the unknown instead of fear, we can experience the awe of mystique.

The word magic was translated from the word Magi; ancient astrologers in Persia. Among them were the Wise Men from the East, who were investigating an unusual astrological planetary formation at the time of Jesus' birth. What is seen as miraculous by one group, can be seen as a natural phenomenon by another.

What we term as "magic" is a deceptive act that creates an illusion for the sake of entertainment or cunning. What the audience sees is a disguise of what actually happens. Magic and scientific magnetism have been confused with each other to the detriment of our understanding and to the promotion of our fears.

It is regrettable that our familiarity with hypnotism comes mainly through the illusion of stage entertainment. We need to understand magic and hypnosis from their practical and beneficial sides. This is different from the usual magical and mysterious sense that we have been led to believe is real.

Relatively few people realize that we are mesmerized every time we become engrossed in a TV program. We are already hypnotized, making it easy for exaggerated advertising to lure us into purchasing merchandise purely by the persuasion of believing what we see and hear. How easy it is to fall into hypnotic sleep while watching TV.

The simplest definitions of hypnotism are suggestion and persuasion. When we agree to a suggestion or are persuaded to comply with any idea, we have succumbed to at least a mild form of hypnotism. Self-hypnotism is the self-persuasion that we engage in much of the time.

We are in a state of hypnosis more often than not. When we are absorbed in the pages of an interesting book, we are in a beginning stage of hypnotism. When driving a car with a part of the mind miles away, we are driving in a mild state of hypnosis.

The belief held by some individuals and religious groups that hypnotism is mentally detrimental because it alters the normal state of mind, is puzzling. When captivated by any charismatic speaker, we are listening in a state of hypnotism.

Chapter One in Michael H. Greene's, *Program Your Own Life* is entitled "Most Everyone is Hypnotized Every Day."

> ". . . Many states have laws banning stage hypnosis or hypnosis being done by anyone other than a qualified practitioner. All the same, non-

professional hypnosis still goes on and will continue as long as mothers lull their babies to sleep with lullabies, as long as ministers and rabbis lull their congregations down into a nice, hypnotic state and give explicit directives, and as long as there is a magnetic politician who mesmerizes his or her constituency."

All hypnosis is basically self-hypnosis. We agree to agree with whatever we are persuaded to believe and do. The persuasion can come from others or from within ourselves. The average person has less fear and suspense concerning the acts of con-artistry that we encounter everyday, than when considering treatment with a practicing hypnotherapist. We should be more fearful of the detrimental persuasions we accept every day. The inappropriate acts we might be persuaded to commit on romantic moonlit nights should cause us more fear and concern than a hypnotherapy session with a certified therapist.

We experience various degrees of depth into hypnosis through our relationships with each other. Although we usually don't recognize it as such, one person's control over another is a form of hypnosis. Although some people are more susceptible to a deeper hypnotic state than others, we cannot be hypnotized against our will.

The word occult simply meant hidden until the seventeenth century, when it was labeled "evil spirituality" by opposing religions. Today *occult* is the word used by one religious group to accuse another through damnation of their practices. The fact is overlooked that during its first three hundred and fifty year history, Christianity was considered a cult.

Austrian philosopher and scientist, Rudolf Steiner (1861-1925), referred to his esoteric teachings as occult and refused to eliminate the word from his writings. The word occult originally referred to mystical knowledge, or gnosis, and he felt it was still appropriate.

He set a goal for members of the Anthroposophical Society that he founded in Switzerland in 1912. He advised them to develop their individual innate spiritual capacity for higher-self knowledge. He believed that this mystical ability had been suppressed by the religious over-emphasis on devotion and materialism.

Among his many scientific warnings was his prediction that when animal protein is fed to vegetarian animals they will go mad. Is this the unheeded answer to "mad cow disease"? His teachings were based on blending with Nature, rather than combating the opportunities it presents.

The modern association of the word myth is usually related to a fictitious story, an imaginary character, a legend or a fable. The myths that exist in every historical culture are stories that serve to explain, in story form, the phenomena of human existence and life's experiences. Myths are based on reality that can be more easily accepted and subliminally understood in story form. The original rendition may change over time, but myths are based on human experience and human beliefs in super-natural control.

This usual distortion of facts over the years was brought to my attention when I researched my family tree. The family myths were basically true, but down through the generations, some of the stories had been twisted or misrepresented.

Mysticism is the doctrine that spiritual knowledge can be attained through meditation and intuition, without the medium of human reasoning. It has been over-shadowed by main-stream religion's emphasis on group control through fundamental Scriptural interpretation.

The Jewish mysticism contained in the Kaballah (Cabala), the secrets of early Christian Gnostics, the writings by later Christian mystics and other splinter groups, throughout history, have been considered secret (occult) or unfathomable. Their teachings are often considered archaic or beyond interpretive understanding.

Western religions require worship through their various interpretations of obedience toward a Living God. Eastern philosophies are mostly practiced through an emphasis on individual recognition and communication with the spiritual *knowledge* that exists beyond the rational human mind.

The Western division between religion and science makes it difficult for us to recognize the close association between mysticism and magnetism. An awareness of the earth's magnetic field led the Chinese to invent the compass—a boon to sailing navigation. Scientific investigation into the role of magnetism in bird and animal migration has prompted speculation that the backbones of vertebrates serve as a catalyst to draw in and utilize magnetism within the mammalian mind and body. The spinal column is viewed by some scientists as a conduit for mental and spiritual magnetism as well.

In *Mind Over Matter: Higher Martial Art*, the *tai chi* master Ming Shi, who also appeared on Bill Moyers' PBS series *Healing and the Mind*, describes ancient Eastern mysticism as "the philosophy of nature as an organic whole, in which nature and humanity are united, and the idea of universal laws governing the totality of the universe."

Albert Schweitzer wrote, "Mysticism occurs whenever a human being sees the separation between the natural and the super-natural, between the temporal and the eternal, as overcome."

MATERIALISM, Matter, Money, Technology

> *"The mind of man is demeaned by his greed for gold."*
> Author unknown

Blaming materialism, money and technology for the woes of humanity seems to be a favorite past time among those most accustomed to the benefits of modern living. St. Paul spoke of the problems money can bring. Unlike the usual quote, "money is the root of all evil," his Biblical words were, "For the *love* of money is the root of all evil…" (1 Timothy 6:10).

Materialism and progress are often blamed or used as scapegoats for the ills of humanity. Technology causes more and more changes that would not have come about without its influence. On the other side of the coin, these changes have afforded humans the joy of countless conveniences and luxury. To live without them would be much more difficult than most people imagine.

Despite the fears of progress, the technical inventions used for probing into the past and the future may yet save humanity from disaster. Past and present discoveries that can be used as warnings and protection against pending disasters may prove to be a salvation for the continued future of humankind.

Momentary insights exist over and above the world of *things*. To become more aware of how to best utilize space, motion and creative thought—as well as how to enjoy the material and physical world—is a challenge for all of us. Rudolph Steiner said, "Today, people in general are little inclined to detach themselves from the claims of the material world and seek the spiritual directly in the physical world around them…"

Some religious beliefs hinge on keeping the material and spiritual *status quo*. About materialism and progress, Jesus said, "But seek first the kingdom of God and his righteousness, and all these things shall be added to you." (Matt. 6:33) When we think through integrity and act virtuously and compassionately, we will be rewarded with more than just our needs. It lends new meaning to Matt: 6:30: "Now if God clothes in such fashion the grass of the field, which today is and tomorrow falls into the fireplace, is he not much more mindful of you. O you of little faith." John 10:10 reads: "…I have come that they might have life, and have it more abundantly."

MEDITATION, Prayer, Contemplation

> *"Meditation allows us to be free from the bonds of unease and fear."*
> Thich Nhat Hanh
> *Breathe! You Are Alive*

Meditation helps us see the extra-ordinary in a non-ordinary way. The difference between prayer and meditation has been defined as: prayer is a petition to an external God, while meditation is an awareness of Spirit or the God within. Simply said, "Prayer is talking to God; meditation is listening to God."

It has been disputed but many researchers feel that sleep, meditation and hypnosis provide similar benefits. Each covers a broader scope of usefulness than is generally realized. The term meditation is becoming better understood. Much of the former skepticism is subsiding.

Heart specialist, Dr. Dean Ornish says that:

> "Meditation is the art of paying attention, of listening to your heart. Rather than withdrawing from the world, meditation can help you enjoy it more fully, more effectively, and more peacefully."

There are broad meanings and many methods of meditation. The difference between the level of meditation you or I might experience and the level of mindfulness realized by an Indian guru, yogi or anyone advanced in meditation, is likely to be light years apart. It is said that the ultimate experience of meditation is not verbally explainable because there is nothing in our earthly experience with which to associate what happens.

The levels of thought required to arrive at a deep meditative state are sometimes described as: first, relaxation; then concentration; followed by contemplation; ending in meditation. These levels are sometimes compared to levels of sleep, using the Greek words *beta, alpha, theta and delta*. Relaxation is associated with the awake state called *beta*; concentration and dozing off or beginning meditation is *alpha*; contemplation and actual sleep or the meditative state is *theta*; while deep sleep and profound meditation reflects a *delta* sleep state. Highly adept meditators can reach the *delta* sleep level and remain fully cognizant of everything that happens around them. The levels of hypnotism parallel these stages also.

Ways to meditate and methods of instruction for meditation are numerous. During the workshop on *Stagefright*, author Dr. Robert Triplett led a meditation in which we experienced the meaning of a statement in his book, "the core essence of the extremes is found in the union of the two."

> We were directed to close our eyes, relax and mentally go to (visualize) an ideal place to experience our meditation. He suggested an open sunny area, facing a wooded or concealed area in front of us. We were instructed to look toward our right and imagine that something *fearful* (animate or inanimate) would emerge from the forest; a wild animal or whatever appeared without our trying or prompting the results. Just let it happen. We were told to observe while communicating with the animal, or whatever appeared, and see what and how it would relate to us. Then we were to tell it to return while watching it disappear from sight.
>
> The same instructions were given about seeing something *pleasant* appearing from the left. Again we were to communicate as before and let the animate or inanimate vision recede.
>
> At this point we were to visualize a huge triangle in front of us with the fearful manifestation reappearing at the right corner and the pleasant one on the left end. We were to envision the two as they began to climb upward toward the peak of the triangle.
>
> As they slowly climbed, we were to compare their differences and how these extremes affected us. As the two climbed and came closer

together on either side of the triangle, we were instructed to observe their likeness and how they could help each other and us. When they merged at the top, we were told to simply watch the intermingling and observe whatever symbol or design resulted. Then we were told to meditate on how the whole experience related to our lives.

During the many times I have instructed or personally used this meditation, whatever materializes as well as the conclusion of the vision have always been different. We can learn much about ourselves and our experiences during this meditation, while reviewing it in retrospect, or by discussion and feedback from others.

Tri-tuning transforms us to the first level of meditation. It is a natural form of meditation-in-action. The level that each of us reaches in meditation is an individual matter. No two meditations will be identical. In *Zen Seeing, Zen Drawing, Meditation in Action,* Frederick Franck sees his meditation-in-action as "hand and eye in unison" and quotes ninth-century Zen master Daie: "Meditation in a state of activity is a thousand times more profound than that in a state of quietude."

When meditation practices were introduced to the West, emphasis was put on relaxation. Meditation was often thought of as mere relaxation. This conclusion probably resulted from the necessity for instructors to emphasize relaxation for Western students to find balance. We tend to be hyper. An extreme swing to relaxation releases the tension to the opposite—a collapsed state. Easterners sometimes tend to be overly relaxed and need to seek the balance of alertness. The aim is to become balanced with both a calm and action response.

Dr. Deepak Chopra explains that relaxation has been misunderstood in the West. He points out that the yogis are quite relaxed already. They are seeking a clarity of mind; action through relaxation, not action *or* relaxation. He says it is not our thoughts, but the gaps between thoughts that reveals a world beyond the mundane.

The Holy Men of India aspire to live in a meditative state. Meditation isn't limited to sitting or lying quietly and undisturbed. Meditation-in-action is the ability to remain imperturbable and clear minded in the midst of chaos.

Simple meditation is not the frightening or difficult practice that it is sometimes reputed to be, and neither is hypnosis. The fact that thoughts come to mind when meditating and that we are aware of what we think or say during hypnosis, doesn't mean that we aren't meditating correctly or that hypnosis is supposed to be mysterious.

Simply think of nothing in particular. Put your mind in neutral and give it a rest from its usual "roof-brain chatter," a phrase used by Unity minister Rev. Robert Marshall. When thoughts or worries come to mind, simply allow them to disappear. Return to "thinking of nothing in particular."

Putting the mind in neutral balances the right and left hemispheres of the brain. While meditating, categorize any thoughts as coming from either the left (mathematical) side of the brain or the right (creative) side. Release each thought and bring the mind back to neutral (neither left nor right brained thoughts). This may give you an idea of whether you are predominately right or left brained and will enhance the ability to meditate.

When instructed not to allow yourself to think while meditating, remember *Tohei Sensei's* words, "It is impossible not to think." The brain is a thinking machine. He often said, "There is a difference between *think nothing* and *don't think*." Trying not to think creates mental stress; thinking nothing means neutral thinking. Thinking of nothing is simply not engaging in any particular thought.

In *Awakening of the West*, Stephen Batchelor explains that—

> " non-thinking does not deny either thinking or non-thinking but transcends them in a higher unity....The distinctive goal of any Buddhist contemplative tradition is a state in which inner calm (*samath*) is unified with insight (*vippissama*). The practice of mindful awareness is a first step in the direction toward inner awareness and personal freedom."

Imagine watching a blank TV screen. See any thoughts that invade the mind as projected onto the screen, without censure, and see them disappear. Let your mind return to the blank screen. Don't try *not* to have thoughts. *Allow* yourself the luxury of a peaceful mind, however short that time may last. Practice will lengthen the time span of meaningful meditation.

The father of Zen, seventh century *Hui-Neng*, said,

> "If we cannot enlighten ourselves, we have to seek the guidance of pious and learned masters. Those, however, who can enlighten

themselves, don't need such extraneous help. Why? Because of our innate wisdom through which we can liberate ourselves."

MIND/BODY COORDINATION

> *"Because the mind moves the body, its workings will be reflected in the body."*
> Koichi Tohei, *Book of Ki*

The term mind/body coordination, which I have called calm alertness or alert calmness, also has been expressed as relaxed attention or calm and action. It is quiescent exhilaration and serene enthusiasm. You may add your own terms of complementary opposites.

In *Stagefright,* Robert Triplett refers to this sense-of-being as calm enthusiasm, energetic calmness and settled strength. Anne Bancroft uses terms "relaxed yet attentive, free and yet concentrated" to describe mind/body coordination in *Zen Direct pointing to reality*. Deepak Chopra calls it restful alertness. Maria Arapakis expresses this concept in her title as, *Softpower! How to Speak Up, Set Limits, and Say No Without Losing Your Lover, Your Job, or Your Friends*. Mihaly Csikczentmihalyi describes the *Flow*...that results from mind/body coordination as the merging of action and awareness. Robert Simon Siegel defines it in his title, *Six Seconds to True Calm*. On his Behavioral Systems audio tapes, Michael Greene instructs clients to "relax and pay attention."

These expressions of a unified mind and body describe the first step toward joining with the spirit of tri-tuning, or what *Tohei Sensei* called mind/body coordination with *ki*—to become one with the *ki* of the universe.

NATURE, Oneness, Recycle, Miracles

> *"Accuse not nature, she has done her part; do thou but thine."*
> John Milton, *Paradise Lost*

In the West, definitions of Nature range from the earthy mundane to the entire physical universe. From a religious viewpoint, nature is sometimes seen as the state in which man is unredeemed by grace.

From a metaphysical standpoint, Nature is a many-faceted word. Balance and Oneness are its largest facets. Nature regulates the rebalancing act of its chaotic extremes. Balance serves as Nature's elastic glue of Oneness that holds the cosmos together with a flexibility that allows for expansion and contraction.

In *The Message of the Divine Iliad,* the late Walter Russell said that we will advance toward our spiritual goal when we realize that Nature takes only what is given. "Giving and regiving equally," is the basis of the cosmic law of love.

> "Likewise, when we practice the law of *rhythmic balanced interchange* in all transactions between the opposites of Nature, we shall have advanced so far physically that our entire civilization will be assured of its eternal continuity instead of being continually condemned to periodic destruction."

He believed that when we "cease to over-balance order with chaos and expecting the impossibility that chaos will crystallize into unity…" we will find peace and happiness. He adds that fear, hate and anger cause the development of toxins that destroy any imbalanced body.

This is Nature's rebalancing act that the twentieth century word, *recycling*, describes. Nature has been recycling on a grand scale since time immemorial. When we look at Nature from the perspective of sacrifice and adaptation, balanced by abundance and joy, we can understand it from the point of Oneness. What is now referred to as Holy, meaning from God or to God, originally meant—One, whole or everything included. Sacrifice and recycling for the sake of balance is a part of nature's laws.

Plant life is recycled through animal life. Plants sacrifice themselves as food for animals. Animal excrement replenishes plant life. Nature cycles and recycles everything, including our human intentions and inventions.

Most of the ancient religions were more in tune with the relationship between oneness and the *all*; the integration of all Nature on earth as well as in the cosmos.

The all but forgotten motto of the United States, E pluribus unum—out of many, one—is another way of saying "unity out of diversity."

An understanding of Nature in its holistic (whole) sense can bring renewed understanding to the meaning of Oneness.

Atone and alone are derived from the word one. Taken apart they mean "at one" and "all one." We need not feel alone so long as we remember that we are "all one." Succumbing to separation theories leaves us lonely, resentful and filled with fear.

Oneness in this sense does not mean one true religion, one world government or a universal goal that everyone should think alike. It is the unity of diversity. As we move toward a possible global form of government, we need to guard against power and control mongers. Changing from a fighting and slave conscience to a global triality conscience can help to set us free from any such threat.

To the Western world of religion, the word "miracle" is normally defined as an event that defies known scientific laws. It is credited to the supernatural, especially as an act of God. A more in-depth understanding of the relationship between Nature and a miracle can be recognized through a statement by St. Augustine. "Miracles happen, not in opposition to Nature, but in opposition to what we know of Nature."

St. Francis of Assisi, the Patron Saint of Ecology, saw the balance and beauty of Nature. He criticized those who would dominate rather than respect it.

OPPOSITES, Positive, Negative

> *"Nothing is ever final in humankind's experience.*
> *Beyond every ending, there is always a fresh beginning.*
> *Beyond every seeming failure, there is always a new opportunity.*
> *Beyond every door that closes, there is always another,*
> *waiting to be opened."*
> Winifred Wikinson Hausmann
> *Fresh Beginnings*

When we think of the world as bad, we are no longer conscious of the good. What we see as bad or good becomes our "truth." Usually we hold these truths until some opposite change causes us to adapt new so-called truths. A key word in Carl Jung's writings is "enantiodramia," meaning that eventually everything goes to its opposite.

One analogy of this conscious and unconscious mental tension can be seen by dissolving salt in water. When the saturation point is reached and nothing appears to be happening, the state of dynamic equilibrium is balancing the equal number of crystals forming and dissolving. An excess of either water or salt would create imbalance.

The same can be seen in either male dominance or extreme feminism. Without teamwork, the balancing and rebalancing required for harmony in the relationship does not exist. The swing of extremes exist all through our everyday lives. It is our awareness of their natural existence and the way we approach them that determines the outcome of conflict or harmony.

Like the "child" category of Transactional Analysis (TA) mentioned in Chapter Four, there are times when it is healthy to be relaxed, lazy or euphorically playful. This "out-of-mind" state has been labeled by some as *non-ordinary reality*. It is the gleeful ecstasy of a child being swung round and round, or the enlightenment of a profound idea. It might be the sheer pleasure of lounging in a hammock or the quiet joy of reading a book. Any simple experience of non-ordinary reality is relaxing, refreshing, exhilarating or enlightening. When Billy Jean King was asked how she won her famous match against Bobby Riggs in 1973, she didn't really know, except to say, "I was playing like I was out of my mind."

At the opposite end of the TA spectrum there are the "parent" concerns, including the stress of worry, the over-zealous drive for better days or the grief and sorrow of plans gone awry. There is also the satisfaction of having taken on the challenge of parental responsibility. These are the so-called *ordinary realities* of life.

The "adult" role represents the *extra-ordinary reality* (sometimes also referred to as non-ordinary) that happens when we put the opposites in perspective without fighting or trying to flee from the challenges of life. It is experienced when the "parent" in us can appreciate and join our "child" need for exhilaration, in a responsible "adult" manner.

Our every thought or action is potentially constructive and destructive. Oxygen, the most essential element, not only sustains life but also destroys it through oxidation. Even Nature's devastation by volcanoes or hurricanes has its place in the eco-system. The reaction between volcanic fiery heat and cold water, probably was the birth action for what has become life as we know it. Everything is both destructive and constructive; creating both chaos and order. Without the destruction caused by hurricanes or water erosion that play their part in the natural eco-balance that created them, such wonders as the Everglades in Florida and the Grand Canyon in Arizona would not exist.

When we practice tri-tuning, we begin to put the opposites into perspective without fighting change or fleeing from its unrecognized benefits. We flow with the scheme of things.

The paradox of opposites can be recognized by Marcus Bach's definition of Apocatastasis: "The serendipitous secret that in every seed of seeming tragedy is hidden the fruit of glory and reward." In *The World of Serendipity* he also quotes from the Persian story, *The Three Princes of Serendip*. "Until tomorrow becomes today, men will be blind to the good fortune hidden in unfortunate acts."

PEACE

> "Salute the day with peaceful thoughts,
> and peace will fill your heart.
> Begin the day with a joyful soul,
> and joy will be your part."
> Frank B. Whitney

Everyone, at some level of conscience, desires the peace that passes all understanding. Yet, we lament, "Peace, peace, there is no peace." In Mother Teresa's words, "If we have no peace, it is because we have forgotten that we belong to each other."

The universal law of opposites is: in war the seeds of peace are sown and during peace the seeds of war begin to sprout. When problems are covered over instead of being resolved, they grow into weeds of conflict. If conflict is not somehow turned into harmony in its infancy, some form of chronic discord results. The influence of one person's peace of mind can be the catalyst of encouragement to dissolve tyranny in the minds of others. A spirit of non-dissension is needed to restore the peace—before war, or conflict in some form, breaks out.

POSTURE

> *"Posture is affected by, and affects, every aspect of out lives."*
> Robert Cooper

Awareness of, and practice to maintain, correct posture is high on the list of the best habits we can develop. It will not only improve general physical health, it will help promote mental and emotional health as well. The world reads our potential actions through our posture. Our attitudes and mental dispositions are reflected through posture.

In the armed services, plans and actions are referred to as posture or posturing. Posture, in actuality, means correctness. The *seiza* (sitting posture) characteristic of the Japanese means "correct posture." It encourages a straight back and forms a habit that is automatically carried out as erect posture when standing.

Though much has already been said about posture in Chapter One, volumes of helpful information can be added to show its relationship to tri-tuning and to potential human achievement. The upright stance and standing erect enabled humans to develop the wide range of articulated speech that we enjoy today. There are various theories, though none substantiated, why humans stood straight compared to the great apes.

Monkeys can learn sign language and how to use computers, proving that they understand much more than they can articulate. An attempt to speak human languages leaves them nervous and frustrated. It is the anatomical positioning of the human back, neck and head that permits our wide range of verbal ability.

When we slouch or allow our posture to collapse, we lose the natural mind/body coordination that helps us make the most of our energy. Is it possible that chronic poor posture over generations will genetically reverse the position of the human voice box, sending us backward in evolution? According to Darwinian theory, everything evolves or revolves according to its need by the organism; the law of natural selection.

Health-wise, stooped posture crowds the lungs, heart and diaphragm. It puts the burden of supporting the head on the neck muscles, rather than on the natural human skeletal structure. Poor posture reflects insecurity, lack of confidence, low self-esteem and a feeling of estrangement from, or fear of, other people.

Stand tall by feeling the gravitational stability of the earth under your feet and an inspirational tug of your head toward heaven. Excess pressure of one vertebrae resting on the next will be relieved and the dexterity of body will be improved.

POWER, Force, Control, Competition

> *This will be a better world when the power of love replaces the love of power."*
> Author unknown

I have avoided the words power and control. They portray a "fighting conscience" rather than a triality conscience. Used in a manner of cooperative leadership with virtuous integrity, they can be very beneficial. When power and control are misused, sooner or later everyone suffers.

We are misled into thinking that success depends upon power and control. A controlling person tends to be rigid, defensive and subconsciously fearful. When the word power is replaced by a sense of cooperative management, a softer picture of gentle strength emerges.

Competition is usually played out to an extreme. To some it means aggression, while to others it can be terrifying or intimidating. Like anything else—power, force, control or competition can be used selfishly, over-protectively or honestly. Both fair-minded leaders *and* followers are equally important if there is to be individual and organizational success. Competition can stimulate growth and efficiency or it can tempt competitors to cheat and steal.

Whether power is used beneficially or detrimentally is determined by attitude and integrity. Control is necessary when responsibility is lacking. A triality conscience, with holitude, helps us choose what is best for ourselves and everyone concerned.

The word force infers control, which invites power. All three words—power, force and control—promote a fighting conscience that induces and combats slave consciences, if not performed through holitude with a triality conscience.

SPIRERGY

> *"There is no them and us...there is only us—
> and yes, we are responsible for each other."*
> Slavenka Drakulic

Spirergy is a newly coined word derived from the in-depth meanings of spirit and energy. It is a way of expressing *cosmic essence*; the unexplained universal *all*. Spirergy is an English translation for the Japanese word *ki*. It is known as *chi* in Chinese. The word *prana* has a similar meaning in Indian *Sanskrit*. All three define the essence of life; the sustaining of life and the changing life cycles.

SPIRIT, Religion, Inspiration

> *"A merry heart doeth good like a medicine;
> but a broken spirit drieth the bones."*
> *Holy Bible,* Proverbs 17:22

Spirit, as used to define *ki* in this publication, is more closely associated with such altruistic meanings as the "Spirit of St. Louis," or the spirit of friendship and compassion toward each other. It is only remotely related to deities or sensational phenomena. In this same vein, Lord Chesterfield (1694-1773) wrote:

> "Spirit is now a very fashionable word. To act with spirit; to speak with spirit, means to act rashly and to talk indiscreetly. An able man shows his spirit by gentle words and resolute action; he is neither hot nor timid."

Spirit, like love, has many meanings to different people. Its original meaning in ancient cultures was breath. What we know as life-sustaining oxygen, they recognized as being the ultimate necessity for sustaining life.

Spirit is now associated more with emotions, both fearful experiences and quiet solitude. It is expressed through both tyrannical preachers and in the spirit of battle with devastating weaponry. It is also known as the peaceful comfort and communion that is associated with whatever name is applied to the Unknown.

A resent differentiation between being religious or spiritual refers to members of Western main-stream denominations as being "religious." The fringe groups and individual views, some referred to as "occult," fit into the category of being "spiritual." The former tend to follow group-minded doctrinal beliefs, while the latter encompasses a variety of holiness and/or inspirational concepts. The word inspired means "in spirit." To be spiritual, says Brother David Steindl-Rast, is to be really alive.

A breech between the late psychiatrists Sigmund Freud and Carl Jung came about because Jung did not agree with Freud's scientific idea that matter is the first cause of things. In *The Writings of C. G. Jung* by Raymond J. Langley, he relates that Jung's double cause, matter *and* spirit, dismisses the spatial idea that God is "out there" and relates it to the New Testament quote that "the Kingdom of God is within you." Langley adds that:

> "If one can adopt this point of view, he can believe in God without viewing the relationship between God and man in terms of a master/slave relationship.... For Freud, religion was misunderstood biology: for Jung, the father-figure [God] was misunderstood religion."

Dr. Jung saw Nietzche's cry that "God is Dead," as the need to relocate God within. Jung claimed that only by acknowledging that man's nature is a two-sided coin of matter and spirit, can the body and spirit achieve harmony with each other.

Western ideals concerning God and spirit seem to parallel civilization's relationships between lords and their subjects. Totalitarian control created a relationship of power and fighting, versus either a worshipful subservience or a resentful relationship, between master and servant.

The various beliefs and human worship of God or gods, down through the ages, seems to parallel a slow evolution—from the group mentality of small clans banding together for protection—to the independence afforded by freedom to think and hold personal conclusions. However, at the point where freedom collides with the need for social conformity, control becomes an issue in every culture. When spirit is separated from Nature and Nature is separated from societal guidelines, Oneness becomes splintered. Then the necessity for spiritual *inter*-dependence throughout the cosmos becomes clouded over by human logic.

Spiritual *attunement* can be experienced more easily and naturally through a mind/body/spirit awareness of balanced integration than through separation of spirit and Nature. The Mahatma Gandhi said, "Every act has its spiritual, economic and social implications. The spirit is not separate. It cannot be."

STAGE FRIGHT

> *"It doesn't matter if you're afraid inside, so long as you act as though you aren't."*
> -from the movie, *The Sleeping Princess*

Many actors claim that without the adrenaline rush of fear experienced before a performance, they could not face the audience. A minister who tried relaxation techniques, said his sermon fell far short of what he could do when nervous and tense. These examples appear to negate the idea that tri-tuning reduces fear.

Knowing how to tri-tune did not automatically rid me of stage fright when I began teaching *Ki Development*. Prior speech training did not overcome the fears associated with my feeling of inadequacy to teach a strange new subject. Inexperience overpowered my ability to tri-tune and required extra practice to maintain a tri-tuning state-of-being.

I was still questioning whether the hyper-stressed method of enduring stage freight was essential when I happened to see a TV interview of Barbara Mandrell by Barbara Walters. When asked about stage fright, she said that as a child singer she had not experienced fear. She wondered what other performers were talking about when they spoke of stage fright—until she resumed her career a year after her automobile accident in the 1980s. She had started performing when she was so young she didn't know what it was to be scared. Before her accident, Barbara had performed naturally, neither stressed nor collapsed. Similar to a baby's eagerness to walk or clasp your fingers without fear of falling, she was naturally tri-tuned while singing and acting.

To get beyond the normal fear of performing before a group, knowledge of our subject is our best deterrent to stage fright. The lack of confidence in these instances is the mind or body's way of warning that, "I'm afraid we're not capable of this performance!"

After years of practice, Olympic performers or professional actors can confidently accomplish feats that during their early stages of practice would have been impossible even to attempt. Correct persistent practice eventually catapults us to the stage of excellence.

Our bodies and minds relate what they think we are capable of or comfortable with. That message is transmitted through the brain and nervous system. We improve when our mental confidence gives encouragement to the body, which allows it to perform naturally as we repeatedly practice toward perfection. When the mind and body are in tune, a blend of confidence and practice improves the performance.

Speech instructors sometimes use the slogan, "I can't teach you to get rid of your butterflies, but they can be trained to fly in formation." When forced, the body will perform. It will respond more accurately when a spirit of free-flow with mind/body coordination is added. When the audience senses this *free-flow*, they too become a part of the interchange of *energy* that flows between viewers and performers.

Stage fright was placed at the top of a list of fears when over 3,000 inhabitants of the United States were polled. Almost half (41 percent) responded that they were most afraid of speaking before a group. In *Stagefright, Letting It Work For Your,* Dr. Robert Triplett urges victims of this #1 fear to transform their energy by giving up protective measures. He assigned names to the contrasting thought personalities in our minds. They included The Doubter versus The Believer, or the Weakling versus The Risker, etc.:

> "Although the two groups [of opposites] show contradiction, each valued sub-personality depends on its polar opposite for manifestation. . . . To develop good judgment, we must observe proficiencies as well as deficiencies. . . . When we give in to fear, its energy taps into the energy of courage and as they merge, 'a sense of joy bursts into bloom.'"

Dr. Triplett calls this state of tranquillity an "energetic calmness, an attitude of vibrant composure. It displays a kind of settled strength in which calmness is impregnated with enthusiasm." In a workshop that I attended, he instructed performers to get a clear picture of themselves performing and to say silently three times, "I see myself to be calm and alert." I was thrilled to hear him use the "calm and alert" expression that I was using in my *Ki Wellness* classes.

In this workshop he asked a harpist, who was trying to deal with stage fright, to play and then describe her fears. Then he told her to play again and *try* to be afraid. When she finished, she laughed. Her fear had all but disappeared. He explained how "fear and courage fit together, also, in that courage involves a willingness to risk danger. Were there no danger, there would be no need for courage. One acknowledges the other."

Also, during this seminar, he used a guided meditation for blending the opposites that is fully explained under the Part II topic, MEDITATION.

In one of her many lectures, author and founder of Hay House, Inc., Louise Hay recounted how she evaluated her very first speech. She mentally congratulated herself on what she had accomplished, *before* listing the ways she could improve her next talk. She gave herself credit for the courage to see it through and concluded that she had done well for a first attempt. She added that if she had dwelled on the shortcomings of her performance and put herself down, she would have approached her next speech with fear and doubt.

She advises not to give power to stress. "Stress," she says, "is another word for fear. Ask yourself, "What am I afraid of?"

When self-evaluating, or critiquing someone else's performance, follow the "sandwich" technique used in speech classes. Begin and end with encouraging compliments and praise. For the sandwich filling, list the ingredients of what happened and what can be improved upon during the next public appearance. Add suggestions for that accomplishment.

The sandwich technique of critiquing is an ideal for encouraging anyone to see both their accomplishments and ways to improve a situation. It is a particularly useful way to correct and guide children, as well as for self analysis.

When we learn to approach our fears in the manner recommended in these examples, we complement the opposites instead of fighting and ridiculing ourselves or the world. Rather than trying to get rid of fear through overconfidence, practice experiencing the ecstasy that comes naturally from the balance of alertness and calmness. In other words, practice tri-tuning with a triality conscience.

Suggestion: In any stressful situation, ask yourself, "Why am I afraid?" You may be surprised at some of your "gut feeling" answers.

THANKS

"Beggar that I am, I am even poor in thanks."
Shakespeare, *Hamlet*

Over and above the times we normally say "thank you" to others and give thanks for our good fortune, consider how often we overlook opportunities to lift someone's spirit by acknowledging our gratitude to them. In turn, thanking someone else helps us feel better too.

There are times when it can be difficult to say thank you, especially when responding to a compliment. If we agree to our worthiness of praise, the acknowledgment can make us feel boastful. If we answer in a self-demeaning way, such as "Oh, it was nothing," or "I thought I performed terribly," both parties experience uneasiness.

To some people, saying "thank you" can be embarrassing. When the poor are given gifts for which they cannot reciprocate, they are sometimes too embarrassed to comment. Most of us could stand lessons in expressing our gratitude. Practice saying "thank you," if only mentally or prayerfully. Give thanks for anything in your daily life that you could not possess or accomplish without the aid of something or someone's efforts.

Jesus questioned the fact that only *one* in a group of ten that he healed, returned to thank him. To the one, he simply said, "Arise, go; your faith has healed you" (Luke 17: 11-19).

Often we fervently pray about a condition that is causing us stress, pain or devastating fear? When the prayer is answered to our satisfaction, how much time do we spend in gratitude? Compare the wasted energy used in worried prayer with the amount required to give thanks? Saying thank you or feeling thankful takes a minimum of energy.

The Japanese word *intoku* means "good done in secret." *Tohei Sensei* defined *intoku* as "acting without seeking attention and praise, to act without any hope of reward."

In this regard, the dolphin or porpoise would be an excellent symbol. They are the only animal known to help humans with no apparent expectation of receiving something in return. Humanity, as a species, cannot boast of that same benevolence.

Unity minister Rev. Bob Marshall advises parishioners to give thanks for each bill they can afford to pay. If a new house or car is desired, his advice is to thank the old home or vehicle for the services it is rendering. There is no end to what we can knowingly be thankful for, much less the unrecognized blessings we are receiving every moment.

Author of *Ki in Aikido,* C. M. Shifflet, sees *Aikido* as "the art of Thank You;" the ideal relationship between the *uke* and *nage*. She adds:

> "Practice saying 'Thank you!' verbally and internally at every possible opportunity. The person who taught you to read, the unseen army that keeps water running through your pipes, all the bad things that never happened, all the people who have helped you see something you could not see for yourself."

For one day, become aware and give mental thanks for every minor and major gift or event, seen and unseen, that benefits you in any way. When you get into your car, thank the unknown people who did their job correctly to provide you with the transportation necessary to reach your destination. Imagine getting on an airplane and mentally thanking all those whose responsible actions make a safe flight possible. If we take that suggestion of thankfulness seriously for a whole day, we can become more aware of our blessings.

The Japanese have a single word for blessing the food before meals. *Iteidakimasu* means "thanks to everyone and everything that has contributed to this food as nourishment for my body." Western table blessings sometimes include so much prayer that is extended into other subjects, that gratitude for the food itself becomes obscured.

The habit of blessing food presumably is a carry-over of the elaborate rituals of thanksgiving by primitive peoples who believed that animals and vegetation appeared or were provided for them through super-natural powers. Misunderstanding has caused these practices to be labeled as "animal worship" and belief in false gods.

There is a theory in the metaphysical world that the blessing of food, verbally or silently, can change its molecular structure according to the receiver's needs. A thank you and giving thanks to whomever or in whatever manner we express gratitude, creates natural tri-tuning. A sense of holitude will deepen our expressions of gratitude toward others and to ourselves. Instead of responding to personal success with normal egotistic thoughts of self-praise, a silent "thanks" to ourselves along with a *feeling* of joy can go a long way toward developing self-esteem and self-appreciation.

We can improve our habits of thankfulness. When playing a competitive game or performing a task, for instance, instead of condemning ourselves when we fail, we can thank ourselves for what we did achieve. When we feel mentally pompous over some achievement, saying "thank you" acknowledges our humility toward help from other sources—from the Unknown, God, Jesus, a higher power—whatever name gives us comfort.

When we fall short of our expectations, we can assure ourselves that we did our best, instead of lamenting the failure. Saying "thank you" silently to ourselves will boost us, just as our praise of others encourages them.

THOUGHTS

> *"Thought is pure energy...A thought is forever."*
> Neale Donald Walsch
> *Conversation with God, book 1*

Nothing exists that didn't begin with a thought. This may come as a surprise since it is so easy to think a thought. The most complex inventions and the loftiest of ideals all began with a thought. Every idea sows the seed for future thoughts and wishes. Our thoughts not only create material things, they influence other thought forms as well. To what extent we cannot be certain. We create and continually recreate the world, individually and collectively. Ralph Waldo Emerson summed it up. "The ancestor of every action is a thought."

Thoughts determine action. Words reflect conscious and subconscious thoughts. When we utter innocent comments such as "I hate (what or whomever)," our subconscious mind takes it literally. Likewise, we need to be careful when we make a wish. Our wishes have a way of coming true and some desires return to haunt us. We need to consider all possibilities and probabilities, which necessitates thinking, and our conclusions should be weighed against the possible repercussions of our thoughts.

We have a marvelous brain capacity to entertain, weigh and choose our conclusions. Once we speak, our thoughts are not retractable. At that point we can only ask the pardon of others and forgiveness of ourselves. Not only our words affect the rest of the universe; our thoughts also travel. If this were not so, prayer would not be effective.

Thoughts are things. We must live with the thoughts we hold in our minds.

Where do thoughts come from? Are our brains attached to an invisible cosmic communication system? Some scientists suspect that the cosmos might be one all-inclusive *thought*.

TIME

> *"Time goes, you say? Alas, Time stays, we go."*
> Austin Dobson
> *The Paradox of Time*

Time is a manmade reminder that helps us keep on schedule. Otherwise, time is a variable that speeds by quickly when we're having fun and stands still when we're bored. Time passes, relative to our perception. Whatever is interesting and rewarding to us, somehow mentally speeds time. Two people, performing the same task, can experience the same amount of time differently.

The only time that actually exists is *now*. We cannot change what has passed or guarantee the future. Each moment is an opportunity to change for the better. When we are not in the moment, we may be regretting the past or fearing the future. In a state of haste or procrastination, we do not fully experience or completely enjoy anything. From a linear perspective, when we are in the present we disregard past lessons and future repercussions. When we blend the past, present, and future—we are *in the moment*.

Whatever we do for our health at present saves time and suffering in the future. When we exercise to insure future health or deep breathe while waiting, we are saving time. When we meditate in motion, instead of getting all tied up in our emotions, we are insuring a better disposition.

One of the most disappointing responses from *Ki Wellness* students is "I didn't have time to practice tri-tuning." My response, "You don't have time to save time?"

If there is a #1 advantage of tri-tuning, it is saving time. When we are stressed due to the subtle fear habits we carry around with us, we do not perform to the utmost of our ability. The students would not need to make excuses if they had practiced mind/body coordination with spirergy. It is a matter of developing the habit of *remembering* to tri-tune. Admittedly, this is a challenge for all of us.

TRIALITY CONSCIENCE, Relationships

> *On this day: Mend a quarrel.*
> *Search out a forgotten friend.*
> *Dismiss a suspicion and replace it with trust.*
> Author unknown

A triality conscience is the natural result of tri-tuning the mind, body and spirit. In this state-of-being, we can be in favor of something without feeling the need to throw out its opposite. We never graduate from learning the art of tri-tuning or the developing of a triality conscience. Always, we are at various stages of endeavor; either commencement, involvement or completion of a particular phase of our personal growth. We gain confidence to face new challenges from what we have already accomplished.

To develop a triality conscience, we start where we are. We need to be aware of our shortcomings but with a minimum of self-guilt and punishment. Instead of being devastated by our mistakes, we can use our stumbling blocks as stepping stones. A triality conscience allows us to appreciate life's challenges; to see the imperfections of others, and ourselves, in an encouraging light.

By his collection of stories, *The Book of Virtues,* William J. Bennett revived the old-fashioned word—virtue—that deserves inspirational renewal. So long as we live by a fighting and slave conscience, revolution will overshadow any attempts for harmonious evolution. Fear expressed through greed can be called hell on earth. It is similar to the situation depicted in St. Jerome's vision when he was granted his wish to see the difference between Heaven and Hell.

> The people in Hell were starving and desperate, despite the fact that they were sitting at an infinitely long table spread with all sorts of food. Ten-foot long forks were permanently attached to each of their arms. They couldn't feed themselves, so they were frantically trying to snatch food from each other.
>
> St. Jerome envisioned the same situation in Heaven, but the people there were smiling and happy. Instead of desperately trying to feed themselves, they were feeding each other across the table.

TRI-TUNING, Interdependence

> *"The ordinary arts we practice everyday at home are of more importance to the soul than their simplicity might suggest."*
> Thomas Moore

Learning to tri-tune is simple. Remembering to tri-tune is the challenge. Tri-tuning is a state-of-being; a basic tool that makes it easier to improve ourselves and our actions. Many programs teach us how to mentally deal with such fears as anger, hate, vengeance, stress and anxiety. Tri-tuning is a single-minded, yet 3-dimensional, way to re-balance and attune mind and body with spirergy. It is an interdependent way of coordinating and uniting; an alliance of concerted fusion with the interlocking of spiritual concordance. Tri-tuning is a subtle activity that reaps natural, but profound, results.

There are tri-tune symbols in almost every religion, including the Christian version of Father, Son and Holy Spirit. In Buddhism, three encircled curved droplets represent the Buddhas, the Scriptures and the Monks. These emblems of encouragement inspire us to be better than we are. (*Refer* to the TRI-TUNING SYMBOL.)

We aren't likely to develop every new tri-tuning habit as quickly as we had hoped. Each of us has individual drawbacks and shortcomings. Some habits are more difficult to replace than others and each experience is different for each of us. The objective is to enjoy the practice of this three-in-one sense-of-being and become familiar with the *feeling* of being tri-tuned. Then it can be retrieved at will. After continued practice there will be a point at which *each* tri-tuned habit will become second nature.

From our normal linear view, mind and body are at opposite ends. We tend to use one opposite to fight the other. Visualize the following opposites: rigid/limp, alert/calm, attention/at ease.

Imagine tri-tuning as a triangle of mind/body/spirit. All three components are required to fulfill the goals of triangular views of: rigid/limp/limber; alert/calm/alert-calmness; attention/at ease/spirergy.

Recall the 3-D glasses used in the 1960s that brought movies into three-dimensional perspective. They were a modern version of the earlier hand-held stereoscope. The more resent hologram, developed through physics, has been compared by quantum physicists to the possible three-dimensional workings of the mind. Michael Talbot, in *The Holographic Universe*, reveals that "what is even more astounding is that some scientists are beginning to believe that the whole universe itself is a giant hologram."

Our eyes project three-dimensional pictures onto the brain. Ironically, we reason by a two-dimensional dualistic code of ethics that bestows on us a cultural license to fight for or against everything. We constantly fight the opposites and try to defend ourselves from one or the other side of a dispute.

As humans, we have the mental ability to bring the inevitable extremes of life into harmony. We can balance the sufferings caused by the self-destructing chaos that we create.

Publications such as Michael Talbot's *The Holographic Universe* and Stanislav Grof's *The Holotropic Mind,* put us in touch with the latest three-way revelations concerning the human brain from the standpoint of holography. From the latter mentioned book:

> "We are seeing the emergence of a new image of the psyche, and with it an extraordinary world-view that combines breakthroughts at the cutting edge of science with the wisdom of the most ancient societies."

Tri-tuning sets the stage for considering both sides of a situation, gleaning what is useful with an open mind, instead of a narrow, one-sided, defensive mind. So long as we remain tri-tuned, we are carried beyond the fear of separateness, into a world of harmony and peace of mind. It is a matter of going with the flow of what we know is appropriate at the moment.

With a tri-tuning outlook on life, we don't throw out or destroy anything. Neither do we excuse due punishment. We are responsible for our actions. Tri-tuning recognizes the good in the bad and the bad in the good. Stress is a necessary part of our existence and so is relaxation. Tri-tuning teaches us to put them in perspective and use them in complementary ways.

Tri-tuning may sound like what is referred to as "like a Pollyanna" or "being a Patsy." Before drawing such personal conclusions, be certain you have given it a fair test. Instead of forming a unilateral triangle, tri-tuning is viewed through triad combinations.

The beauty of tri-tuning is its allurement toward a responsible sense of "live and let live." We begin to recognize that our balls of knowledge have shadow sides that we don't always understand. Others might see that obscure side and help us see it clearly. Dr. Carl Jung said, "One does not become enlightened by imagining figures of light, but by making the darkness conscious."

Instead of the usual unilateral triangles that we tend to live by, tri-tuning is an equilateral triangle. We allow our muscles to move naturally and our minds to react calmly. This brings the vibrations of mind and body in tune with the vital pulse of the cosmos. (*Refer* to Illus. #3.)

Developing tri-tuning as an art parallels Chris Evert's comment that her father taught her how to play tennis, but she had to teach herself how to win. We can be taught how to tri-tune but how much we practice putting it into good use—is up to each of us.

TRUTH, Absolute

"We can disagree on issues and still work together."
General Colin Powell

I have avoided the word truth. From a tri-tuning viewpoint, truth is relative. Truth is all too often usurped as a means of control or persuasion to a particular brand of beliefs or laws against an opposite, or different, determination. Ultimate or absolute truth is still beyond human comprehension. None of us is "all knowing" about any *ball of knowledge.*

Many religions proclaim the words of a particular doctrine to prove a special brand of truth. Within each so-called truth, various interpretations of that particular creed are held by some of its members and by splinter groups of that same religion. When ancient writings are interpreted according to a present-day perspective, rather than through the local customs of the time and place of their origin, truths are distorted.

Tri-tuning doesn't compel everyone to think alike, believe alike or act alike. Nature, which includes the entire cosmos of universes, is made up of a vast diversity. Recognizing the unity in diversity, rather than establishing a particular and absolute "truth," places respect before domination. The relative world, in which we live, is in a state of constant flux and re-balancing of the opposites. The pendulum swing balances one extreme with its opposing counterpart. Each seeks its corresponding opposite.

It seems to be a normal human reaction in every era to look upon present social norms and accepted knowledge as gospel truth that will remain forever. Somehow, even the most educated professionals tend to hold onto particular present-day fallacies thought to be indisputable truths. Yet, when we look back only five hundred years, we wonder how those who thought the world was flat could have been so unenlightened.

What seems perfectly natural in one culture is completely foreign to another. It must have been innate human kindness that allowed the Indians and European settlers to interact at all. Such accounts as *The Education of Little Tree* by Forrest Carter leave us wondering how they could tolerate each other. The difference between their mind-sets were in many ways farther apart than the Eastern and Western cultural differences we are experiencing today.

Historically, there has been a splintering off from basic religions to form new "truths." This doesn't mean that an old or new religion should be discouraged. A religion doesn't continue to exist unless it is considered beneficial to at least some of the followers. Harm comes when one religious group tries to regiment everyone into believing that its brand of truth is the only true religion. The fear invoked and the devastating roles sometimes played out by group members, are injurious to the non-members that these challengers set out to convert, ridicule or destroy.

The word *truth* has been used to indicate various means of perfection. Phineas Parkhurst Quimby (1802-1866), referred to his healing art as "truth," meaning the restoration of health. His techniques, or means of restoring truth, evolved from hypnotism to simply helping people find the mental causes of their illnesses by conversing with them. He referred to health and illness as "truth and error." He considered disease to be an error in belief, and truth as cure by the mind. When the error is corrected, truth takes its place. He claimed that mind was spiritual matter and could be changed. Though mostly self educated, his spiritual and healing theories initiated what is now know as the New Thought movement. Such denominations as Christian Science, Science of Mind and Unity of Missouri, all sprang from this origin of thinking.

In this same sense of using words as explanation, **Zoroaster** described what he believed to be man's dualistic nature as the deities "Truth" and "Lie" to explain his beliefs in the hereafter. Truth is used as a symbol for perfection.

Over the centuries, human spirituality has swung from ancient beliefs in absolutism to what is now referred to as the *uncertainty principle* of physics. This slow evolution has brought humanity from the dominating hierarchical group control based on proclaimed truths, to the flexibility of individual democratic freedom of thought. Some philosophers gave up the basic idea of absolute truth centuries ago as it became more evident that we live in a universe consisting of ever-changing chaos and order.

Until humanity recognizes spiritual ways to utilize more of our potential mental capacity, we will fall short of increasing our present earthly balls of knowledge to all-knowing infinite wisdom. While we are a part of the Divine knowledge, we have yet to understand and cognitively develop our full potential of Infinite wisdom. We live more by pretense than actual knowing.

Taoist, Lao Tzu said, "To know that you do not know is the best. To pretend to know what you do not know is disease."

WESTERN RELIGION

> *"Alas, you can never be open to the teachings so long as you are closed to everything save your own truth."*
> Neale Donald Walsch
> *Conversations with God, Book 1*

Many religious people have attended services all their lives, but have relatively little notion of the historical drama of change that Western religions have undergone. Many adult beliefs are based on a childhood Santa Claus image of God as a supra-human man who punishes bad deeds and rewards good ones. Although the Santa Claus god myth is a simple way for children to learn about universal giving and receiving, as adults we can replace childish fantasies with mature intellect and intuition. Knowledge of the factual history of religion should parallel our mental maturity. It is good to know the uncensored facts about our family beliefs and religious backgrounds.

The major religions of the Western world—Islam, Judaism and Christianity—have a history of both influence upon, and antagonism toward, each other's beliefs. All three worship the same Living God but the disagreements concerning belief, worship and territorial power have caused periodic strife and warfare since their historical beginnings.

The common roots of all three go back to the Biblical patriarch, Abraham. Hagar, the mother of his first son Ishmael, was an Egyptian handmaid for Abraham's supposedly barren wife, Sarah. When Sarah bore Abraham's second son, Isaac, she demanded that Ishmael and his mother be driven into the desert. Moslems (also spelled Muslims and Muslems) claim that Ishmael's mother was also Abraham's wife and that the twelve tribes of Ishmaelites in north and central Arabia are Abraham's legitimate descendants.

Islam, (meaning "to surrender to the will or law of God,") the fastest growing religion in the world, is based on the revelation (the Koran), revealed to Mohammad during his 22 years of prophecy (610-32 CE). Mohammad examined Christianity and declared Jesus to be a great prophet along with Old Testament prophets, but he declared all of them outdated.

Some of the basic tenets of all three branches of Western religion reflect **Zoroastrianism**. Despite the similarities between Muslim,

Christian and Jewish religions, disagreements have kept them warring much of the time. Christianity's blackest mark was the bloody and unsuccessful crusades during the eleventh, twelfth and thirteenth centuries.

When early Christianity was espoused by Roman Emperor Constantine the Great in 312 CE, its European expansion grew as one body until the Reformation Period. In the 1500s, growing discontent divided Christianity into Protestant and Catholic (meaning universal, that which is to be believed always by everyone, everywhere) factions. During the New World exploration, many Catholics settled around the Gulf of Mexico and into North and South America. Of the many European Protestant denominations that sprang from disagreement over Biblical interpretation, all were represented as a major part of the migration into North America during the 1700's.

The increase of Protestant denominations represented in America created a unity of diversity. There was some control and persecution of various sects during the British Colonial period, so the guarantee of full religious freedom was not realized until the Constitution of the United States was ratified after the Revolutionary War. Religious freedom from state authority was something new in the entire Western world.

We are experiencing a trend among the main-stream religions to merge denominations and beliefs. Like merging corporations, bigger appears to be better. Religious belief contends that if everyone thinks alike, conflict will be reduced. This idea runs counter to the original democratic ideal of religious freedom and individual thinking.

When our family joined a new Lutheran congregation in the 1960s, I was impressed by Rev. Henry Schumann's emphasis on the fact that he did not expect any member to agree with every word of Lutheran doctrine. He encouraged each one to choose his or her own conclusions. Referring to the causes of the Protestant Reformation, he emphasized a hope that no religious denomination would ever again, gain the dominating power that the papacy of the Christian Church in Rome had held over Europe for more than 1,000 years. This close-minded political and religious control led to the inevitable Renaissance Period and to the Reformation out of which most Protestant Christian religions arose.

Records show that by the fourteenth century, most of European land was owned by the Roman Christian Church. It was the biggest land ownership in history. Anything outside the Roman Christian faith was considered as anti-Christ. Many dissenters; scientists, philosophers and politicians were killed. In 1616, Galileo recanted concerning his idea that the earth revolved around the sun, so that he could proceed secretly with his discoveries.

What a difference it would make if more religious emphasis were put on respect for, and an interest in, other people's religious preferences rather than domination. Instead, many think it is their duty to convince everyone to think that their particular belief is gospel truth. The benefits of *respect* for each other's religions would far surpass any merit of mesmerizing everyone to believe alike.

We can disagree with our neighbor's spirituality and still live together with love toward one another. As Jesus admonished, even toward our enemies. If we become too close-minded, we become prisoners of our own beliefs. If we attempt to convince everyone to believe one doctrine or follow one creed, we activate an opposite extreme. The examples of this tradition have inevitably and historically ended in division. A freedom of choice through responsible individuality creates harmony.

WIN—WIN

> *"If I help you win, then I win too."*
> Denis Waitley, *The Double Win*

Denis Waitley, who began serving as Chairman of Psychology of the United States Olympic Committee's Sports Medicine Council in 1980, explains the usual confusion about his concept of a *Double Win*. "The real winners in life get what they want by helping others get what they want. Independence is replaced by interdependence."

Denis Waitley does not see competition as the problem. He feels that competition in business, politics or sports helps to sharpen skills.

At the same time, it exposes poor workmanship and greed. Competition can bring out the best in us. He says,

> "What is missing in today's win-lose society is the spirit of cooperation and creativity; a feeling that it is more important to help everyone develop his or her potential as a human being rather than simply to get on the score board and add another win to the victory column."

He concludes that values are no good until given away; that by sharing them (our expertise) to help others, we keep them—creating a double win.

The usual stress associated with the "thrill of victory or the agony of defeat" is so ingrained in our psyche that either is over-shadowed by a tinge of fear. When we see competition as a challenge for success rather than facing an *enemy*, we can deal with the shadow side through better preparation for the next experience.

In a win-win atmosphere, controversial issues can be brought up without the threat of being ridiculed. Instead of hiding problems under the table until they hopefully disappear, these situations can be discussed in a rational and understanding manner. With a win-win sense-of-holitude, family and relationship conflicts would not be left to fester into incurable situations. With a double win, the fear associated with a win-lose attitude can be turned into satisfaction for all concerned.

We can win by losing. Thomas A. Edison referred to his failures as gaining the knowledge of what wouldn't work. Despite delays by his many failures, he repeatedly struggled toward successfully completing his inventions.

A mind-set change is needed to replace the usual defensive fear-filled roles of "win-lose" and "winner-takes-all," with a win-win sense-of-holitude. To achieve this goal, we must begin by admitting where we stand and what we can do to replace our win-lose fears. Even with that awareness in mind, we will be tempted to blame others and ourselves for our predicaments until these habits are replaced. When we are bent on winning, a contrasting mental voice will remind us, "but you might lose," and it will hold us in the grip of fear. To attain success from a triality perspective, the only place we can begin is here-and-now.

The following two poems: *The Need to Win,* an archery version by an unknown author and an everyday parallel by the author of this book, entitled *The Need to Prove Ourselves,* reveal what happens when we are not mind/body coordinated.

The Need To Win

When an archer is shooting for nothing
He has all his skill.
If he shoots for a brass buckle
He is already nervous.
If he shoots for a prize of gold
He goes blind
Or sees two targets—
He is out of his mind.

His skill has not changed. But the prize
Divides him. He cares.
He thinks more of winning
Than of shooting—
And the need to win
Drains him of power.

The Need to Prove Ourselves

When we coordinate mind and body
Anything is easier.
If we try too hard—
Weakness prevails.
Determination makes us nervous.
When pride is involved,
We get uptight,
We fall apart.

Our skill has not changed,
Knowledge is the same.
Expectation divides mind and body.
We think more of praise
Than just doing our best—
And the need to impress
Drains us of spirergy.

The win-lose game keeps us stressed or limp. The win-win game encourages a Musketeer motto, "one for all and all for one," sense-of-holitude. This attitude will gain admiration from our associates and the self-satisfaction that we did our best for ourselves and each other.

PERSONAL TRI-TUNING

> *"There are no clear and final answers, there are only discussions and thoughts and silent wonder filling each moment."*
> Brian Andreas, *Strange Dream*

This alphabetical list of topics and suggestions represents some of the unlimited ways that a sense of tri-tuning can benefit our lives and help us to develop a triality conscience. So long as we live by a fighting or slave conscience, we waste our energy trying to eliminate the opposite of what we want. An attitude of holitude will generate a triality conscience. Everyone is endowed with a personal *ball of knowledge* that can be tri-tuned, enlarged, improved upon and shared with others. We influence each other more through our deeds of kindness than from our dictates of control.

You may find different solutions for problems concerning the topics discussed above. The way we relate to and deal with each other's differences is more important than the differences themselves. We can enjoy our similarities when we respect each other's differences. To enhance others while bettering ourselves is the most rewarding goal we can set for ourselves. The fair-mindedness of a triality conscience will enable families, friends, businesses, governments and organizations to air problems honestly, without fear of undue reproach.

Warning: When we seek a solution through tri-tuning, while others are perceiving the same situation from a fighting or slave conscience, our motives may be misunderstood. Opponents may jump to an opposing extreme which they will consider to be the only positively correct viewpoint that must be defended at all cost. When our view is presented, they will try to make us appear negative and argumentative. Our suggestions will be taken as a threat. They will make a stand and defend their position at all cost.

During each confrontation it is easy to lose our tri-tuning sense-of-being and join into the conflict defensively. Also, we may not have been as securely tri-tuned as we thought, which could have been detected through our tone of voice. We may have forgotten about the blending and mending way of acknowledging the other person's position before we presented our own. Suddenly, we realize that we've blown any possibility of having our well-researched solution accepted.

This is the obstacle that most of us face as we attempt to practice tri-tuning. The longer we have lived with our undesirable fighting and slave habits, the longer it will likely take to replace them. Reviewing and acknowledging our usual reactions may tempt us to blame and shame ourselves. We may fall into the trap of self-guilt and punishment. As a preventative, we can rehearse our tone of voice and the art of blend and mend to help bridge the gap of fear about future misunderstanding. Each practice will bring us closer to our goal of personal growth.

We know from prior experiences that it isn't easy to replace our defensive and controlling, or our timid and withdrawn, habits with new actions based on courage and grace. Knowing that we can change our habits *more easily* through tri-tuning, is encouragement enough to keep us practicing to improve ourselves and to lift others.

You may be overwhelmed by the many desired changes that come to light when you begin to know yourself through tri-tuning. When these changes seem insurmountable, remember the Chinese proverb, "A journey of a thousand miles begins with the first step."

Our intention to maintain tri-tuning and improve our habits may not bear bountiful fruit as quickly as we wish, but the attempt will be more satisfying than remaining in the unhappy mire of conflict. We will eventually win, if we can learn to accept this challenge with the same natural innocence we experienced when we learned to crawl before we learned to walk. We *can* enjoy the entire experience.

If you enjoy learning in a group setting, form a group as a means to tri-tune your everyday lives. This will provide you with partners to test the instructions. Tri-tuning as a family venture will help solve the problems that may have been pushed aside for fear that feelings might be hurt or conflict escalated. Practice tri-tuning with a friend or spouse as a partner.

The *Tri-tuning Tips* newsletter (*See* AFTERWORD p.235) will offer you an opportunity to share tri-tuning experiences and to get answers to questions that arise when reading this text, or while practicing to tri-tune your life.

When we tri-tune with a triality conscience, we consider all sides of any situation. We are naturally inclined to make decisions through an attitude of holitude. In other words, we balance our responsibilities equally with our rights. Another way to live the Golden Rule is to "extend the same rights to others that we claim for ourselves."

A Review of the Tri-tuning Tests and Skills in Part II:

1. Comparing Ordinary Deep Breathing, p. 124
2. Whole-body Breathing Exercises, p. 124
3. Tri-tune Your State-of-Being, p. 141
4. Retrieve the Sense of Tri-tuning, p. 142
5. Subconscious Reaction Ki Test, p. 151
6. Sad Face and Happy Face Ki Testing, p. 154

208 ▲ Tri-Tuning

PART III

PART III

Creating a Better World

"We have it in our power to begin the world again."
Thomas Paine
Common Sense, 1776

My Introduction to Ki and Aikido

Blessed are the flexible for they shall not break."
Author unknown

I HAD DOZED OFF when the interview with *aikido sensei* George Leonard began on the *Alive and Well* Public TV program. It was Thanksgiving Day, 1981, but a stormy relationship had turned my day into a lonely holiday. *Sensei* Leonard's explanation of *ki* kept nudging me to open my eyes and watch his *aikido* demonstration. I had never heard of *ki* or *aikido,* but something about the way he was describing the association of body, mind and spirit brought me fully awake.

For years the curiosity about *who* we are, the purpose of humanity on earth and *how* to better ourselves, had lured me to explore the many subjects that attempt to explain our physical and metaphysical world. What he was saying about *ki* and *aikido* seemed to be the all-inclusive physical, mental and spiritual perspective on life for which I had been searching. From my experience, most programs specialized. They were either mental, listening to a lecture; physical, such as Hatha yoga with the meditation and spiritual aspects excluded; or a particular religious belief—some proclaiming absolute and unquestionable truths.

Sensei Leonard's analogy of an *aikido* technique demonstrated how, for one thing, if national leaders would use the philosophy of *ki* to settle international disputes, we could be living in a safer world. He explained how each of us is a part of the universal interconnected web, notwithstanding the fact that each of us has unique individual identities.

That program sent me on a quest that led to my calling the Japanese Embassy in Washington, D. C. They referred me to George Simcox, Chief Instructor for the Virginia Ki Society. During an hour-long phone conversation he referred me to *Tohei Sensei's* publications. I returned to Florida and, after a year of reading to become at least vaguely familiar with the *martial arts* and *Eastern philosophy* in general, I happened to attend the *Ki Development* Seminar in 1983 (*Refer* to Part I, Chapter Four, My Introduction to Ki International.)

Creating the Future

"Today is the tomorrow we created yesterday."
Author unknown

George Leonard's LET Program (Leonard Energy Training) tapes give advice about how to utilize *ki* by "expect nothing, be ready for anything."

Expect Nothing; Be Ready for Anything

To put this phrase into practice:

1. **Close your eyes and have a partner *ki* test your stability from the front, back or either side.**
2. **Not knowing where each test might be, it will be easy for your partner to push you off balance from any direction if you are not mind/body coordinated (tri-tuned).**
3. **Tri-tune and have your partner test again with the same amount of pressure.**
4. **If you concentrate primarily on mind/body coordination with minimal awareness on the testing, you will remain stable no matter where you are tested.**

Exchange places with your partner. Repeat the test and discuss how the phrase "expect nothing, be ready for anything," can be of value in your lives.

What we expect to happen, momentarily and throughout our lives, is sometimes what we get—but it can result from what we have unconsciously caused to happen. However, it may happen in a *way* that we least expect. Like King Midas, we often wish for what we later regret.

To a large extent our lives are self-fulfilled prophecies. What we fear becomes reality. Being fearful, panicky and uncoordinated leaves us devastated and unable to think clearly or act appropriately. There is a vast difference between fear and caution.

Sometimes what happens is the opposite of what we had expected. In either extreme, caution and courage are substitute words for the actual meaning of "expect nothing, be ready for anything."

> A young man, off to New York City to fulfill his dreams of becoming an actor, was naively grateful when a stranger in Grand Central Station offered to carry his luggage. When the stranger took off with his largest suitcase, he realized that he had innocently *expected* a helping hand.

Naive positive thinking can create a state of always assuming goodwill by others. Such expectations can be balanced by calm/alert (precautionary) actions through tri-tuning. This intuitive ability, carried out with compassion, was borne out in the TV episodes of Kung-Fu.

Fear is the body's warning signal of possible danger, just as pain is the body's expression of illness. Neither of these indicators are to be ignored. They are best dealt with through calm/alert speculation, rather than rash conclusions. "Expect nothing" means—do not presume or assume; be ready for whatever might come, but with caring.

Theodore Roosevelt said, "Do what you can with what you have, where you are." When we practice living life to its fullest by making the most of what we have, we are more likely to be "ready for anything."

By acting on the value of these premises, we can help reduce much of the mass hysteria that results from minor or catastrophic local or world events. When we use these two slogans with cautious compassion, we can face potentially disastrous situations with brave flexibility. A sense-of-holitude can improve humanity's general attitude toward prejudice. We are constantly confronted with decisions concerning our feelings about: other races, creeds or living statuses; our opinion about those who promote new ideas or report phenomenal happenings; our judgmental and hysterical reactions concerning disease epidemics—the list could go on and on.

In the 1500s, news that the world is round was just as preposterous and controversial as today's unbelievable UFO claims. Instead of an attitude of blame and shame, or guilt and punishment, we can broaden our outlook from tunnel vision to cautious consideration of new possibilities. We can retain our skepticism without ridiculing or punishing those with new ideas.

The millennia fears that are stirred up toward the end of each 1000 year period, cloud a time when celebration and inspiration could swing mankind into a *new direction* with renewed hope. In the year 999 CE, few crops were planted in Europe. It was predicted that the world would come to an end at the turn of the new millennium. During the next few years many starved because of the resulting food shortage. For those who died as a result of millennia fears—their world did come to an end. Self-fulfilled prophecies cause more conflict than so-called natural disasters.

The dreamers of things to come have the faith that, "after the final no, there comes a yes. And on this yes the future of the world depends." The reality of this quotation by Wallace Stevens is justified through what happened after Wilbur Wright wrote in 1901, "The secrets of flight will not be mastered in our lifetime or in a hundred years."

It is considered normal to think of the world as a hard, unforgiving place where we have to fight our way to success—or succumb to failure. Century fears, seasonal fears and momentary fears obscure our clear vision. Energy is wasted on fear, instead of cautious preparation for whatever might occur. It is easy to put the blame on nature, God or a supposedly supernatural event. We tend to forget that *our* collective thoughts and actions have created most of what we approve of, as well as what we abhor.

Around the turn of any new millennia, the doomsday clamors get louder. There are warnings of planetary shifts, rising of ocean tides, temperature and weather changes, earthquakes that will cause continental changes and volcanic eruptions. The rational fact that volcanic eruptions are constant occurrences and that other cataclysmic reactions have happened before and can happen again at any moment, does not always dispel these fears. Some of these predictions are holdovers from the past, while others are present day prophesies.

Many of these promising and warning messages are credited to religious deities who are concerned about humanity's less than noble actions. Usually the messengers of impending disaster accompany their predictions with a bottom line of promise: *If the human race will improve its conduct, many predicted disasters will not occur.*

Whether we believe in these reports or not, less brutality will occur if each of us is less violent. Like the Hundredth Monkey story in Part II under Change, when enough of us improve our thoughts and actions, locally and globally, our brothers and sisters around the world will be drawn to do the same. Any time is a good time to *personally* improve our integrity and our value systems.

Catastrophes have always occurred and will continue to happen without warning. We have little means of preparing for unpredictable events, except to become serene and content within ourselves. Who can say to what extent our thoughts and actions affect everyone and every happening in the entire world?

The fact that a local or global disaster could strike at any time, gives us little reason to be chronically fearful. Fear merely saps our energy that could better be used for sensible preparation that could avert the dreaded possibilities. Common sense physical preparation for natural disasters and the attaining of spiritual atonement (at-one-ment), need not be accompanied by hysterical fear of damnation and punishment.

I recall how in the 1950s, during the Communist nuclear threat, a neighbor was chronically fearful about the possibility of a bombing attack. When, as mothers of pre-school children we gathered at the playground, she would steer the conversation to her fears. No manner of reasoning could console her. I sometimes reflect, concerning the energy she wasted on her fears. I wonder whether her young daughter was ill-affected in later years by the mother's chronic fears.

We continually experience new fears as inevitable changes cross our paths. The advantage of using our stumbling blocks of change as stepping stones toward a promising future, can be stagnated by fear. Learning the art of adapting appropriate change is one of the greatest millennium gifts we can give ourselves, our children and each other.

Still more baffling is the dilemma that we cannot know which change is an advantage. New medications can be lifesaving, while the possible side-effects might be killers that invade other parts of the body. What we think is good, may temporarily show its opposite side, yet eventually turn out well after all. Faith that everything happens for the ultimate best, can minimize frustration when we face life's pro and con decisions.

As we exit the industrial and technological ages and take our places in the "information age," we are being bombarded with new problems. Progress through technology is hurling us into more dangers than our present knowledge has prepared us to face. Situations that stayed relatively the same over years, decades and sometimes centuries in the past are now changing within years or even months. The American Indian saying that the earth will live forever is now replaced by there's no such thing as the same old way. While every era has dealt with the chaos of some change, adapting to the quickened pace of change is the challenge of the future. *Future Shock* author, Alvin Toffler, warns that in the twenty-first century those who are not willing to *learn, unlearn* and *relearn* will be considered illiterate.

From humanity's historical beginnings to the present, we have inherited hierarchical types of government; chieftains, monarchs and emperors. They were either protective or cruel to their subjects, according to their personal whims. By taking advantage of the information age, each of us can be sufficiently informed. We can take the responsibilities that once were dictated by an elite few who held totalitarian authority.

A certain degree of group authority is necessary for personal and communal safety in all eras of time. We make constant decisions between conformity and individuality. Should I do what my child or spouse expects of me, or shall I pursue my own desires? We are faced with constant decisions, between doing what we think is best and obedience to group control. Conformity to group living needs the balance of individual integrity, which is also essential to group harmony. We vacillate between the extremes of independence and dependence, when by adding *interdependence* as a triad much of the conflict could be replaced by harmony.

As human population has increased over time, the fears associated with a fighting versus slavery conscience have incited territorial warfare to become a normal way of life. Some ethical rules of war have been adhered to, but the cunning and conquering parts of Machiavellian-type strategy also have been heralded. They are fought in the name of religion, ideals and territorial demand.

Scientists tend to excuse violent behavior as aggressive human instinct. Biologist Lewis Thomas corrects the usual interpretation of "survival of the fittest," to mean "those fitting in best with the rest of life." Mary Perkins, author of several Baha'i Faith publications, substantiates this quote in *Growing into Peace*. She refers to the anthropological discoveries of peoples in remote communities who lead peaceful lives. This challenges the belief that aggression is natural. "Where aggressive behaviour is rewarded it increases. When it is practised regularly, the tendency to act aggressively increases. Where it is not rewarded, it is hardly evident at all."

Accessibility to new knowledge, made available through the information age, can help blot out global empowerment of lords over subjects, the rich over the poor, and con artistry over the innocent. More facts are readily available to everyone. Nevertheless, the benefits from freedom gained through accessible knowledge depend on the integrity that must be carried out by each individual and by the group. As we become individually responsible, we will have less need to depend on others to interpret the facts for us. While a little knowledge can be a bad thing during the transition of change, a spirit of the thirst for wisdom can be gained through individual freedom.

The seeds of democracy and fair play that have been planted here and there throughout the ages, have spread slowly. No republic has yet matured to its full potential. Just as it takes a village to raise a child, it takes responsible villagers to raise the child as a respectable and reliable citizen of the village.

By the same token, both responsible citizenry and honest government are required to maintain a successful democracy. The potential for virtuous thoughts and courageous deeds are contained within each of our minds. Responsibility is the best fertilizer to promote the growth and maturity of freedom into full blossom.

Turning Fear into Care

> *"Those who bring sunshine into the lives of others, cannot keep it from themselves."*
> James M. Barrie

So long as we resort to fighting or slave consciences, we will easily be persuaded to join the panic stricken. In that hypnotic state, we become vulnerable followers of any banner that resembles "fighting." One charismatic "doomsdayer" can set off fast-spreading assumptions equal to the destruction of a wildfire in dry timber. Fighting alarmists are not always on soapboxes. They appear among us as fear-filled gossips, "wolf" criers, con artists and whiners. President Reagan lifted hope out of fear with such reminders as "If we do not listen to the nay-sayers, this will be a good year."

With the fusion of a mind/body/spirit focus, we can ignore the scapegoat preachers and teachers of doom and gloom. *Ki* is involved in every thought we think and every act we commit. When we use *ki without* mind/body coordination we are in a state of fighting or a slave conscience. When we are mind/body coordinated with *ki*, it is much easier to act with courage and compassion.

The numerous acts of kindness performed each day have been a source of encouragement for us all. Imagine the difference it will make if each of us sets a goal to replace just one detrimental habit. The seeming impossibility that the lion will ever lie down with the lamb, could be seen as possible.

In the Galapagos Islands, most animals have no fear of humans. On one island, however, some animals were killed until about one hundred years ago. On that island, to this day, the fear of man is instinctual among its animal inhabitants.

Using that example, is it little wonder that so many forms of human fear linger unnecessarily for many generations? The wisdom within the collective balls of knowledge, as well as our own balls of knowledge, can produce a genetic increase of awareness through the information age. We can sweep the cobwebs from our mental attics that are filled with dusty outmoded fears. With each harmonious accomplishment, we can experience the Biblical promise of the "peace that passeth all understanding" (Philippians 4:7).

Without individual and cultural stability, we tend to react like drunken sailors, sailing on treacherous waters, churned by the opposing winds of persuasion. Fate tosses us from one side of our swaying ship to the other. Seeing and analyzing both sides of any situation, balances and stabilizes our personal decisions through a sense of knowing. While "we can't control the wind, we can adjust our sails."

During World War II, hope was kept alive by the encouragement of President Roosevelt's words, "There is nothing to fear but fear itself." He helped to turn world fear into caring with his Four Freedoms; a declaration of the United States foreign policy, presented to Congress on January 6, 1941. The four freedoms were: freedom of speech and expression everywhere in the world, freedom for every person to worship God in his own way, freedom from want, and freedom from fear everywhere in the world. They served as a source of inspiration for peace-seeking minds around the world.

The Allied Forces, and later the Marshall Plan, helped to carry out unprecedented peace negotiations and restorations after World War II. The opposite extreme, the walled-in strategy of Communism, is now feeling the repercussions of a reversed pendulum swing. (*Refer to Part II, FREEDOM.*)

We tend to presume that if governments weren't corrupt; if other nations would conform to our particular political and cultural tastes; if parents and teachers acted the way we think they should; and if relationships posed no problems—this would be the best of all possible worlds. We forget that governments are directly or indirectly a reflection of us, particularly in a democracy.

Whether ruled by dictators or living within a democracy, politicians and citizens reflect a mixture of integrity and corruption. Other cultures have just and unjust reasons for their seemingly peculiar actions that may go beyond the scope of our particular cultural *ball of knowledge*. Problems within any relationship, domestic or global, are two-sided situations.

Furthermore, what one citizen views as beneficial, another sees as wrong doing. A successful democratic community is one where everyone carries his or her own weight as much as possible. What any government hands out, gives it equal control over the receiver. Even in democracies, being responsible and helping each other is better than expecting hand-outs from worshipful heads of government or its agencies.

The freedom to disagree and the responsibility to consider both sides is the foundation of democracy. The next step toward freedom is to get beyond the win/lose and the majority wins type of scenarios, to a win-win complementary system inspired by the founders of the American republic in 1776.

Two founding fathers of the fledgling United States of America, John Adams and Thomas Jefferson, who served as our second and third presidents, did not communicate for twelve years because of their increasingly opposite views on the ideals of government.

In the Ken Burns TV documentary on Thomas Jefferson, there is reference to a friend of Adams,' who expressed his pleasure about their renewed friendship, but described Adams and Jefferson as the North and South Poles of the Revolution.

Adams advocated a strong central government. Jefferson favored more power among the states. Each considered the right of self government to be the most valuable issue. Both men sensed in each other, values they lacked in themselves. Adams needed Jefferson's idealism to redeem himself. Jefferson needed Adams' realism for grounding.

Their renewed correspondence continued until, ironically, they both died on July 4, 1826. That day was the Fiftieth Anniversary of the signing of the Declaration of Independence. They were the last living signers.

Ken Burns revealed that in one letter, Adams had inquired:

"My dear Mr. Jefferson,
If you could, would you go back to your cradle and live over your [73] years again? Would you want to live it?"

Jefferson answered Adams:
"Yea, I think with you that it is a good world on the whole, framed on the principle of beneficence and more pleasures than pain dealt out to us. There are indeed [those] who might say nay, gloomy and hypochondriac minds, despairing of the future. To those I say, 'How much pain have cost us the evils which have never happened?'

My temperament is sanguine. I steer my bark with hope in the head, leaving fear astern."

Historical events, as well as fables, remind us that some rulers down through history have been just, while others have been motivated by greed. Thankfully, some have striven for excellence within themselves and have inspired those who inherited their leadership.

The word *serendipity*, popularized in the 1960's by a folk-song group—*The Serendipity Singers*, means—the unexpected good fortune that happens while searching for something else. It was coined in 1754, by Horace Walpole in his version of a Persian fairy tale, entitled *The Three Princes of Serendip*. The Kingdom of Serendip was the ancient name for Ceylon, now Sri Lanka, off the coast of India. Examples of serendipity include Columbus's discovery of America when he expected to land in the East Indies or such instances as a college student, while studying to be an engineer, finds physics to be a much more satisfying calling.

In Elizabeth Jamison Hodges' version of the Persian story, she defines serendipity as the unexpected rewards received by the three princes for their kindness, knowledge and humility. The following is a synopsis of *The Three Princes of Serendip*:

> The king of Serendip sent his three sons across a monster infested sea to the mainland. They were to search for the magic formula contained in a 100-line poem called "Death to Dragons." During their search, they were to gain character, wisdom and the right to rule. The first prince was to increase his logic; the second, to understand knowledge and art; the third prince was to learn courage, peace and government.
>
> Search as they might, only fragments of the poem were found. Many times the princes were delayed because their services were needed by those who tried to help them in their search. The king's declining health forced him to give permission for his sons to return home before finding the entire secret. The extent of their findings was:
>> "Though the treasure saline be,
>> You will not scoop it from the sea.
>> And often from the sight is hidden,
>> Such magic not by wishes bidden.
>> One may seek but cannot borrow,
>> This mystery lying close to sorrow."

The three princes arrived at the sea only find it impossible to cross because there were even more sea dragons. When a golden bird, that had appeared in the sky during each of their troubles times, dropped liquid from a cylinder in its beak—the monsters vanished forever.

Without giving away the secret formula, I will say that it was a product of the compassionate deeds performed by the princes, in spite of the fact that their help took away precious time from their search for the magic secret.

In *The World of Serendipity,* the late Marcus Bach (an uncle to the author of *Johnathan Livingston Seagull,* Richard Bach) enlarged on the meaning of serendipity, describing it as "…involved in all life, at all times, as part of nature's law."

All of our life's experience is serendipitous. Sometimes we are so pompous about our successes that we overlook the many accomplishments that come to us through serendipity. Rather, we give all the credit to our egotistic conscious efforts but blame ourselves when we feel we have failed.

Changing the World by Changing Ourselves

Something we were withholding made us weak, until we found it was ourselves."
Robert Frost

Each of us creates the individual world in which we live. We contribute to the world at large by our thoughts—individually and collectively. Our thoughts motivate our actions. Nothing exists that wasn't originated by a thought, whether it is considered to be Universal mind, God or our own thoughts. Our everyday thoughts and actions determine the continuous re-creation of the world and our individual worlds.

When we assume that our values and actions don't touch others, that our vote or opinion doesn't count—we need to stop and observe the cause and effect of our every action. Mother Teresa said, "Duty is a very personal thing. It is what comes from knowing the need to take action and not just a need to urge others to do something."

A stone tossed into a calm lake causes a ripple effect. A second stone tossed nearby sends ripples that overlap the first. Though unseen, our thoughts ripple also. They have visible and invisible effects upon us, our relationships and, ultimately, influence the entire universe. The intersecting ripples in our lives can be seen as chaos or as challenge. They can be dealt with through harmonious interactions that the late Walter Russell defined as *rhythmic balanced interchanges*. (*Refer* to Part II, NATURE.)

From a fighting or slave conscience point of view, we are in chaos when we overplay our roles of independence or dependence. When we assume the challenge of interdependent roles, our lives will be more balanced and harmonious.

What affects one, for good or ill, ultimately affects everyone. Each of our "simple acts of kindness" helps to counter the overwhelming number of intentionally harmful and unintentionally injurious deeds committed in the world each day. Imagine what it would be like if each day everyone would perform just one more "random act of kindness" and one less "act of malice" than the day before. Each compassionate act would help lessen our own fears and help others overcome their anxieties.

Prayer is believed by most people to be effective. Defensive and controlling thoughts that may or may *not* be considered as prayer—are also powerful. Ironically, our fearful thoughts affect others. Then they boomerang, playing havoc on us as senders. Each of us contributes to what psychiatrist Carl Jung called a collective unconscious; the similarities of universal understanding and the practices that he believed to be innate in all human cultures. (*Refer* to Part II, CONSCIOUSNESS.)

When we focus by tri-tuning—the integrating of mind, body and spirit—we can weigh a situation with split-second accuracy instead of jumping to uncoordinated fearful or egotistic conclusions. The following story is a comparison that *The Inner Game of Tennis* author, W. Timothy Gallwey, uses to explain his alternative process; "a process by which actions flow spontaneously and sensibly without an ego-mind on the scene chasing positives and trying to reform negatives." (*Refer* to Part II**,** MIND-BODY COORDINATION.)

He compares three kinds of tennis players to three men riding in a car on a city street early in the morning. One man is a positive thinker who enjoys his life as a playboy, filled with self-esteem because of his superior game. The second man is a negative thinker who constantly analyzes himself and his game. The third man, who plays Gallwey's Inner Game, is learning to let go of value judgments, to enjoy things as they are and do "what seems sensible at the moment."

> A beautiful, but completely nude, young woman crossed the street in front of them while they waited at a stoplight. The *first* man indulges in the sight with his mind racing through personal fantasies, reminding him what a great lover he is. The *second* man is embarrassed and sees her as an example of the increasing decadence; miniskirts, topless dancers, bottomless dancers and now, nudity on the streets. The *third* man simply watches, judging neither good nor bad, but notices that her eyes are closed. Realizing that she is sleep-walking, he gets out of the car, puts his coat around her before waking her and offering to take her home.

However your imagination chooses to end the story, it serves to remind us how quick we are to misjudge what happens around us because of our conditioned, but uncoordinated or fixed, mind-sets. As a tennis pro, Gallwey teaches that:

> "The first inner skill to be developed in the Inner Game is that of non-judgmental awareness. When we 'unlearn' judgment we discover, usually with some surprise, that we don't need the motivation of a reformer to change our 'bad' habits. There is a more natural process of learning and performing waiting to be discovered. It is waiting until we are ready to be shown what it can do for us when allowed to operate without interference from the conscious strivings of the judgmental ego-mind." (*Refer* to Part II, EGO)

All of us simultaneously interact as instructors and students—all the time. We influence each other every minute, interchangeably, as teachers and learners. When our children throw tantrums or adults treat us unfairly, we feel threatened. All too often we react defensively. Either we lose our tempers or withdraw, instead of patiently acting in a way that is helpful to others as well as to ourselves.

As parents and teachers we tend to reenact our own rearing. Both the nurturing and harmful cycles of family habits repeat themselves again and again. Our slave and fighting consciences keep us on an ever-escalating course of destruction.

Children's actions can teach us patient perseverance, tempt us into irresponsible permissiveness or trap us into abusive control. The way parents respond, either teaches the children habits of self-discipline and fair play or it generates future tantrums and misbehaviors that form warped adult personalities.

In the 1950s and '60s there was an extreme swing in prescribed parental discipline of children, from strict rules of obedience to uncontrolled permissiveness. A tempting sound for children in those days was the ringing of a bell by the Good Humor ice cream salesman. Ice cream companies with sales routes were plagued with calls from irate parents, demanding that they not come onto that street during the caller's particular family mealtime.

Responsibility for a matter controllable within families was seen as a responsibility of the community. The parental fear of psychologically ill-affecting the minds of their children by discipline, created disrespect toward their responsibilities to society. Habitual lack of self-control in childhood extends into adulthood. Child abuse, such as "baby shaking" so extreme that baby's necks are broken, draws questions about how much self control was learned by that abusive parent during his or her childhood.

When children do not receive responsible adult guidance, they instinctively ask for it—sometimes in devious ways. The extreme swing from strict cultural discipline to the permitting of uncontrolled childhood behavior, brought with it the opposite adverse qualities that now plague our culture. It is alarming to hear Paul Harvey report that bankruptcies declared in 1997, outnumbered the total number of graduates from all schools in the United States. A lack of childhood guidance by parents and society equals adult mismanagement.

So long as we limit ourselves to a two-dimensional world of fighting the opposites, we will be out of balance with ourselves and the entire cosmos. When we remember to tri-tune we can allow life to happen naturally, rather than using undue force to make things happen. We can be in tune with the *all*, not fighting our way. (*Refer* to Part II, HABITS.)

Beyond the freedom to be responsible, provided by democratic nations, there are those who feel that government should protect them against all stress and personal problems. It seems to be a human trait that the more we get, the more we expect. Somehow we feel entitled to the utopian rights that we seek. Government and Nature can provide our necessities, but only successfully through the natural give and take of rights and responsibilities.

We are not always willing to share the rights with others that we demand for ourselves. A hunger for freedom from oppression lured our forefathers to strange new continents. They did not always extend those rights to their neighbors. A fictional TV drama, set in New England during the witch-hunt days in the 1600s, is a typical example.

> A woman thought to be a witch lived alone on a wooded hillside above a quiet, peaceful New England village. One year the inhabitants began dying from an unknown disease. The town fathers gathered and decided that everyone should wear a certain style of cross on a chain around their necks to ward off the evil spirits that were no doubt causing the plague.
>
> Time passed but the deaths did not cease. In desperation another town meeting was held. Someone suggested that the witch had cast a spell on the town. Others agreed to that possibility. The accusations escalated into a fearful fury. The townsmen armed themselves, ascended the hill and murdered the supposed witch without question. Only when making certain she was dead, did they notice that she too was wearing the very same style of cross on a chain around her neck.

Group fear of the unknown creates irrational reactions. Humans, super-humans and objects declared to be sacred, have been worshipped throughout the ages. These beliefs are largely based on what is unknown or what is declared to be truth. Many stories, like the following South Seas island tale, show how fear of what is misunderstood enslaves the human mind:

> During an ocean voyage on a nineteenth century sailing ship, the sextant was washed overboard along with many of the crew. The captain and remaining sailors sighted a small inhabited island. They learned that generations before, a similar fate had left a wrecked ship that lay rotting in the harbor.
>
> To their amazement, the sextant from the wrecked ship had been enshrined as a symbol of worship. When the captain attempted to examine the sextant, he was quickly subdued by those guarding the sacred relic.

The sailors learned that while attempting to rebuild the now decaying ship, the former crew had established families. Disputes concerning the foreigner's disrespect for native taboos, had led to an eventual killing of the entire crew.

The natives, including offspring of the dead sailors, had observed how the sexton had been guarded as a treasured instrument. They concluded that it held some kind of magic that would guard them from evil spirits in the ocean. Its value as a sacred object to be worshipped was so strong that no amount of persuasion could convince the sailor's descendants of its actual use.

As the crew neared the complete restoration of their ship, the impatient captain and crew plotted to steal the sextant, instead of waiting to hopefully gain the trust of the islanders. In their fruitless attempt, they were killed and the ship was burned.

The sacred sextant was retrieved and placed again where it was worshipped for its unknown magic.

What cannot be defined during a particular era is contributed to the unknown in the form of deities or magic. The masses are subjected to the power of their assumed conclusions.

Everyday the control of power undermines the opportunities to blend and mend; ways of turning fear into care. We resort to control and fighting, instead of looking at both sides of a situation for the solution. (*Refer* to Part II, POWER.)

A better world will come from the bottom up the chain of command as well as from the top down. Just as a chain breaks at its weakest link, we can't blame government, executives, professionals or bosses for everything that goes wrong—especially in a democracy. No matter what roles we play in life, ditch digger or CEO, each improvement in our actions and reactions will render a more acceptable domino "cause and effect" for everyone. Martin Luther King, Jr. advised that "our goal is to create a beloved community and this will require a qualitative change in our souls as well as a quantitative change in our lives."

So long as we limit ourselves to the two-dimensional world of fighting the opposites, we will be out of balance with ourselves and the rest of the universe. When we can remember to tri-tune we will "let it happen" rather than "make it happen." (*Refer* to Part II, HABITS.)

Doing Our Best in the Best of all Possible Worlds

> *"He proved admirably that there is no effect without a cause ... in this best of all possible worlds."*
> Voltaire, *Candide*

We always do the best we can; not necessarily as well as we could have done or should have done, but the best we could do at that particular moment. At a given time, what we think of or what we do is the result of an accumulation of everything that has happened before. Our world is as good as it can possibly be, considering what was passed on to us and what we have contributed.

In *The Celestine Vision*, James Redfield summarizes our personal liberation by forgiveness in these words: "The key to forgiveness is simply acknowledging that everyone was doing the best he or she could at the time."

"It seemed like the thing to do at the time," is an honest reasoning for our every thought or action. Putting an emphasis on blaming and shaming ourselves or others, simply adds to our guilt trips of self-punishment or vengeance. Rather, we can consider the premise that everyone does his or her best at any given moment.

This does not excuse the karmic laws of the universe—that we are responsible for the results of our actions. The mental energy that we waste on needless blame and shame can be better used to plan for future improvement. This way of thinking keeps us in the flow of life and personal growth; playing our parts in the drama of the cosmos.

How we react depends on both our heredity and our environment. Life is what Nature gave us, plus what we give ourselves. The value of our free-will lies in our willingness to become aware of what we could have done, choosing what will be most commendable in the future and developing that decision into a subconscious habit.

The twentieth century could be called the "century of conveniences." Think of something you routinely do today. Imagine how you would have accomplished that same routine in 1900. Imagine cooking a meal on a wood stove or getting to and from employment in a rural area. Going to a store to buy the few items that weren't handmade, entailed either taking the time to walk the distance, saddling a horse or hitching it to a wagon. Life was not so simple as today or as easy as it is now assumed to have been.

Now, simply finding a parking space is considered a legitimate cause of undue stress. The horse would have needed to be protected from the elements, fed and watered, curried and properly cared for much of the time. Horses couldn't just be parked and forgotten until the next whim to, like a car, simply turn a switch and drive off.

Think your way through several such differences between the convenience of today and the complexities of life in the past. The number of accomplishments we can achieve today, in a much shorter time than yesteryear—is phenomenal. It's debatable whether we can legitimately refer to the past as the simple life or the "good ole' days." They could better be referred to as the days of "good common sense" and "self-reliance."

By the mere touch of a remote TV button, we can now get weather reports that a century ago farmers foretold mainly by experience and intuition. We can phone someone on the other side of the world in less than a minute; a communication that would have taken days or weeks a century ago. A frozen meal can be purchased and microwaved in minutes that would have taken hours or days to prepare. Are we justified in complaining of little time or what a terrible period this is to be alive? We are quick to complain about the least inconvenience and slow to appreciate what we could be enjoying.

Scientists theorize that standing upright freed human hands. Dexterity of the hands stimulated brain enlargement which, in turn, increased technological ability. The gift, or what some call the curse, has come full circle. The human brain has created the convenience of a magical button-pushing and knob-turning world. The brain power required to know which button to push and why, may stimulate the brain even further.

The down-side of brain-hand evolution is that while it has provided the capacity for hand-tool extensive, the increased brain power is used to develop massive destructive weapons. It is speculated by some scientists that when pre-historic civilizations developed to the point of highly-technological knowledge, they were annihilated by the destructive use of their own inventions.

We are at the point where we must ask ourselves whether we will allow *matter* to get out of hand (excuse the pun) or whether we are willing to correct what we are mentally and spiritually equipped to accomplish. That is, develop the human harmony necessary to enjoy freedom and responsibility as the means to preserve humanity rather than to annihilate ourselves. We have allowed the speed of technology to draw us into frenzied stress, away from the necessary balance between the material world and the virtues of spirit.

Among others with similar warnings, Dr. Deepak Chopra often states that the possibility of a harmonious life dwells in the quiet gaps between our thoughts. Survival of the human species is up to us. We have the physical, mental and spiritual capacity to rebalance and enjoy our world. (*Refer* to Part II, BALANCE.)

An ideal goal for the twenty-first century: become aware of and utilize our hidden virtues to enhance both our material and spiritual worlds. Scientists see the next century as a challenge to learn the secrets of how all molecules, genes and the environment move together to build something as complex as human behavior. It is seen as clearly more than synergistic sums of its parts. Scientists debate whether the universe is actually one big *thought*, of which we are but a minute—yet consequential—part.

Harmony between mind, body and spirit is possible. The human mind, in conjunction with Universal Mind or Thought, is already equipped for that accomplishment. All we need is to become aware and develop it. We can be "swinging on a star" in a more spiritual sense of the phrase.

We have evolved from cultures dominated by kings and subjects, to democratic leaders and the freedom of individualism. Slavery has been declared illegal throughout the world. Despite the poverty that still exists, there is more opportunity than we realize and more advantages than we seize. It is time for reevaluation of our personal roles as contributors to a better world.

Those who ridicule others who are more affluent, should study statistics of the good will that is passed along every day to those less fortunate. President George Bush said,

"Today, millions of Americans, the quiet Americans, the selfless Americans, are giving of their time and themselves, and they work at day care centers and inner city schools, homes for the elderly—anywhere there's a need, any time they are needed—making a difference in the lives of those for whom the American dream seems an impossible dream."

Of his proposed thousand points of light, it is said that a candle does not lose its light by lighting another candle. We *can* help each other through our parts.

Each of us can help others in hundreds of ways each day without over-stepping the bounds of privacy. One generation can plant trees so that the next generation will have shade and sufficient oxygen, in appreciation for the benefits that past generations have provided for the next. Review in your mind the things that you would not be enjoying now, if someone hadn't already made a sacrifice. Think of ways you can benefit someone else, now or in the future. As Helen Keller said, "When we do the best we can, we never know what miracle is wrought in our life or in the life of another."

As children, we played a mischievous game called "pass it on." One child would hit or push another and insist that they do the same to someone else. If that game were tri-tuned, it could have been seen as the "passing on" of something of value to someone less fortunate than ourselves. They, in turn, could pass something they owned on to someone in more need than they.

Diana, Princess of Wales, spoke in an interview about the need to be needed. She lifted herself from the ashes of personal disappointment and despair by reaching out to those less fortunate. Her life of material luxury proves that neither childhood nor adult needs and suffering are limited to the poor. It was not only the money that she was able to raise, but the ways she personally touched the lives of others, that endeared her to so many. When asked about the dangers surrounding the charities she promoted, her answer was, "I'm not frightened when I do good."

Each of us, royalty and commoner alike, has our part to play in the medley of life. We can, each in our own way, carry on Princess Diana's legacy by emulating her example of promoting love and care for humanity.

Now is the only time we have to learn from the past and to mold the future. The *present* is the only moment we have to evaluate change and review our actions. At this moment, we can mentally act out a virtuous deed. We can promote that thought—without blaming or shaming ourselves, or others, even after we miss the mark again and again. When we are in the present, we are in the *Presence*.

A means to manage change is contained in Rev. Rinehold Neighbor's prayer, known as the Serenity Prayer. It was originally worded, "God give us the grace to accept with serenity the things that cannot be changed, courage to change the things that should be changed, and the wisdom to distinguish the one from the other."

How we handle our fears determines our courage. Our courage depends on how we use the wisdom we accumulate by experience. We are instruments in the orchestra of the cosmos; contributing both harmonic or discordant sounds. We are either in tune with the music of the spheres—or in discord; at one with the all—or separated. A fighting conscience renders the notes too sharp. A slave conscience makes the music too flat.

However, we do live in a universe where the safety valves of extreme are a necessary measure to restore the balance between chaos and order. Scientists are finding that our earth is not exactly symmetric. If it were, we would not exist. The universe is not intended to exist in stagnant perfection. As the Eastern saying implies, "There is perfection in imperfection."

Tri-tuning is not about perfection. It is about improvement.

There are sharp and flat notes in the symphony of the spheres. When we allow ourselves the luxury of going with the flow of our personal musical score of life, there is a *knowing*—when to play sharps, flats, syncopate or when to interject discordant notes—appropriately. A concerted effort puts us in tune with the universal Director.

Close your eyes for a moment and imagine a world in which each person tri-tunes one extra time every day. Compare this image to a normal day's events in the world.

Tri-tuning would elevate the fulfillment of Jill Jackson's lyrics and Sy Miller's music to their *Peace Song* that invites peace on earth, but reminds us that peace begins with us. (*Refer* to Part II, PEACE.)

We have more in common with the cosmos than we might suppose. Scientists have discovered that our bodies are composed of the same elements as planets and all heavenly bodies. These elements are common components in the earthly mineral and plant kingdoms, as well as the animal kingdom. All of the cosmos is *made* of star dust. A holographic, three-dimensional universe exists within every living cell.

We are innately better than we think we are, and potentially better than we act. Each of us, just as we are and in our own way, is a *star.*

All Is Well

> *"Every small task of everyday life is part of the total harmony of the universe."*
> St. Theresa of Lisieux

Every experience in life can be viewed as a blessing or a blessing in disguise. We can be seekers of our hidden blessings. A triality conscience of holitude can serve as a personal Jiminy Cricket conscience for each of us.

Realizing that all of life is a blessing, frees us to understand that we do our best and that *all is well*. The ancient story of a Golden Temple helps us recognize how easy it is for fear to cause us to hide and forget our blessings—even from ourselves.

> Long ago and far away, the celebrations of happiness in a harmonious village were centered around an ancient but beautiful Golden Temple. As time passed, the people began to take their prosperity for granted. Less and less care was given the building and the festivals became anything but harmonious.
>
> One day a stranger appeared, with the warning that distant invaders were burning, ravaging and conquering villages as they advanced. Realizing that the gold decorations on and inside their Golden Temple would be stolen, they decided to quickly camouflage the temple with a covering of dirt and plants. With their cooperative effort, the task was finished a few months before the invaders struck. The temple had been disguised by what appeared to be just another hill.
>
> The town was ravaged. The conquerors killed any villager who resisted. They set up their own government, enslaving those who

survived the attack. As slaves, the people became somber. The invader's festivals included treachery that made the former aggressive behavior look like child's play. Any exposure of the Golden Temple was secretly covered over and its existence was mentioned only in whispers. Over the years the story became a myth that was all but forgotten.

Generations later, when digging after a torrential rain, one of the slaves struck metal. To his amazement it was solid gold. Recalling the legend of the Golden Temple, he covered the area and secretly began to ask questions. The rumor spread among the slaves. The possibility that the myth was based on a true story, gave the villagers secret hope and courage. Vague memories about the original happy celebrations began to surface. They could barely hide their joy when they banned together to whisper about possible solutions to their slavery. The people began to trust and help each other.

While they continued to plot ways to gain freedom, their ruler and his warriors set off to conquer a distant land. When the villagers heard that the ruler had been defeated and his soldiers massacred, they reclaimed their village from the ruler's representatives who remained behind. The Golden Temple was uncovered and restored. With a renewal of trust in each other, their festivals again reflected thanksgiving and harmony.

Our bodies have been referred to as the *temples* for our souls. Neglect of our body temples invites all kinds of external invaders and internal turmoil.

When, as a body of people, we neglect our responsibility to the group and to Nature, our individual freedom becomes threatened. Slavery, in its many forms, intervenes. Nations, local governments, organizations and families, rise and eventually fall in accordance with their honesty and benevolence or as a result of their unfair and greedy actions.

When we overcome fear through caring and caution, a fighting or slave conscience is no longer necessary. Solutions to our problems will mysteriously present themselves, seemingly out of nowhere.

Whether any experience is considered a blessing or curse, depends upon the perception of each observer. If, during the twenty-first century, doubters can rediscover the enlightenment that way-showers have shared throughout history, the bliss experienced during all previous times will be surpassed.

In an old revival song the words were repeated, "It is well, it is well, with my soul." Whether we think of our life essence as soul, spirit or virtue—when we affirm that "all is well," we create well-being within and among ourselves. This contentment provides not only physical health, but mental and spiritual wellness as well. Through the tri-tuning of mind, body and spirit, fear is put in perspective. This sense-of-being permits us to Live Beyond Fear.

A Review of Tri-tuning Skills in Part III:

1. Expect nothing; be ready for anything,   p. 210

234 ▲ Tri-Tuning

Afterword

Tri-tuning Tips, a periodic newsletter, is available to help answer questions and give readers a chance to share their tri-tuning experiences. *Tri-tuning Tips* can assist individuals, couples, families and groups to expand upon their tri-tuning experiences. To receive the first issue free of charge, send your questions, comments, corrections, suggestions or accounts of personal tri-tuning experiences to:

Universal Quest Publishing
P.O. Box 1393
Vero Beach, FL 32961

(561) 562-3031   hildaper@sunet.net

Return the portion below or a photocopy of the page.

Please send me a free first issue of the *Tri-tuning Tips* newsletter.
My comment, question, suggestion or tri-tuning tip is:

_____
_____
_____
_____
_____
(continue comments on the other side)

Please indicate how you wish your name and location if printed in Tri-tuning Tips:

_____

Name: _____

Address: _____

_____

City: _____ State: _____ Zip: _____

Phone(s): _____

Universal Quest Publishing   P.O. Box 1393   Vero Beach, FL 32961

236 ▲ Tri-Tuning

Glossary of Foreign Words

Foreign words and phrases can not be fully defined in a few paragraphs. The following brief explanations do provide a general understanding of some Eastern words and the context in which they are used in the text. For easy cross-referencing, bold italics will indicate that the word is included in the following alphabetical listing.

NOTE: In the Japanese language, syllables are rarely accented. Each syllable receives the same emphasis.

Acupuncture
This ancient Chinese medical procedure dates back to at least 1500 BCE. Acupuncture involves the insertion and manipulation of thin needles to affect the "vital energy" or ***chi*** flow along invisible meridians in the body. Acupuncture corrects and balances the flow of ***chi*** for the healing of diseases and for use as an anesthetic.

When introduced to the West, its effects were viewed as a psychological response until acupuncture was proven to be equally effective on animals. Since the discovery of the nerve receptors, enkephalin and endorphins in 1975, some neurophysiologists suggest that the electrical stimulation of acupuncture needles serve as a natural block to the body's signals. Like any other type of medical treatment or healing, acupuncture is not a cure-all. Each person's body make-up is different and its reaction to various modalities, including Western medicine, can differ from one moment or period of time to another.

Aiki   (I-key)
Aiki is a Japanese word used by ***Morihei Ueshiba*** to express the spiritual side of ***aikido***; the martial art he founded. It is a way to cultivate the ideal sense of love that an aikidoist should demonstrate in everyday life as well as at the ***dojo***. Aiki has been defined as the laws of the universe and the principles of life.

Ueshiba Sensei's spiritual dimension became his central thrust. He was influenced by ***Zen Buddhism*** and his native ***Shintoism***, particularly the popular pre-World War II sect, *Omoto-Kyo.* **Ueshiba Sensei's** martial art was called *aiki-budo* before he renamed it ***aikido.***

Aikido (I-key-doe)

Many aspects of the martial art aikido evolved from Chinese warrior sword and knife tactics to forms of unarmed combat. These warrior techniques were brought from China into Japan, beginning about 800 CE. Rudiments of aikido can be traced through the Takeda family, who had instructed *samurai* warriors for generations.

It was from the Takeda family that **Morihei Ueshiba,** founder of modern aikido, learned some of the art that he blended with other martial arts. After World War II, he changed the traditional martial art purpose from felling the opponent to obliterating the idea of an opponent.

The basis of aikido is harmony, which is the essence of the fundamental creative energy force or ***ki***—united with the mind and body. Dividing the Japanese word ***budo***—***bu*** means to stop the spear and fighting—***do*** is the way or path. Together they mean respect for life. Like most ideals, its meaning expresses a goal not always achieved.

In *Aikido and the Dynamic Sphere* by A. Westbrook and O. Ratti, aikido is described as "a modern discipline of harmony between opposites on a universal scale."

Jim Wilson, author of *An Illustrated Introduction to the Martial Arts,* states that the:

> "...main schools of aikido philosophy maintain that the secret of this art is the oneness of mind, spirit and body and that the supreme state is to be at one with Nature and the Spirit of the Universe....Aikido is the perfect balance between physical and mental control, balance and perfectly timed relaxed movement."

He further describes aikido as a deeply spiritual activity as well as physical defense and exercise. He advises those who desire a form of self-defense plus insight into themselves and others to "study the beautiful art of aikido."

Buddha (bu-da)

Buddha is a ***sanskrit*** word meaning "to know." Attaining *buddhahood* involves an awakening or enlightenment. A Buddha is a person whom others regard as having great divine wisdom. Gautama Siddhartha (563-483 BCE), the original Buddha, was born in northern India to royal parents. It was predicted that he would either become a wise king or a spiritual leader. Wishing for his son to follow him as king, Gautama's father lavished him with earthly pleasures and tried to hide from him the sorrows and sufferings in the world.

When the young Gautama accidentally learned what the outside world was really like, he remained troubled about human suffering. Despite his father's efforts and although he had married a princess who bore him a son, Gautama—at age 29, left home in search for enlightenment. His ultimate goal was to achieve what the *Hindus* and *Jains* of India call *nirvana*.

According to tradition, after many unfulfilled spiritual quests, he sat under the *Bodhi* (Bo—tree of wisdom; bodhi—state of consciousness beyond definition and limitation) tree until he was spiritually awakened, thus attaining *nirvana*.

Thereafter, *Buddhahood* was granted to those considered by another Buddha to have reached *nirvana*. Also a *Bodhisattva,* one who reaches the state of illumination but chooses to continue in the state of *sansara* (in the wheel of reincarnation, outside of *nirvana*), can bestow *Buddhahood*.

Buddhism

Buddhism is the philosophical system or religion experienced and taught by *Gautama* **Buddha.** His answer to the human problems of suffering and sorrow were presented as his Four Noble Truths: 1) ordinary life is suffering; 2) suffering is caused by craving, attachment and grasping; 3) *nirvana* provides cessation of suffering; 4) the path to *nirvana* is the Noble Eightfold Path which includes: Right (meaning appropriate) View, Right Thought, Right Speech, Right Action, Right Vocation, Right Effort, Right Mindfulness, and Right Contemplation. These are called the spirit of Buddha's Middle Way between extremes.

For several hundred years, beginning in the fifth century BCE, Buddhism over-shadowed *Hinduism* and was a contemporary to *Jainism* in India. About the first century BCE, a split caused the conservative *Theravada* Buddhism to migrate into Southern India, Ceylon (now Sri Lanka), Burma, Thailand and other Southeast Asian countries. *Mahayana* Buddhism spread to China, Tibet, Korea and Japan through the *bodisattvas*; those who practice to reach the stage of ***nirvana*** and help others attain that spiritual level.

In China, around the turn of the first millennium CE, several schools of Buddhism were co-mingled with *Confucianism* and **Taoism**. *Pure Land Buddhism* evolved in China and spread to Japan as *Jodo*. Those who followed the teachings of *Amitabha* **Buddha,** were promised an afterlife with him in the Pure Land beyond.

The school of Buddhism brought to China from India that became known as *Ch'an (***Zen** in Japanese) is mainly credited to a *Bodhisattva* named *Bodhidarma*. Having brought the philosophy and 18 self-defense exercises he became known as the First Patriarch of *Ch'an*. After the fifth patriarchal descendant of the ancestor, *Bodhidarma, Ch'an* Buddhism split into what was called the Gradual Enlightenment School in the north and a Sudden Enlightenment School in the south.

The Sudden School followed the teachings of *Hui-neng* (638-713 CE), the last Chinese patriarchial descendant of *Ch'an Buddhism* in China.

Ch'an was translated as **Zen Buddhism** in Japan. Several schools of **Buddhism** spread to Japan where they were merged to some degree with the native religion, **Shinto**.

Budo (pronounced bu-doe)

Bu means **martial arts** or martial concerns. *Do* is the way to deal with those concerns. The Japanese word "*do*," and the Chinese word *Tao* mean a spiritual way or path; the state of *te*, or grace.

Chi, Qi (chee)

Chi is the English spelling for the sound of *Qi*, the Chinese word describing the elusive energy that sustains life. When in balance, the human body is healthy. It is believed that imbalance in the two body hemispheres causes illness which, with the balancing of chi, can be healed through **acupuncture,** Chinese herbs and **Tai Chi** exercises.

Chi is also associated with the Chinese art of Feng Shui that has become popular in the West. This ancient Chinese way of dealing with chi flow in the universe and its effect on human emotions and health, determines the best direction for the positioning of structures and the planning of their interior and exterior design.

Nancilee Wydra, author of *Feng Shui: The Book of Cures,* says, "It explores the relationship of person to place and provides simple, easy-to-implement solutions for inauspicious conditions of an environment that can tip a balance in our favor."

Dojo (doe-joe)

A dojo is the practice room or training center for learning martial art techniques. Halls used for spiritual exercises and *meditation* in **Zen** monasteries are also referred to as dojos. Originally, dojo was a Buddhist term that referred to the place where Shakyamuni Buddha attained the Way (awakening).

Eastern philosophy

Eastern religions are referred to as philosophies because the term religion is based primarily on a particular group consensus of "I believe" which is, ideally, strictly adhered to by its members. Eastern philosophies allow a broader scope of individual revelation, with the emphasis on personal experience of spirituality. While Easterners are more group oriented as a culture, a personal union with an all-encompassing eternal spirit is mostly an individual matter.

Indian philosopher, Sarvepalli Radhakrishnan said, "***Hinduism*** requires every man to think steadily on life's mystery until he reaches the highest revelation." This statement defines the typical goal within various Eastern philosophies as they spread north, east and south from India, through China and into Japan.

Eastern nations did not tend to ravage each other's lands over spiritual conflict to the extent that religious wars occurred in the West. Eastern philosophies, though basically the same, differ greatly in specific views.

This parallels the pattern of various followers of the major Western religions—Islam, Judaism and Christianity—who worship the same Living God. Their sub-groups (such as Shiite Moslems, Jewish Mystics known as Cabalists, or Christian Scientists), interpret God differently than their respective main-stream groups. The same is true of the various sects of Eastern philosophies.

Although the followers of mainly **Hinduism, Buddhism,** *Confucianism* (ethical teachings) and *Taoism*, more readily share each other's ideologies, their practices also differ vastly. Just because **ki, chi,** and **prana** are basically the same concept, does not mean that they are interpreted, defined or practiced identically within Eastern philosophies.

The methods for opening of *chakra* energies (invisible wheel-like vortices of energy in the human body) in Indian tradition, differ from the balancing of *chi* (Qi) meridians in Chinese **Taoism.** Neither the idea of *chakra* nor meridian energy is a basis for the transference of *ki* in *kiatsu*. While all of these modalities are based on universal energy, different theories and techniques are used in each modality.

Hinduism prevailed in India from about 1500 BCE to about 500 BCE when it became over-shadowed by **Buddhism, Jainism** and Islam. *Brahmanism,* the upper caste of **Hinduism,** was restored around the first century BCE and **Buddhism** was virtually driven out of India. **Buddhism** survived through its spread north into Tibet and south into Ceylon (now Sri Lanka), Burma, Thailand and Malaysia. At the turn of the millennium it also appeared in China and was carried into Japan, beginning in 552 CE.

Hara (ha-ra)

Hara in Japanese and *dantian* in Chinese, are words used to define the vital, but non-specific, center in the human abdomen. Karlfried Graf Dürckheim, in *Hara, The Vital Centre of Man*, describes the hara as:

> "nothing other than the physical embodiment of the original Life center in man....From experiences gained through Hara one comes to see that it contains a hidden 'treasure of life,' which is man's birthright, which was lost in the evolution of his consciousness and which he must discover and practice as a pre-requisite for all higher development."

Tohei Sensei refers to the hara as the *"one point,"* basically in the center of the abdomen. His **Ki** Development program for learning and testing mind/body coordination with **Ki**, verifies Dürckheim's expression "third factor."

Dürckheim defines the hara as neither body nor soul but "the whole man, that is, the sum total of those apparently separate functions in which the individual exists as a whole." The first factor is erect posture, second correct breathing and third, "The interrelation of tension and relaxation prevailing within him."

Hinduism

What Westerners call Hinduism, is the oldest known major spiritual philosophy. Its roots go back to 1500 BCE or possibly even before the Indo-Aryan tribes invaded the Indus River Valley in southwestern India. They left religious literature called the *Veda* or knowledge, which became known as *Brahmanism.*

From the *Vedas* come the highly developed metaphysics and mystical writings called the *Upanishads* about 850 BCE. The *Brahman* is seen as universal soul or godhead. The *Brahmans* (the highest Hindu caste) are considered the caretakers or high priest teachers. The goal is the blend of *Atman* or Universal Self (pure consciousness) with the indwelling Self of man, which expresses "that art thou." This union frees the individual from repeated lives and deaths caused by **karma**. The practice of **yoga** also was recorded in the *Upanishad* literature.

Hindus were divided by two ways of viewing the world. One, drawn by the *Vedas*, who sought the sacred and profane rewards of children, health, wealth and a good rebirth. The other drew upon the *Upanishad* principles of seeking release from the world of desires.

The *Bhagavad-Gita* describes a mediating third path of devotion to ultimate reality that the world is an illusion. The most popular of the Hindu gods are: *Shiva*, the destroyer; *Vishnu*, the creator; and the Goddess, *Devi* who as the prime mover commands the male gods to do the work of creation and destruction.

Buddhism held a Middle Road belief between the two extremes of Hinduism. It did not prevail in India, mainly because of the strong Hindu belief in the *caste* system, which held each person to a particular birth *caste* during that lifetime.

Jainism (jine-ism)

Jainism was founded by Nataputta Mahavira (599-527 BCE), called *Jina* (Spiritual Conqueror). Jainism, which is similar to and contemporary with **Buddhism,** still claims a small following today. Its parent sect was *Brahmanism*, a **Hindu** sect. As strict adherents to nonviolence, their reverence for animal life is extreme.

They believed that *karma* produced embodiment of the soul which could be freed by practice of the three "jewels:" right faith, right knowledge and right conduct. Despite the **Jains** adherence to the institution of caste, Mohandas Gandhi followed some of their precepts.

Karma is the law of cause and effect, that extends reward or retribution for the merits or demerits we create by our thoughts, words and deeds. Rather than reward and punishment, it is seen as "our actions returning to us."

In its relationship to *reincarnation*, the karma that is not balanced out in this life will be rectified during a subsequent rebirth. The purpose of life is viewed as the means of gaining a personal way of getting off the wheel of repeated *incarnations* by uniting with the *Infinite*.

Ki (key)

The word ki, defined as **spirergy** (spirit-energy) in this writing, has different levels of meaning. If limited to motion, as *chi* moving along meridians, it deals more with the movement of vital life energy within the body. On a broader scale, reflecting Einstein's quotation, "Everything is energy," the molecules in a rock or a piece of plastic change slowly—but are a part of the ever-changing energy. Every cell, including our body cells, lives through a birth, life and death cycle of never-ending change.

Ki is the Japanese word for this unexplained life-giving, life-sustaining and the ever-exchanging motion and matter that make up the universe. *Tohei Sensi* defines ki as the "infinite gathering of infinitely small particles" that make up, or is, the universe. He also equates ki with "what Westerners call God."

In explanation, I add that this may be considered blasphemy to those who limit God to personified or super-human status. Most believers, however, see the One Living God as everywhere and in everything; all knowing—omnipresent, omnipotent, and omniscient. This, too, includes everything. The Jewish faith defines the One God as "God is One," meaning all-inclusive.

Tohei Sensei related that during a speech in Oregon, he said that "the purpose of all religions is to bring forth the universal mind." He was asked by a minister in the audience whether Jesus, Moses or the Buddha would have passed the ki tests? When he answered, "Of course," the minister asked what proof he had of this? *Tohei Sensei* explained that without unifying mind and body to access the universal mind, their accomplishments would not have been possible.

Quoting Gautama Buddha, "Above and below, I am the Honored One," and Jesus' saying that he was the Son of God, *Tohei Sensei* summarizes that we are all potential Buddhas and all children of God.

Relating *ki* to the *one point,* he believes that each person contains the center of the universe in the lower abdomen. The universe condensed becomes ourselves, and when further condensed, it becomes the *one point*. This point of centering or focus brings us to a sense of Oneness with the All.

Kiai (key-I)

Kiai is an accumulation of unified *ki* expressed with a penetrating staccato sound followed by silence. Instead of the expected pronunciation, ki-ai, the intensified result is a quick "ye-e-e-e" sound or "ee-yay-ee" sound as described in William Reed's *Ki, A Practical Guide for Westerners.*

Kiai is a yell sometimes used to accompany a strike or throw. Without mind/body coordination with *ki*, repeated practice of sounding a kiai can cause throat soreness. This response, made popular in Hollywood Oriental martial art films, is intended to stop a man in his tracks.

Any build up and release of emotionally coordinated *ki*, whether shouted or inaudible, is a powerful release. In *Illuminated Spirit,* by Dan and Jackie DeProspo, Dan relates that his softly voiced *kiai* to Onuma *Sensei*, his *kyudo* (Japanese archery) master, while on his death bed, momentarily quickened the pace of his heart monitor. This soft, but penetrating, sound was a parting endearment of respect for his dying *sensei*.

Ki-aikido (key—I-key-doe)

Ki-aikido was developed by **Koichi Tohei** in Tokyo, Japan. This school of *aikido* martial art training emphasizes the awareness, explanation and use of *ki*. Ki-aikido differs from the original *aikido* mostly because of an emphasis on the explanation of mind/body coordination and the extension of *ki* through **Ki Development** training.

Kiatsu (key-aut-sue)

Kiatsu therapy training is an energy-healing art, using the philosophy of *aikido,* that occurred to **Koichi Tohei** when he became ill on the battlefield while serving in China during World War II. It differs from massage-like treatments, as there is no manipulation or constant movement on the client's body. Kiatsu is a transference of universal energy (*ki*) to the client, increasing the vital life-flow that promotes the body's self-healing processes.

Just as a weak battery is aided by the boost from a fully charged battery, a sick person needs a re-start of the body's self-generator to promote and restore health. Kiatsu treatments provide *ki* which the body utilizes where *ki* (life energy) is lacking. Unlike most healing therapies, kiatsuists do not attempt to out-guess the body's infinite wisdom. Healing energy is extended to painful areas or over all the body (except male/female private anatomy). The client is systematically treated by the extension of *ki*. The body utilizes life energy to heal just as it determines how and where to use the energy metabolized from the breath we breathe, the food we eat or the revitalizing sleep we get.

Emphasis is put on the transference of universal energy to the client. *Ki* is mentally extended through the kiatsuist's fingers and thumbs into the body, soothing externally and penetrating internally where the body directs and utilizes the energy. Clients who are not overly skeptical about unseen energies, are aware of and enjoy the added *ki* energy. Those who are apprehensive at first, many times are amazed at the effective results. Others may not be aware of the energy and wonder if anything is happening.

I was introduced to Kiatsu at Maruyama Sensei's seminar described at the beginning of Chapter Four. One of my periodic migraines was threatening when he demonstrated kiatsu that evening. He treated me for about fifteen minutes.

When I joined my friends for the drive home, something about my appearance must have changed. They asked if I was sure I could drive. My answer was; "Yes, I can drive, but we might fly right over the treetops like E.T." That was the best way I could describe the euphoric state I was experiencing.

I enjoyed a restful night's sleep, after suddenly being relieved of the usual constipation associated with my migraines. The next day, I was able to continue the seminar instead of having to suffer through the customary one to three days of painful confinement.

Kiatsu is a natural response. When we bump an elbow or stub a toe we automatically place our hand on that spot. It is interesting to note that the greatest percentage of the human brain matter is geared toward the activity of the hands—there is healing power through the hands!

From an acupuncture point of view, the heart meridian ends in the palms of the hands. Think of the comfort of touch: a baby in a mother's arms, a pat of encouragement, a helping hand extended to a child or a romantic touch. This same energy is known to assist premature babies who thrive on touch and massage. These facts have only recently been realized by Western medical caretakers. Or, I should say, been revived. When I entered nurses training in the mid 1940's, patients were given nightly back rubs. They were considered mentally soothing and relaxing, as well as physically stimulating, for both the prevention of illness and for healing.

All of these actions express a triality conscience; a turning of fear into caring. Dolores Krieger, founder of Therapeutic Touch, says that compassion toward the client is an important and necessary part of any healing therapy.

Kiatsu can be used for self-healing. When tri-tuned, healing energy flows to oneself or others, as directed. When injured or in pain, instead of reacting with fear, mentally direct your healing energy to that area. Which is the most likely to stimulate the healing process: the woman who examines her breasts with healing energy in mind or one who is filled with fear of finding a lump? The body is in a constant state of self-healing.

Talk to your body and learn to listen to its messages. You will develop a sense of appreciation and respect for your body and its communicative signals.

Ki Development

This program was founded by **Tohei Sensei** as a means of teaching his **ki** principles: 1) keep **one point**, 2) relax completely, 3) keep **weight underside**, 4) extend **ki**. They explain mind/body coordination with **ki** extended, which can enhance our every thought and action in daily life. In some **ki-aikido dojos**, an hour of Ki Development practice precedes the hour of **aikido** practice. In other **dojos**, it is blended with the **aikido** practice.

Those who do not wish to practice aikido, can use the Ki Development instructions in this and other publications. My Westernized **Ki Wellness** program combines ki development skills, ki meditation, ki breathing, self-healing and discussions about the philosophy of **ki** through both Eastern and Western mind-sets.

Ki no Kenkyukai (key-no-ken-que-ky)

Ki no Kenkyukai, translated Ki Society International, was established by **Tohei Sensei** in September, 1971, to teach the principles of mind and body unification. On May 1, 1974, he set up headquarters at 101 Ushigome Heim, 2-30 Haramachi, Shinjuku-ku, Tokyo, Japan, 162. There he taught *Shin Shin Toitsu Aikido*; the art of **aikido** with mind and body unification, based on his **ki** principles.

In addition to the Tokyo school, *Ki no Sato*, or "Homeland of Ki," the new Ki Society World Headquarters opened on October 28, 1990, a half-hour drive north of Tokyo. At that time there were 15,170 Ki Society members in Japan and approximately 100,000 members around the world. Mailing address: Ki no Kenkyukai H.Q., 3515 O-Aza Akabane, Ichikai-Machi, Haga-Gun, Tochigi-Ken, Japan, 321-34. Tel: 0285-68-4000.

Both are nationally recognized schools in Japan for **ki** research. There are Ki Society branches in more than twenty countries. The address of the chief instructor, U.S.A., Kashiwaya Sensei, is: Seattle Ki Society, 6106 Roosevelt Way, N.E., Seattle, WA 98115. Phone: (206) 527-2151.

Ki Testing

Ki testing was devised by ***Tohei Sensei*** as a means of muscle or kinetic testing to determine whether the mind and body are coordinated. When the test shows weakness or instability, it is proof that the mind and body are out of sync. When we practice **tri-tuning**, in everyday life, it becomes a ***ki*** skill.

Many names are associated with muscle testing. One scientific term of explanation is contact reflex analysis. (*Refer* to Part II, KINESIOLOGY)

Ki Wellness

Ki Wellness is my Western version that expands on the merits of ***Ki Development,*** to include and demonstrate how Eastern philosophy can be better understood by Westerners through a blend of Eastern and Western mind-sets.

Martial Arts

Martial techniques exist all over the world. What we know as specifically Oriental martial arts, originated in various Eastern countries. In time, they were passed down, merged and changed. New organizations with varied techniques continue to surface.

Traditionally, basic Oriental techniques of the martial arts such as *kung fu, karate, kendo, judo and **aikido,*** were closely guarded secrets until after World War II. The ancient training at the Shaolin Monastery (Temple) in China was based on the tactics originally brought from India by *Bodhidharma,* a *Mahayana Buddhist.* They were disclosed only by word of mouth for fear that this knowledge might fall into the hands of bandits. Anyone familiar with the ultimate power of these techniques can understand their precautions.

The techniques included in this book represent a kindergarten stage of the philosophy upon which the martial arts are based. In Thomas Cleary's translation of Ming Shi's *Mind Over Matter: Higher Martial Arts,* he explains that the simultaneous use of mind and body "is still not the highest lever of refinement of consciousness." Beyond the next level, "using consciousness, not strength," is a more advanced state where even consciousness is no longer used. Conscious intent is eliminated in order to exercise "total awareness of supranormal consciousness and physical being." This highest level of exercise, where the "nonintentional is supreme and consciousness without conscious intent is true consciousness,"—is the ultimate realm of experience.

Nage (nau-gay)

In practice, the aikidoist (attackee) is the nage who learns to throw the *uke* (attacker). Since an aikidoist does not attack, a partner must play the role of *uke* who, at the same time, learns to roll out of the nage's *aikido* techniques without injury. The nage learns to throw; the *uke* learns to flow.

Nirvana (near vauna)

Nirvana is a **Sanskrit** word literally meaning to "extinguish" the flames of earthly desires and achieve absolute peace. It is the goal of **Jains, Hindus** and **Buddhists;** the escape from the rounds of **reincarnation** or transmigration and release the soul (atman) from the senses and from worldly illusions. In **Zen Buddhism**, this state of enlightenment or direct perception of knowingness is expressed in Japanese as *satori,* meaning **Buddha** mind or seeing into one's own nature.

One point

"One point" is the phrase coined by **Tohei Sensei** to express in English what he realized on the battlefield in China during World War II. His first experience in battle left him in shock to think that he could be so frightened after all his practice of the **martial arts.** "I surrendered to the universe, the decision whether I would live or die." This helped to release his fears. He also found that rather than hardening the *hara* as some ancient *senseis* had taught, or forgetting the abdomen, his courage and confidence were heightened when he concentrated his mind in what he phrased the *"one point."*

Chuck Norris, defines the *tai-ten* (*hara*) as the "one point" or "the gravitational center of the body," in his book *The Secret Power Within—Zen Solutions to Real Problems.*

This invisible center of the human body structure, is not part of the human anatomy. It is a centering that can be pinpointed and recognized somewhere in the lower abdomen, depending on personal anatomy and bodily position. Some say two inches below the naval but, with practice, each person can sense his or her center of balance. It also changes with body position for body balance. When sitting *seiza* (Japanese style) the **Hara** becomes external, below floor level.

There is scientific speculation that it relates to the connection between the brain and nerve endings in the abdomen. The term "a gut feeling" is another expression for the mind/body connection and the balance that is produced by coordination of mind and body.

Prana

Prana is a **Hindu Sanskrit** word meaning breath, or more specifically, the life force that permeates and constantly recreates the universe. The word prana is familiar to Westerners mainly through one form of *yoga* called *pranayana* (breath-way).

Reincarnation

There are varied Eastern beliefs about how the soul reincarnates on earth and the role it plays between lives. One variation is the **Hindu** version of *transmigration*, the passing of a soul from one state, or body, to another—possibly to a lower life-form. Most religious groups, including Western religions, have held some form of belief in reincarnation at some period in their history. The belief in reincarnation by some early Christians disappeared with the smoke from the burning of early Christian writings. When the Christian Bible was formulated in the fourth century CE, under the supervision of Roman Emperor Constantine, all sacred writings not included in the New Testament were destroyed.

Sanskrit

Sanskrit is any written form of classic old *Indic* language, including the *Vedic* **Hindu** religious scriptures; the Brahamanas, which included the *Vedas* and *Upanishads*. The *Vedas* are the source of the ancient *Ayurvedic* medicine now promoted by Dr. Deepak Chopra and others.

Sensei (sin-say)

Sensei is the Japanese word for doctor and teacher. Because word order is different from that used in English, rather than Professor Tohei, it becomes Tohei Professor. Teachers are highly regarded in Japan and are considered to be on equal status with doctors.

Shintoism (shin-toe-ism)

Shinto, meaning the way of the *kami* gods, is the native religion of Japan. The most majestic of these spirit dieties are *Nihongi*, a sky father and *Kokiki*, the earth mother. The Emperor, supposedly a god-man, is believed to be descended from a long family line beginning with the sun goddess, *Amaterasu Omikami,* who sent her grandson down from heaven to have dominion over the tribes.

Shintoism has existed continuously, throughout Japanese history. It has also co-existed along with several sects of **Buddhism,** *Confucianism* and Western religions. After World War II, the new Japanese constitution included religious freedom.

It is customary for **Buddhist** retreat centers in Japan to include a Shinto Shrine, and Shinto centers to include a **Buddhist** Temple. The *torii* gate at the entrance of every Shinto Shrine (place of individual worship) signifies the openness of the religion itself.

Tai Chi (tie-chee)

Tai chi is the practice of slow body movements performed as healthful meditative exercises and as preparation for the *tai chi chuan* martial art. Tai chi has been practiced, with new systems added, for over 5,000 years. Some tai chi movements express animal movements and are so named.

The objective is to practice in harmony with the chi (***ki***, in Japanese). Because this chi is so much a part of the innate feeling nature of Orientals, there is little explanation of how to harmonize with this universal ***chi***.

In the West, tai chi is usually taught in the same repetitive manner as in the Orient, with little if any explanation of how to experience ***chi***. Westerners are expected to absorb and recognize the chi through repeated practice and to personally achieve mental transformation. The instruction is often limited to "follow me."

Chinese grow up with an awareness of chi and its uses. Without the innate awareness of chi or ***ki,*** dormant in Western cultures, the real value of the chi can easily be overlooked or misunderstood from the limited Western point of view. Despite this handicap, tai chi has become popular and significantly effective in the West, particularly among the older generations and those who desire a less strenuous type of exercise.

Taoism (Dow-ism)

The word *Tao* means the *way* or path to Reality; the order or way the universe works. According to tradition, Taoism was handed down from the philosophy of *Lao Tzu* (meaning Old Master), a curator of the imperial records during the *Chou* Dynasty in the sixth century BCE. He resigned his post in disgust and was on his way into the unknown west to flee society and meditate. The gatekeeper at the last outpost recognized *Lao Tzu* and begged him to write down the main tenets of his philosophy. After composing the *Tao te ching,* the bible of Taoism, he was never seen again.

Taoism paralleled *Confucianism*, but placed more emphasis on spirituality and personal health. *Confucianism* is a code of ideal civil behavior and the political ethics of government, rather than a spiritual religion. Taoism flourished but veered somewhat from the philosophy *Lao Tzu* had prescribed.

A co-existence developed between Taoism, *Confucianism* and **Buddhism** in China, around 200 CE. A Taoist by the name of *Chang Ling* borrowed some ideas from **Buddhism** and established Taoism as a religious order. After about the nineteenth century CE, Taoism was again swayed from the *Lao Tzu* pattern and deteriorated into sorcery, fortune telling, charm selling, magic and alchemy.

The eventual splits and changes within all three Chinese philosophies left China mainly with Neo-Confucianism until the Communist take-over during and after World War II. A Western interest in Taoism, has given it a booster shot of resurgence, especially in Chinese medicine which has been practiced in China for thousands of years.

Tenkan (ten-con)

Tenkan is a Japanese word to describe the turning techniques in **aikido**. They are accomplished by circular motion or spinning turns (demonstrated in Part I, Chapter Four, under Aikido Tenkan Technique.)

Tohei, Koichi (toe-hay, co-ee-chee)

Koichi Tohei was born January 20, 1920. Though a sickly child, he received a black belt in Judo at age fifteen. During a bout of pleurisy from over-training, he strengthened himself through ***Zen*** and *misogi* (purification) training, which included breathing exercises. In 1939, he enrolled to study ***aikido*** under its founder, ***Morihei Ueshiba***.

He served as a Japanese Officer in China during World War II, where his ***martial arts*** training helped him to overcome battle fright. He also used the concept of ***ki*** to heal his own and fellow-soldiers' illnesses. Over the years, he developed this healing technique that he named *kiatsu* (finger pressure with *ki*).

After World War II, the disappointment of failed business ventures lured him to rejoin ***Ueshiba Sensei*** for a career as an ***aikido*** instructor. In 1969, he was awarded the tenth degree, the highest black belt rank available in ***aikido***. He became the Chief Instructor and later was president of the World Aikido Federation.

He began traveling, first to Hawaii in 1953, to teach ***aikido***. In 1971 he founded ***Ki no Kenkyukai***, translated Ki Society International. In 1974, he separated from the Aikido Federation and founded *Shin-Shin Toitsu Aikido* (***aikido*** with mind and body coordination). In 1980, he organized ***Kiatsu*** therapy training as a two-year certified course.

On October 28, 1990, he opened the New Ki Society World Headquarters Campus on the twentieth anniversary of the founding of Ki Society. He called the training center *Ki no Sato*, meaning "Homeland of Ki," as it is located on the property where Tohei Sensei spent his youth.

Ueshiba, Morihei (Uuh-way-she-ba, More-e-a)

Morihei Ueshiba (sometimes spelled Uyesshiba), was born December 14, 1883, at Wakayamama Prefecture in Japan. As a young boy he witnessed the beating of his father by opposing politicians. Though he was a sickly child, he vowed to learn the ***martial arts*** so he could help himself or anyone else in such a situation.

After excelling at many ***martial arts***, he realized that as his strength diminished with age, younger martial artists would defeat him. He meditated on methods to replace brute strength. Eventually, he named his spiritually inspired revelations—*aikido*, meaning "...the true *budo*, the working of love in the universe...."

He died in 1969 at age 86, still practicing the art he founded. Students called him *O'Sensei*, meaning Honored One.

Uke (uuh-kay)

The uke plays the role of an attacker to provide the *aikidoist* (*nage*) with a partner for throwing practice. An *aikidoist* is not an attacker, but a partner plays the role of *uke* to give the other aikidoist a means to practice *aikido* techniques. It is said that the *nage* learns to throw and the uke learns to flow (roll).

Weight underside

Weight upperside and weight underside are not common English expressions. They are the very fitting terms used by *Tohei Sensei* in *Ki Development* training. They are used to describe the unnecessary amount of stress we habitually allow to build up in our upper bodies and how to release it. When we keep weight underside (release shoulder tension), we maintain a comfortably erect posture and a light, but flexible, body that induces mental clarity.

Stress causes our weight to become upperside; the "he-man" or "macho" Western image. When we shrug by lifting our shoulders, we become stressed and must rely on brute strength. When we keep the body weight underside, we are stable and immovable when *ki* tested.

Keep Weight Underside

Stand in naturally erect posture and raise one hand to shoulder height with your arm parallel to the floor. If a partner can push your arm up (testing from under the wrist), your body-weight is upperside. If not, you have weight underside, showing that you are mind/body coordinated.
If he/she cannot push your arm down (testing from the top of the wrist), you are also stable with weight underside. If he/she can push your arm down, you are not mind/body coordinated.

If the testing is done properly (no shoving or jerking), the tester can feel the partner's strength or weakness. Change positions and compare. This is the test used by **Sensei** Simcox in Chapter Three, Teaching Ki Development to Westerners.

If I had instructed you to lift your arm instead of your hand, you would have been more likely to also lift your shoulder and weaken your entire body. Experiment with these *ki* tests and apply the practice of weight underside in your daily activities to minimize stress.

Yin/Yang (yen/yaung)

Yin/Yang is a term in Chinese Taoist philosophy. The yin/yang symbol represents the positive and negative polarities in the universe. The two opposite-colored curved droplets are seen as balancing and complementary, not a value-judgment in the good and evil sense of positive versus negative ascribed to in Western cultures. The yin-yang concept is carried out in Oriental arts and skills.

Yoga

Yoga is a **Sanskrit** word meaning yoke or union. Its goal is a oneness with oneself; the link to unite with the *Universal Spirit* or *All*. It is a releasing of the ego to attain *nirvana* or absolute peace.

Its main scriptural source, the *Bhagavad Gita,* was written about 300 BCE, but yoga was being practiced long before, in the second millennium BCE. A number of forms of yoga have been introduced down through the ages. In the West, familiarity with yoga has been limited mostly to *hatha* (physical) yoga exercises. This is unfortunate. Without the inclusion of the spiritual side of yoga, much of its value is lost.

Zen Buddhism

Zen in Japanese and *Ch'an* in Chinese express the **Sanskrit** term *dhyana*; the consciousness of a **Buddha**. Traditionally, the concept that came to be known as Zen Buddhism in Japan, was initiated by *Guatama* **Buddha** himself. During one of his daily discourses to a crowd of twelve hundred at Vulture Park he remained silent for some time, after which he held up a flower. Many onlookers became disgruntled. One person smiled, understanding that words are no substitute for the unmediated here-and-now experience of observing the living flower. Buddha said, "Here is the true way and I submit it to you."

This form of absolute Reality within *Mahayana* **Buddhism** in Northern India was a quest for the One beyond many; a universe beyond all opposites. It kept alive the Hindu revelation that when man realizes his non-dual identity, he is delivered from suffering and death.

This tradition was introduced into China in 520 CE, by *Bodhidharma.* As a missionary monk, he taught spiritual development at the Shaolin Temple through eighteen martial exercises to promote health and vitality.

The Zen (*Ch'an* in China) concepts that evolved through *Mahayana* **Buddhism**, were closely related to and influenced by **Taoism.** In both, the realization is that we cannot be separated from God except through our thoughts, which cause our suffering. Taoism, or Reality, "is sensed as a flowing movement, a power like the wind or water. It is sometimes termed 'the Way of things' and one who is in accord with it is said to be in a state of *Te* or grace." Also from *Zen Direct pointing to reality,* Anne Bancroft adds that the method of realization is "called *Wu-wei,* or non-assertion, which is very similar to the Buddhism freedom from craving." Under the Taoist influence, *Ch'an* released its *Hinduist* desire to escape the ordinary world of physical form in preference to becoming world transforming.

A split between the Gradual Enlightenment School and creation of the Sudden School of *Ch'an* is credited to Hui-neng (638-713 CE). He became the Sixth Patriarch (or Ancestor) of Zen in China. It is said that upon hearing words from *The Diamond Sutra* (scripture), "Depending upon nothing, you must find your own mind," he attained instant enlightenment—though he was a poor illiterate woodcutter.

Hui-neng entered a *Buddhist* monastery and was assigned kitchen work. *Hung-jen,* who was the Fifth Patriarch, realized that including the educated scholars, *Hui-neng* was the only one who had reached the understanding of *Buddhahood* (**nirvana**). His story is related in *The Diamond Sutra and The Sutra of Hui-neng,* translated by A. F. Price and Wong Mou-lam.

An assignment given the monastery scholars to determine the ancestral succession was to write a stanza about freeing oneself from incessant rebirth. Shen Hsui, the most learned monk, wrote:

> Our body is the *bodhi* tree,
> And our mind a mirror bright.
> Carefully we wipe them hour by hour,
> And let no dust alight.

Knowing this to be inferior, *Hui-neng* dictated his version of wisdom to the young boy who had read the poem to him:

> There is no *bodhi* tree,
> Nor stand of a mirror bright.
> Since all is void,
> Where can the dust alight?

This convinced the Patriarch that *Hui-neng* had reached enlightenment—the realization that everything in the universe is the essence of mind itself. He was also aware of the danger from jealous scholars. *Hung-jen* secretly gave *Hui-neng* his robe and begging bowl; the material inheritance from the Sudden Enlightenment school. The esoteric inheritance was transmitted heart to heart—to the one who realized the *dharma* (universal law). Thus, the Fifth Patriarch, *Hung-jen* helped the Sixth Patriarch, *Hui-neng* leave without notice.

Among the angry monks who trailed him, one insisted that he came only to learn the secret of the *dharma*. *Hui-neng* explained,

> "Refrain from thinking of anything....When you are thinking of neither good nor evil, what is at that particular moment, your real nature [literally, original face]....There are good ways and bad ways...but enlightened men understand that they are not dual in nature. Buddha-nature is nonduality."

Zen Buddhism is a discipline of individual action rather than worship. Holding no doctrine or diety worship, Zen is a path to personal awakening of the self—to the Oneness of the Universe. The achievement of *satori* (Japanese word for the state of enlightenment), is ultimately the same experience as **nirvana** in **Sanskrit**.

The teachings are realized through meditation and intuition rather than discussion; an emptying of the mind from any particular thought, rather than focusing on a thought or the desired result. *Satori*, or ***nirvana***, an awakening of the spirit within, is a personal experience. Ultimate enlightenment is beyond explanation. It is said that if you can explain a meditative *experience* to someone else, you have not reached ***nirvana***. The epitome of meditation is beyond interpretation by human association or vocabulary because there is nothing existing on earth for association or comparison to the experience of ultimate realization.

Students at Zen schools are committed to combining meditation with a considerable amount of manual labor. *Hui-neng* had combined labor and meditation because he wasn't allowed to take time off from his manual chores. Zen meditation is an active, living meditation as well as quiet, postural meditation. It is comparable, in a sense, to **Ueshiba Sensei'**s goal of "living life as a prayer."

The philosophy and practice of Zen has contributed to the skilled accomplishments in Oriental arts and crafts: painting, calligraphy, the ***martial arts***, ceremonial tea preparation and drinking, *haiku* poetry, architecture, *ikebana* (flower arranging), bonsai plant designing, and Oriental gardening. Zen Buddhism was introduced into Japan by Buddhist monk Eisai in 1191, where it was ingrained and is still being refined as a part of Japanese culture.

Movie star and martial artist, Chuck Norris, recounts his introduction to Zen, in *The Secret Power Within*, when his Korean karate teacher remarked,

> "Your mind is not here....There is no control when the mind is absent. You must be one with yourself and with what you are doing. While doing something, you are doing it to the fullest. That is true Zen."

Zoroaster

Known in ancient Persia as Zorothustra, Zoroaster was a religious prophet, born (c 630-550 BCE), in eastern Persia. Some historians believe that either he lived earlier or that some of his beliefs had existed before his time. As a young man he began receiving revelations from the godhead, Ahura Mazda. His doctrines are preserved in his metrical psalms, the scriptures known as the Avesta.

Zoroaster's ideas influenced the Judeo-Christian beliefs in demons, angels and the hereafter. Although some scholars feel that his intentions were misinterpreted, he is believed to have originated, or at least advanced, Western dualism through his division of the opposites; the creation of two deities he called Truth and Lie. Just as they had to choose, the belief was that upon death each person must cross the Bridge of Discrimination. There, the followers of Truth would pass over, while the followers of Lie would fall into hell. He prophesied that all evil would be eliminated by an ordeal of fire.

His doctrine influenced the Greeks who, in the fifth century BCE, abandoned their original idea of the oneness of the universe. In the second century BCE, his doctrine had great influence on Western thought through Plato and Aristotle.

The basis of the Western premise was that the mind is separate from the body. It recent years this long-standing conclusion has been challenged by those who advocate the mind/body connection and the *transpersonal* (mind, body and spirit) view by holistic psychologists.

Zoroasterianism

Darius I, probably was the first Persian king to adhere to the Zoroastrian Doctrine, was followed by his son Xerxes I. The religion went in and out of favor over the centuries while Persians were being converted to Islam. Zoroastrianism exists today as a minority religious group in Iran and Bombay, India.

Review of Tri-tuning Skills in Glossary of Foreign Words:

1. Keep weight underside, p. 255

Bibliography

Alan-Williams, Gregory. *A Gathering of Heroes, Reflecting on Rage and Responsibility*, Academy Chicago Publishers, Chicago, IL, 1992.

Amos, Wally, with Leroy Robinson. *The Famous Amos Story, The Face That Launched A Thousand Chips*. Doubleday & Company, Inc., Garden City, New York, 1983.

Arapakis, Maria. *Softpower! How to Speak Up, Set Limits, and Say No Without Losing Your Lover, Your Job, or Your Friends*. Warner Books, A Time Warner Company, 1990.

Ayto, John. *Arcade Dictionary of Word Origins*, Arcade Publishing, New York, Little, Brown and Company, 1990.

Bach, Marcus, *The Chiropractic Story*, DeVorss & Co., Inc., Los Angeles, CA, 1968.

———. *Strangers at the Door*, Abbington Press, Nashville and New York, 1971.

———. *The World of Serendipity*, DeVorss Publications, P.O. Box 550, Marina del Rey, CA 90294., 1970.

Bancroft, Anne. *Zen, Direct pointing to reality*, Thames and Hudson, 500 Fifth Ave., New York, N.Y. 10110, 1980.

Batchelor, Stephen. *The Awakening of the West, Encounter of Buddhism and Western Culture*, Parllex Press, Berkeley, CA, 1994.

Bennett, William. J. ed. *The Book of Virtues*, Simon & Schuster, New York, N. Y., 1993.

Benson, Herbert, M.D. *Beyond the Relaxation Response*, Berkeley Books, New York, 1984.

Berne, Eric, *Games People Play, The Psychology of Human Relationships*, Ballantine Books, New York, 1964.

Borysenko, Joan, *Minding the Body, Mending the Mind*, Addison-Wesley Publishing Co., 1987.

Bradshaw, John. *Home Coming, Reclaiming and Championing Your Inner Child*, Bantam Books, 1990.

Bragg, Paul C. and Patricia Bragg. *Bragg Super Power Breathing for Health & High Energy*, Health Science, Box 7, Santa Barbara, CA 93102 USA., 1995.

Brown, H. Jackson, Jr. *Life's Little Instruction Book*, Rutledge Hill Press, Nashville, Tennessee, 1991.

Bry, Adelaide, *The TA Primer, Transactional Analysis in Everyday Life*, Perennial Library, Harlper & Row, Publishers, Inc., New York, Evanston, San Francisco, London, 1973.

Burns, Ken. *Jefferson*, PBS Video, 1320 Bradock Rd., Alexandria, VA, 1997.
Campbell, Joseph. *The Power of Myth*, Doubleday, 1988.
Capra, Fritjof, *The Tao of Physics,* A Bantam New Age Book, 1975.
Carlson, Richard, *Don't Sweat the Small Stuff...and it's all small stuff,* Hyperion, 114 Fifth Avenue, New York, New York 10011.
Carnegie, Dale & Associates, Inc. *How to Win Friends and Influence People,* Pocket Books, New York, 1982.
Carter, Forrest. *The Education of Little Tree,* University of New Mexico Press, Albequerque, 1976.
Chivington, Paul K. with Laura Elizabeth Keyes. *Seeing Through Your Illusions*, G-L Publications, 2168 South Lafayette, Denver, Colorado 80210, 1983.
Chopra, Dr. Deepak. *The Way of the Wizard, 20 spiritual lessons in creating the life you want to live,* Mystic Fire Video, New York, 1995.
_____. *Perfect Digestion: the Key to Balanced Living.* Harmony Books, 1995.
_____. *The Seven Laws of Success,* Mystic Fire Video, 1995.
Cirlot, J. E., translated from Spanish by Jack Sage. *A Dictionary of Symbols*, Philosophical Library, New York, 1962.
Cranton, Elmer M. *Bypassing Bypass, The New Technique of Chelation Therapy*, Stein & Day Publ., New York, 1984.
Csikszentmihalyi, Mihaly. *Flow: The Psychology of Optimal Experience,* Harper & Row, Publishers, New York, 1990.
DeBecker, Gaven. *A Gift of Fear,* Little, Brown & Co., Boston, New York, Toronto, London, 1997.
DeProspero, Dan and Jackie. *Illuninated Spirit, Conversations with a Kyudo Master,* Kodansha International, Tokyo, New York, London, 1996.
Dobson, Terry with Victor Miller, *Giving in to Get Your Way—The Attackics System for Winning Your Everyday Battles,* Delacorte Press, 1978.
Doftoevsky, Fyodor. *Crime and Punishment,* Bantam Books, NY, 1958, (originally published, 1866).
Dressler, Annetta Gertrude. *The Philosophy of P. P. Quimby,* The Builders Press, Boston, MA, 1985.
Dunn, Halbert L. *High Level Wellness,* R. W. Beatty, Ltd., Virgina, 1961.
Dürckheim, Karlfried Graf. *Hara, The Virtual Centre of Man*, Mandala, An Imprint of Harper Collins Publishers, 1962.

Bibliography

Eadie, Betty. *Embraced by the Light*, Simon & Schuster Audio, New York, 1993.
Ferguson, Marilyn. *The Aquarian Conspiracy, Personal and Social Transformation in Our Time,* T. P. Tarcher, Inc., 9110 Sunset Blvd., Los Angeles, CA, 90069.
Feuerstein, Georg. *Everyone Does It, Not Everyone Knows It,* Article in *Quest Magazine,* Autumn, 1994.
Franck, Frederick. *Zen Seeing, Zen Drawing, Meditation in Action,* Bantam Books, New York, Toronto, London, Sydney, Auckland, 1993.
Friedman, Norman. *Bridging Science and Spirit: Common Elements in David Bohm's Physics, The Perennial Philosophy and Seth*, Living Lake Books, St. Louis, MO 63105, 1994.
Gallwey, W. Timothy. *The Inner Game of Tennis*, Random House, New York, 1974.
Gardner, Joy. *Color and Crystals, A Journey Through the Chakras,* The Crossing Press, Freedom, CA 95019, 1988.
Gray, Eden. *Recognition Themes on Inner Perception,* Inspiration House Publications, Stroudsburg, PA, 1969.
Greene, Michael H. *Program Your Life,* Behavioral Systems, Inc., Rt. #2, Marshall, VA 22115, 1980.
Grof, Stanislav and Hal Zina Bennett. *The Holotrophic Mind, The Three Levels of Human Consciousness and How They Shape Our Lives,* Harper, A Division of Harper Collins Publishers, San Francisco, CA 1990.
Hanh, Thich Nhat. *Breathe! You Are Alive,* Parallax, CA, 1996.
Harpur, Tom. *The Uncommon touch: an investigation of spiritual Healing*, McClellan and Stewart, Inc,, 481 University Ave., Toronto, Ontario M5G2E9, 1994.
Harris, Thomas, *I'm OK—Your're OK,* Avon Books, 1967.
Hay, Louise L. *Conversations on Living*, Hay House, Inc., Santa Monica, CA 90401, 1982.
Heckler, Richard Strozzi. *In Search of the Warrior Spirit*, North Atlantic Books, 1990.
_____. *Aikido and the New Warrior,* North Atlantic Books, Berkeley, California, 1985.
Hodges, Elizabeth Jamison. *The Three Princes of Serendip*, Athaeneum, New York, 1964.
Holloran, Richard. *Japan: Images and Realities,* Charles E. Tuttle Co. Publishers, Tokyo, Japan, 1969.
Holzer, Hans. *Beyond Medicine, The Facts About Unorthodox and Psychic Healing,* Henry Regnery Co., Chicago, IL. 1973.
Jackson, Ian. *The BreathPlay Approach to Whole Life Fitness*, A

Dolphin Book, Doubleday and Co., Inc., Garden City, New York, 1986.
Jampolsky, Gerald, G. *Love is Letting go of Fear.* Celestial Arts, Millbrae, California, 1979.
Keys, Ken, Jr. *The Hundredth Monkey,* Love Line Books, Coos Bay, Oregon, 1991.
Kabat-Zinn, Jon. *Wherever You Go, There You Are,* Hyperion, New York, N. Y., 1994.
Kopp, Sheldon. *Mirror, Mask and Shadow, The Risks and Rewards of Self-Acceptance*, MacMillan Publishing Co., Inc., New York, 1980.
Lamsa, George M. *The Holy Bible, From Ancient Eastern Manuscripts.* Holman Bible Publishers, A. J. Holman Co., Nashville, 1933.
Langley, Raymond J., *The Writings of C. G. Jung,* Monarch Press, A Division of Somon & Schuster, Inc., West 39th Street, New York, New York, 10018, 1970.
Life Magazine Editorial Staff. *The World's Great Religions, Volume I; Religions of the East*, Time Inc., New York, 1963.
MacFarland, Rhoda. *Coping Through Assertiveness*, The Rosen Publishing Group, Inc., New York, 1986.
McKechine, Jean L. and Publisher's Editorial Staff, *Webster's New Universal Unabridged Dictionary,* Dorset & Baber, 1979.
Moyer, Bill D. *Healing and the Mind,* Doubleday, 1993.
_____. *Wisdom of Faith,* Films of Humanities & Sciences, Princeton, NJ, 1996.
Norris, Chuck. *The Secret Power Within - Zen Solutions to Real Problems*, Little, Brown and Company, New York, Boston, Toronto, London, 1996.
Ornish, Dean, *Dr. Dean Ornish's Program for Reversing Heart Disease*, Dr. Dean Ornish, Ballantine Books, NY, 1990.
Palmer, D.D. *The Science, Art and Philosophy of Chiropractry,* Portland Printing House Co, Portland, OR, 1910.
Payne, Peter. *Martial Arts: The Spiritual Dimension*, Crossroads Publishing Co., New York, 1981.
Peale, Norman Vincent. *The Power of Positive Thinking,* Doubleday, New York, 1990.
Perkins, Mary. *Growing into Peace, A Manual for Peace-Builders in the 1990s and Beyond.* George Roland, Publisher, Oxford, England, 1991.
Porter, Eleanor H. *Pollyanna*, a Dell Yearling Classic, 1986.
Price, A. F. and Wong Mou-Lam. *The Diamond Sutra and the Sutra of Hui-neng*, Shambhala, Boston, 1990.

Redfield, James. *The Celestine Prophecy, An Adventure,* Warner Books, Inc., A Time Warner Company, New York, NY, 1993.
_____. *The Celestine Vision, Living the New Spiritual Awareness,* Warner Books, A Time Warner Company, 1997.
Reed, William. *Ki: A Road Anyone Can Walk*, Japan Publications, Inc., Tokyo and New York, 1992.
_____. *Ki: A Practical Guide for Westerners,* Japan Publication, Inc., 1986.
Robbins, Anthony. *Awakening The Giant Within,* A Fireside Book, New York, 1991.
Russell, Walter. *The Message of the Divine Iliad, Vol. I & II,* University of Science and Philosophy, (Formerly the Walter Russell Foundation), Swannanoa, Waynesboro, Virginia, 1971.
Shi, Ming and Siao Weijia. *Mind over Matter: Higher Martial Arts*, translated by Thomas Cleary, Frog Limited, Berkeley, CA, 1994.
Shifflett, C. M. *Ki in Aikido,* Round Earth Publishing, Merrifield, Virginia, 1997.
Siegel, Bernie S. *Love, Medicine and Miracles*, Perennial Library, Harper & Row, Publishers, New York, 1986.
Siegel, Robert Simon, *Six Seconds to True Calm,* Little Sun Books, 1995.
Steindl-Rast, Br. David. *Approaches to Christian Mysticism*, Big Sur Tapes, P.O. Box 4, Tiburon, CA 94920.
Steiner, Rudolf. *An Outline of Occult Science,* translated by Henry B. Monges and revised by Lisa D. Monges, Anthroposophic Press, Inc., Spring Valley, N.Y., 1972.
_____. *Health and Illness,* The Anthroposophic Press, Spring Valley, N.Y., 1983.
Stone, John and Ron Meyer, ed. *Aikido in America,* Frog, Ltd., Berkeley, CA, 1995.
Talbot, Michael. *The Holographic Universe*, HarperPerennial, A Division of Harper Collins Publishers, 1991.
Taylor, Louise and Betty Bryant. *Ki Energy for Everyone,* Japan Publications, Inc. Tokyo and New York, 1990.
Toffler, Alvin. *Future Shock,* Random House, New York, 1970.
Tohei, Koichi. *Ki in Daily Life*, Japan Publications, Inc., 1978.
_____. *Book of Ki: Coordinating Mind and Body in Daily Life*, Japan Publications, Inc. 1976.
_____. *Kiatsu, Ki no Kenkyukai*, H. Q., Tokyo, Japan, 1983.
Triplett, Robert. *Stage-Fright, Letting It Work For You*, Nelson-Hall, Chicago, 1983.
Tzu, Lao. *Tao te ching, A book about the way and the power of the way,* Shambhala, Boston, 1997.

Uchida, Yoshiko. *We Do Not Work Alone, the thoughts of Kanjiro Kawai,* Kawai Kanjiro's House, Gojozaka Kyoto, Japan, 1973.
Voltaire. *Candide,* ed. By Norman L. Torrey, Appleton-Century-Crofts, Inc., New York, 1946.
Waitley, Denis. *The Double Win*, Listen and Learn Series, McGraw-Hill, Fullerton, CA, 1985.
Walsch, Neale Donald, *Conversations with God, an uncommon dialogue, Book 1 and Book 2*, Hampton Roads Publishing Company, Inc., 134 Burgess Lane, Charlottesville, VA, 22902
Walther, David S., *Applied Kinesiology Synopsis,* SdC Systems DC, 275 W. Abriendo, Pueblo, CO 81004, 1988.
Watson, Donald. *The Dictionary of Mind and Spirit*. Avon Books, New York, 1991.
Westbrook, A. and O. Ratti. *Aikido and the Dynamic Sphere*, Charles E. Tuttle Company, Rutland, Vermont, 1970.
Wilson, Jim. *An Illustrated Introduction to the Martial Arts,* Marshall Cavendish Books Limited, London, England, 1986.
Wood, Ernest. *Zen Dictionary*, Charles E. Tuttle Co., Rutland, Vermont and Tokyo, Japan, 1957.
Wydra, Nancilee. *Feng Shui: The Book of Cures,* Contemporary Books, Lincolnwood, Illinois, 1997.

Index

Numbers in **boldface** indicate a quote.

—A—

Abraham, 200
Acupuncture, 34, 237, 240, 247
Adams, John, **218**
Afterword, 235
Aiki, 61, 237, 238
Aikido, xiii, xxi, xxvii, 32, 38-40, 42-44, 60, 87, 92-94, 98, 103, 109-110, 115, 155, 209, 237-238, 246, 248, 250, 253-255
Aikido Federation, 42, 254
Alan-Williams, Gregory, xiii
Alert calmness, xxiv, 13, 21, 26, 30, 190, 196
Alexander, Franz, **35**
Amitabha, 240
Amos, Wally, **153**
Andreas, Brian, **205**
Anger, 3, 58, 90, 101, 118-120, 179
Anthroposophical Society, 171
Apocatastasis, 182
Arapakis, Maria, 178
Aristotle, 73, 260
Arnold, Oren, **xvi**
Atman, 243
Attitude, 61, 66, 156, 163-164, 184
Attune, 3, 9, 187
Awareness, 9, 27, 77
Ayto, John, 140
Ayurvedic, 251

—B—

Bach, Marcus, **28, 132, 182, 220**
Bach, Richard, 220
Bachelor, Stephen, **177**
Bagavad-Gita, 243, 256
Baha'i, 215
Balance, xxv, 19, 33, 56, 71, 120-122, 133, 159, 179, 217, 228

Ball of knowledge, 77-81, 134, 197-198, 205-206, 216-217
Bancroft, Anne, **178, 257**
Barrie, James M., **216**
Bennett, Hal Zina, **132**
Bennett, William J., 194
Benson, Herbert, **29**
Bergson, Henri, 166
Berne, Erik, 105
Bhagavad-Gita, 243
Bible, xxiv, 68, 100, 122, 141, 168, 173, 200-201, 217, 251
Bierce, Ambrose, **62**
Blame and Shame, 27, 107-110, 138, 149, 150-151, 156, 173, 212
Blend and Mend, 98-103, 118, 206
Bodhi tree, 239, 258
Bodhidharma, 240, 249, 257
Bodhisattva, 239-240
Bohm, David, 166
Bonsai, 259
Borysenko, Joan, 151
Bowing, 87-88
Bradshaw, John, **106**
Bragg, Paul, **122,** 126, **139**
Brahmanism, 242-244, 251
Breath, 33, 49-50, 52, 122-127, 139, 193, 207
Brown, H. Jackson, Jr., **20**
Bry, Adelaide, **105**
Bryant, Betty, **49**
Buddha, **51,** 62, 238-240, 242, 245, 250, **257**
Buddhism, xi, 51, 171, 196, 239, 240, 242-244, 249-250, 252-253, 257-259
Budo, 95, 238, 240, 255
Burns, Ken, 218
Burns, Robert, **78**
Bush, George, **228, 229**

▲ 267

—C—

Cabalists, 107, 172, 241
Calm-alertness, xxiv, 13, 178, 189
Campbell, Joseph, **66, 67**, 145
Capra, Fritjof, **34,** 73, 87
Caring, 67, 97, 136, 146, 166, 216, 227, 230, 247
Carlson, Richard, **125**
Carnegie, Dale, 63
Carter, Forrest, 198
Catholic, 202
Cayce, Edgar, 102
Ch'an, 240, 257
Change, 54, 65, 118, 127-131, 214, 220, 225
Chakra, 242, 244
Chi, xxvii, 34, 37, 43, 185, 237, 240, 242, 244, 252-254
China, 36, 41, 43, 47, 62, 113-114, 118, 122, 172, **206,** 235, 238, 240, 246, 252-254, 257
Chivington, Paul K., 122
Chopra, Deepak, **44,** 54, **83, 95,** 136, **160, 169,** 176-178, 228, 251
Chou Dynasty, 253
Chrisander, Count Nils, **168**
Christianity, xi, xxiii, xxv, 29, 36, 64, 73-75, 147, 172, 196, 200-202, 241, 251, 260
Circle, xi, xii, 57, 85
Cirlot, J. E., xii
Clark, Arthur C., **78**
Cleary, Thomas, **70,** 249
Columbus, 219
Competition, 184-185, 203-205
Confucianism, 240-242, 252-253
Conscience, xxix, 23-24, 56, 58, 65, 67, 109, 114, 136, 144-145, 154, 168, 184, 194, 215, 222, 230-231, 239, 247, 249-250
Consciousness, 55, 70, 96, 107, 131-133, 157, 165, 221, 250
Constantine, 64, 201, 251

Cooper, Robert, **183**
Cosmos, xxiv, 7, 8, 152, 179, 185-186, 196-197
Courage, 6, 25, 250
Cousins, Norman, 119
Cranton, Elmer M., 130
Csikszentmikalyi, Mihaly, **146,** 178

—D—

Dantein, 41, 242
Darius I, 260
Darwin, 183
Death, 59, 73, 133-136
Defense, (ive) 5, 13, 16, 95, 99, 136, 144, 184, 238
Deguchi, Onisaburo, 60
Democracy, xxiv, xxix, 114-115, 146-147, 215, 217-218, 223, 228
Deprospero, Dan, 98, 125, 245
Descartes, Rene, 73
Devi, 243
Dharma, 258
Dhyana, 257
Do, 32, 238, 240
Dobson, Austin, **194**
Dobson, Terry, 110-112
Dojo, 50, 56, 87, 237, 241, 248
Doftoevsky, Fyodor, **108**
Drakilic, Slavenka, **185**
Dualism, xxiii, xxviii, 24, 72-73, 96, 97, 107, 122, 136-137, 196, 260
Dunn, Halbert, **164-165**
Dürckheim, Karlfried Graf, **242-243**

—E—

Eadie, Betty, 91-**92**
Eastern philosophy, xxii, xxiii, xxv, xxx, 32, 56, 62, 71, 210, 241-242
Edison, Thomas, 203
Ego, 95, 138, 149, 165, 222, 256
Einstein, Albert, 78, **117, 244**
Eisai, 259
Electricity, xxi-xxii, 9, 38, 71
Emerson, Ralph Waldo, **192**

Index ▲ 269

Enemy, 20-22, 26, 44, 59-60, 64, 66, 89, 95, 100, 107, 120, 143, 203
Energy, ix, xxi, xxiv, xxix, 1, 8-10, 26, 33-34, 82, 127, 139, 143, 157, 162-163, 212, 247
English Conversation, 35, 88, 93
Enlightenment, viii, 236
Epictetus, **28, 149**
E pluribus unum, 179
Eto, Harry, 140
Evert, Chris, 197
Exercise, 44-45, 52, 138-140

—F—

Fair-mindedness, 24, 75, 81, 140, 205
Fear, **xvi,** xxii, xxiv, xxvi, xxix, 1-6, 13-16, 20-23, 26-27, 52, 59, 68, 82-83, 88-90, 95, 98-99, 100, 123, 125-126, 133, 136, 140-144, 152, 155, 162-163, 166, 169, 175, 179, 187-190, 194, 198, 203, 213, 216-225, 233, 247, 250
Feeling nature, 24, 40, 53-54, 61, 93, 112, 195
Feng Shui, 34, 240-241
Ferguson, Marilyn, **151**
Feuerstein, Georg, **165-166**
Fight/flight, xxviii, 21, 123, 141, 158
Flow, xxviii, 21-22, 26, 42, 54, 57, 59, 145-146, 188
Foreword, vii
Forgiveness, 92, 119, 226
Four Noble Truths, 239
Franck, Frederick, 176
Frank, Dan, 109
Franklin, Benjamin, xxii, **117**
Freedom, xxix, 75, 114-115, 146-149, 169, 186, 201, 215, 217
Freeze, 21, 141
Freud, Sigmund, 132, 186
Friedman, Norman, **55, 112**

Frost, Robert, **220**
Fuller, Richard Buckminster, **144**

—G—

Galapagos Islands, 216
Galileo, 202
Gallwey, W. Timothy, **221, 222**
Gandhi, Mahatma, **113, 187,** 244
Garden of Eden, 122
Gardner, Joy, **7**
Gentle strength, 14-15, 19
Gide, André, **xvi**
Gingrich, Newt, 79
Glossary of Foreign Terms, 237
God, xi, xiii, xxv, 60, 67-69, 73, 81, 87, 107, 120, 122, 129, 132, 135, 141, 172, 174, 179-180, 186-187, 192, 200, 212, 217, 220, 241, 244-245
Goodheart, George, 167
Graham, Billy, 69
Gray, Eden, 107
Greene, Michael, H., xiv, **170,** 178
Grof, Stanislav, **132, 196**
Guide to Symbols and Terms, ix
Guilt, 107, 108, 138, 149-151, 194
Gut feelings, 160, 166

—H—

Habits, 3, 16, 22, 24, 57-58, 66, 98, 151-153, 223, 225
Hagar, 201
Haiku, 259
Hall, James Norman, **1**
Hanh, Thick Nhat, **174**
Happiness, 82, 97, 153-157
Hara, 41, 242-243, 250-251
Harmony, xxiii, xxv, 7, 28, 32, 61, 72, 86, 92-93, 96-97, 108, 114, 157-158, 165, 181, 195-196, 214, 216, 221, 228, 236
Harpur, Tom, **135**
Harris, Thomas A., 105
Harvey, Paul, 223

Hatha yoga, 29, 209, 256
Hausmann, Winifred Wilkinson, **180**
Hay, Louise, **189**
Healing and Health, 47-49, 158-163, 247
Heckler, Richard Strozzi, **60**, **83**,110
Heraclitus, **73**
Hinduism, 34, 62, 239, 241-244, 250-251, 257
Hippocrates, **158**
Hodges, Elizabeth Jamison, 219
Holistic, ix, xxii, xxiii, 165
Holitude, ix, 61, 76, 85, 94, 100, 117, 155, 163-165, 184, 203, 205, 211
Holloran, Richard, **31**
Holy, xi, 61, 176, 179
Holzer, Hans, **158-159**
Hsui, Shen, **258**
Hubbard, Elbert, **xvi**
Hui-neng, **177**, 240, **257-259**
Hundredth monkey, **128**, 129, 213
Hung-jen, 257-258
Hypnotize, 6, 169-172, 176-177

—I—

Id, 165
Ikebana, 36, 259
Illustrations:
  #1, mind, body, vital life energy, 8
  #2, mind, body, spirit, 8
  #3, body, mind, intention, 8
  #4, body, mind, spirergy, 10
  #5, calm, alert, calm/alertness, 13
  #6, logic, instinct, intuition, 14
  #7, Leonardo da Vinci, 15
  #8, Testing, 18
  #9, fight, flee, flow, 21
  #10, Revised Ki Symbol, 35
  #11, Original Ki Symbol, 35
  #12, Yin/yang Symbol, 71
  #13, Fight, 93
  #14, Flee, 93
  #15, Blend and Mend, 93
  #16, High-level Wellness, 165
India, 239-243
Information Age, 85, 90, 214-216
Ingersoll, Robert Green, **118**
Instinct, 53, 131, 165
Intention, 8, 69, 158, 166
Integrity, xxx, 23-24
Interdependence, 186, 214
Intoku, 190
Intuition, 14, 53-54, 78-80, 102, 106, 128, 138,165-167
Inyushin, Victor, 33
Isaac, 200
Ishmael, 200
Islam, 29, 200, 241, 260
Iteidakimasu, 191

—J—

Jackson, Ian, **127**
Jackson, Jill, 231
Jainism, 239, 243-244, 250
James, William, **61**
Jampolsky, Gerald, **98**
Japan, xiii, xiv, xvi, xxi, xxvii, 3, 29, 31-32, 34-36, 40, 43, 47, 50, 53, 56, 59, 87-88, 94, 110, 113-114, 125, 183, 191, 210, 235-236, 237-238, 241, 244, 246, 248, 251-253
Jefferson, Thomas, **218-219**
Jesus, **64**, **84**, **100-101**, 108, **168**, 170, **174**, 190, 200, 202, 245
Jiminy Crickett, 231
Jina, 244
Jodo, 240
Johnny Appleseed, xxi
Johnson, Robert, **23**
Johnson, Samuel, **53**
Judaism, xxv, 29, 70, 73, 101, 172, 200-201, 239, 241, 245, 260
Judo, 249, 254
Jujitsu, 32
Jung, Carl, **81**, **131**, **132**, **180**, **186-187**, **197**, 221

Index ▲ 271

—K—
Kabat-Zinn, Jon, **46**
Kami, 34
Karate, 43, 55, 58, 103, 249
Karma, 58, 119-120, 243-244
Kawai, Kanjiro, 31
Keller, Helen, **155, 229**
Kendo, 249
Kenjutsu, 32
Keyes, Ken, Jr., **128**
Ki, ix, xxi-xxiii, xxvii, 32-52, 55-58, 61, 67, 69, 87, 95, 96, 103, 132, 162, 178, 185, 189, 209, 216, 238, 242, 244-246, 248-249, 252-254
Kiai, 125, 245
Ki-aikido, xiv, xxvii, 32, 44, 51, 87, 140, 246, 248
Kiatsu, xiv, xxi, xxvii, 32, 38, 47-49, 52, 94, 163, 167, 242, 246-247, 254
Ki Development, xiv, xxi, xxvii-xxviii, xxx, 32-52, 55-57, 87, 94, 140, 187, 210, 246, 248, 248-249, 256
Kinesiology, 43, 52, 167, 249
King, Betty Jean, 181
King, Martin Luther, Jr., **110, 225**
King Midas, 211
Ki no Kenkyukai, xiii, 31, 32, 248, 254
Ki no Sato, 248, 254
Ki Society International, xiii, xxi, xxvii, xxx, 31-32, 39, 87, 94, 210, 248, 254
Ki Symbol, 35, 87
Ki testing, 43-46, 56-57, 208, 249, 255-256
Ki Tests, (see Tri-tuning Skills), 274
Ki Wellness, xxvii, xxx, 37, 55-56, 101, 103-104, 151, 189, 194, 248-249
Koester, Arthur, **53**

Kokiki, 252
Kopp, Sheldon, **82**
Krieger, Dolores, 247
Krishnamurti, Jiddu, 74
Kung fu, 211, 249
Kuhn, Edvard, 146
Kurosawa, Akira, **74**
Kyudo, 125, 245

—L—
Lamothe, Gerard, viii, xiii, **127**
Lamsa, George M., 168
Langley, Raymond J., 186
Leeuwenhoek, Anton van, 130
Leonard, George, xxvii, 209-**210**
Lincoln, Abraham, **94**
Liang, Ma Yueh, **37**
Ling, Chang, 253
Lister, Joseph, 130,
Logic, 14, 27, 165
Lord Chesterfield, 185
Lord Derby, 138
Love, 32, 82, 84, 98, 99, 106, 141, 162, 168-169, 173, 179, 184, 235

—M—
Machiavellian, 215
Machintosh, Sir James, **117**
MacLaine, Shirley, 125
Magi, 169
Magic, 55, 71, 83
Magnetism, 55, 169-173
Mahayana Buddhism, 240, 249, 257
Mandrell, Barbara, 187
Marshall, Robert, xiii, 177, 191
Martial arts, 32, 36, 40, 47, 56, 58, 59, 104, 113, 210, 238, 240, 249-250, 254-255, 259
Maruyama, Koretoshi, xiv, xxvii, 87, 246-247
Maryland Ki Society, xxvii, 87, 109
Materialism, 54, 171, 173-174
Mazda, Ahura, 260
McCabe, Ed, **126**

McFarlane, Rhoda, **104**, 105
Mead, Margaret, 74, **80**
Meditation, 17, 46-47, 52, 118, 174-178, 189, 193, 241, 259
Menninger, Karl, **144**
Mercer, Johnny, 62
Mesmer, Anton, 33
Meyer, Ron, **32**, 40, **42**, 60
Middle Way, 62, 239, 243
Miller, Henry, **157**
Miller, Sy, 231
Miller, Victor, 112
Milton, John, 157
Mind/body coordination, xxv, xxviii, 2, 8, 29, 39, 47-48, 70, 73, 99, 178, 183, 194-197, 216, 221, 242-243, 249
Mind-set, xxii, xxiii, 7, 28, 30, 47, 54-56, 64, 82, 130, 137, 198, 203, 222, 248-249
Misogi, 254
Mohammad, 201
Monroe, Rev. Miles, 130
Moore, Thomas, **195**
Moses, 114, 245
Moslems, xxv, 20, 200, 241
Mother Teresa, **182, 220**
Mou-lam, Wong, 257
Moyers, Bill, 37, 89, 135, 157, 173
Musketeer, 204
Mysticism, xiii, xxv, 55, 73, 78, 169, 173
Mystics, xxi, 34, 84-85, 91, 172, 241

—N—

Nage, 92-93, 250, 255
Nakamura, Tempû, ix, 39-40
Natural, *defined*, 7, 13, 19, 30, 90, 133
Nature, xiii, xxix, 54, 66, 75-76, 102, 120-122, 133-135, 152, 161, 165, 172, 178-181, 187, 186, 198, 221, 224, 226, 232

Navratilova, Martina, **24**
Negative, xxii, xxv, 62, 81-82, 180
Nehru, Jawaharlal, **xvi**
Neighbor, Rinehold, **230**
Neo-Confucianism, 253
Nevelson, Louise, **18**
New Age, xxv
New Thought, 199
New World, 147, 201
Nietzche, 186
Nihongi, 252
Nirvana, 62, 69, 239-240, 250, 256, 258-259
Nixon, Richard, **108**
Noble Eightfold Path, 239
Non-ordinary reality, 181
Normal, *defined*, 7, 11, 13, 27
Norris, Chuck, **250, 257**

—O—

O'Keefe, Georgia, **106**
Omikami, Amaterasu, 252
Omoto-Kyu, 60, 238
Oneness, xi, xii, xiii, xxv, xxviii, 40, 61, 101-102, 134, 163, 178-180, 186, 238, 245, 258
One point, 41, 44-47, 56, 118, 242, 245, 248, 250-251
Onuma Sensei, 125, 245
Opposites, xxii, xxiii, xxviii, xxix, xxx, 4-7, 14, 24, 53, 56, 68, 71, 74-76, 79, 81-83, 105, 128, 134, 144, 166, 180-182, 196-197
Oprah Winfrey Show, **140**
Ornish, Dean, **100,** 101, 118, **174**
Oursler, Fulton, **xvi**
Ouspensky, P. D., **72**,
Out breath, 49-50, 124-127

—P—

Paine, Thomas, **209**
Palmer, D. D., **167**
Paracelsus, Phillippus, A., **47**
Parmenides, 73
Parton, Dolly, **4**

Index ▲ 273

Pasteur, Louis, 130
Payne, Peter, 33, **104**
Peace, 61, 113, 182, 197, 231
Peale, Norman Vincent, **63**
Peck, M. Scott, **9**
Perkins, Mary, **215**
Pert, Candice, **157, 163**
Petterson, Grove, **xvi**
Physicists, xxi, xxv, 34, 78, 91, 196, 199
Plato, 73, 260
Pogo, 60
Pollyanna, 153-**154, 197**
Porter, Eleanor, 153, 154
Positive thinking, xxiv, xxv, 62-67, 81-83
Posture, 10-13, 18-20, 30, 97-98, 183-184
Powell, Colin, **197**
Power, 74, 113, 184, 225
Prana, xxvii, 34, 185, 195, 242, 251
Prayer, 17, 67, 70, 174, 230
Presence, 69, 194, 230
Pribram, Karl, 166
Price, A. F., 257
Princess Diana, **229**
Protestant, 146, 201-202
Pure Land Buddhism, 240
Puritanism, 47, 148
Pythagoras, **149**

—Q—

Qi, 240
Quakers, 54
Quimby, Phineas Parkhurst, **199**
Quotes on Fear, **xvi**

—R—

Radhakrishnen, Sarvepalli, **241**
Ratti, O., **50, 238**
Reagan, Ronald, **216**
Reasoning, 165
Recycle, xxi, 76, 133, 161, 178-180
Redfield, James, **226**
Reed, William, xiv, xxvii, 40-41, 67-**68,** 245
Reformation, 74, 146, 201-202
Reich, Wilhelm, 33
Reichenbach, Baron Von, 33
Reincarnation, xxiii, 119, 135, 239, 244, 250-251
Relax, 29, 41, 56,
Relaxation response, 29
Repress, 47
Riggs, Bobby, 181
Roach, Al, 156
Robbins, Anthony, 63
Rogers, Will, **81**
Roosevelt, Franklin, **217**
Roosevelt, Theodore, **211**
Russell, Bertrand, **xvi, 1**
Russell, Walter, **168, 179, 221**

—S—

Sage, Jack, xii
Samurai, 58, 238
Sansara, 239
Sanskrit, 34, 185, 238, 250-251, 256-258
Sarah, 200
Satori, 69, 258-259
Save face, 113
Schapero, Neal, **10**
Schumann, Henry, xiii, 201
Schweitzer, Albert, **158, 173**
Scott, Sir Walter, **69**
Seiza, 183, 251
Self-esteem, 3, 26, 62, 69, 97, 184, 192
Selye, Hans, **xvi**
Semmelweiss, Ignaz, 129-130
Sense, 24, 26, 36, 143, 145, 163
Sensationalism, xxv, 55
Sensei, ix, xxii, xxvii, 32, 51, 87-88, 245-246, 250-252, 256
Separation, 137, 230
Seredipity, 182, 219
Shakespeare, **66, 106, 141, 190**
Shakyamuni, 241

Shaolin Temple, 249, 257
Shi, Ming, 37, 70, **120, 130, 173, 249-250**
Shiatsu, 47
Shifflett, C. S., xiv, **143, 191**
Shin Shin Toitsu Aikido, 248, 254
Shintoism, 34, 43, 60, 237, 240, 252
Shiva, 34, 243
Siddhartha, Gautama, 51, 239
Siegel, Bernie, 119, **169**
Siegel, Robert Simon, 178
Simcox, George, ix, xiv, xxvii, 40, 56, 93, **136,** 210, 256
Smith, Houston, **89**
Socrates, **24,** 73
Spirergy, ix, 10, 21, 24, 35-36, 56-57, 69, 100, 117, 185, 195, 205, 244
Spirit, viii, xxi, xxv, xxviii, xxix, xxx, 2, 10, 29, 32-34, 36-37, 72, 85, 92, 119, 132, 140, 145, 158, 161, 167, 185-187, 194, 196, 213, 228, 232, 238, 240, 259
Sportsmanship, 24
Square, xi, xii
St. Augustine, **180**
St. Francis de Sales, **136**
St. Francis of Assisi, **119,** 180
St. Jerome, **195**
St. Paul, **89, 173**
St. Theresa of Lisieux, **231**
Stage fright, 175, 178, 187-190
State-of-being, xxv, 7, 16, 36, 141, 195
Steindl-Rast, David, **186**
Steiner, Rudolf, 171-**173**
Stevens, Wallace, **212**
Stevenson, Adlia E., **145**
Stewart, Potter, **140**
Stone, John, **32,** 40, **42,** 60
Super-ego, 138, 165
Swindoll, Charles, **164**

—T—

Tai chi, 34, 36, 173, 240, 252-253
Tai chi chaun, 252
Talbot, Michael, **196**
Tao te ching, 253
Taoism, xxii, xxvii, xxviii, 34, 62, 70-72, 240, 242, 253, 256-257
Taylor, Louise, **49**
Tenkan, 92-95, 100, 115, 253
Thanks, 88, 190-192
Theosophical Society, xxiii
Theravada, 240
Thinking and feeling, 7, 11, 15, 40, 44, 46, 53
Thomas, Clarence, 109
Thomas, Lewis, **215**
Thoughts, 1, 16, 65, 103, 192-193, 228
Three-dimensional, ix, 1, 104-107, 195-197
Time, 76, 193-194
Toffler, Alvin, 214
Tohei, Koichi, xiii, xvi, xxi, xxvii, **32, 33,** 35, **39, 47, 51, 62,** 87, **93,** 100, **178,** 242, 246, 254
Tohei Sensei, ix, xxvii, xxviii, 32, 33, **39**-52, 62, 67-**68, 93, 100, 102,** 123, 130, 132, **140, 155,** 161, **177-178, 190,** 210, **242, 244-245, 248-250, 254-255**
Tojo, Hediki, 60
Torii gate, 252
Transactional Analysis, 105-106, 181
Transmigration, 251
Transpersonalize, 3, 83, 159
Triality, ix, xxix, 23, 24, 56, 67, 79, 85, 96, 107, 109, 117, 145, 154, 157, 184, 194-196, 247
Triangle, xi, 8
Triplett, Robert, **175,** 178, **188-190**
Tri-tuning, ix, xi, xxiv,xxv, xxviii, xxx, 1-4, 7-32, 35-36, 56-57, 81,

83, 89, 96, 99, 110, 117-118, 131, 141-143, 150, 163, 194-198, 205-207, 230, 247, 249
Tri-tuning Skills/Ki Tests,
  Aikido Tenkan, 92
  Basic Whole-Body Breathing, 49
  Deep Breathing, 124
  Experience Tri-tuning, 16,
  Family Conflict, 95
  Four Basic Principles, 41
  Kiatsu Healing Art, 48
  Ki Exercises, 45
  Ki Meditation, 46
  Kinetic Ki Testing, 43
  Learning to Tri-tune, 15
  Natural Tri-tuning, 19
  Observe Posture, 11,
  Sad and Happy Face, 154
  Sense of Tri-tuning, 142
  Shrugging Shoulders, 12
  Shrugging Test, 19
  State-of-Being, 141
  Subconscious Reaction, 151
  Unbreakable Circle, 57
  Weight Underside, 256
  Whole-Body Breathing, 124
Tri-tuning symbol, xi, 195
Tri-tuning Tips, 206, 235
Trungpa, Chogyam, **65**
Truth, xxiv, xxviii, 77-80, 83, 129, 180, 197-200, 260
Tune-in, 1, 2, 128
Two-dimensional, 196
Tzu, Lao, **72, 199, 253**

—U—

Uchida, Yoshiko, 266
Ueshiba, Kisshomaru, 42
Ueshiba, Morihei, xiii, xxi, **32**, 39, 42, **58, 60-61, 95**, 111-112, 237, 238, **254-255**, 259
Uke, 92-93, 250, 255
Unbreakable circle, 57, 85
Upanishads, 243, 251

—V—

Vedas, 243, 251
Vinci, Leonardo da, 15
Virginia Ki Society, xiv, xxvii, 40, 56, 87, 93, 210
Vishnu, 243
Voltaire, **226**

—W—

Waitley, Denis, **202-203**
Walpole, Horace, 219
Walsch, Neale Donald, xvi, **87, 192, 200**
Walters, Barbara, 187
Walther, David S., 167
Warrior, 58, 59
Watson, Lyall, 128
Weight underside, 41, 56, 248, 255-256, 260
Well-being, xxv
Wells, H. G., 137
Westbrook, A., **50, 238**
Western religion, xxiii, xxviii, 64, 200-202
Westlake, Donald, **156**
Whitney, Frank, B., **183**
Whole-body breathing, 49-50, 123-125
Wilson, Jim, **238**
Wilson, Woodrow, **79**
Win-win, 24, 72, 202-205
Wirkus, Mietek, 163
Wood, Ernest, **70**
World War II, 60, 88, 217, 238, 249, 252-254
Wright, Wilbur, **212**
Wu-wei, 257
Wydra, Nancilee, **241**

—X—

Xerses I, 260

—Y—

Yin/Yang, xxii, xxviii, 62, 68, 70-72, 256

Yoga, 29, 34, 39, 209, 243, 251, 256

—Z—

Zen, 39, 157, 176-177, 237, 240-241, 250, 254, 256-259
Zoroaster (Zorothustra), 73, 199, 259-260
Zoroastrianism, 73, 200, 260

Notes

Tri-Tuning

Notes

280 ▲ Tri-Tuning

Order Form

TRI-TUNING — Harmonizing your Mind, Body and Spirit to Live Beyond Fear

Hilda Neff Perkins

Mail to: Universal Quest Publishing
P.O. Box 1393
Vero Beach, FL 32961

By phone: (561) 562-3031

Return the portion below or a photocopy of the page.

Name: _____

Address: _____

_____

City: _____ State: _____ Zip: _____

Phone: _____ Business Phone: _____

NO CASH Please!

	Price:	Qty.	TOTAL
U.S.A.	$18.95	____	____
Canada	$22.95	____	____

(Florida residents add 6% plus surtax, if applicable.)

Shipping: $3.50
(Add $1.00 shipping for each additional book.)

TOTAL: ____

Send Gift Order To: _____

Address: _____

_____

City: _____ State: _____ Zip: _____

Phone: _____ Business Phone: _____

Make checks payable to: Universal Quest Publishing

Order Form

TRI-TUNING — Harmonizing your Mind, Body and Spirit to Live Beyond Fear

Hilda Neff Perkins

Mail to: Universal Quest Publishing
P.O. Box 1393
Vero Beach, FL 32961

By phone: (561) 562-3031

Return the portion below or a photocopy of the page.

- -

Name: _____

Address: _____

_____

City: _____ State: _____ Zip: _____

Phone: _____ Business Phone: _____

N O   C A S H   Please!

	Price:	Qty.	TOTAL
U.S.A.	$18.95	_____	_____
Canada	$22.95	_____	_____
(Florida residents add 6% plus surtax, if applicable.)			_____
Shipping:			$3.50
(Add $1.00 shipping for each additional book.)			_____
		TOTAL:	_____

Send Gift Order To: _____

Address: _____

_____

City: _____ State: _____ Zip: _____

Phone: _____ Business Phone: _____

Make checks payable to: Universal Quest Publishing